Policies, Institutions and the Dark Side of
Economics

Policies, Institutions and the Dark Side of Economics

Vito Tanzi

Director, Fiscal Affairs Department, International Monetary Fund, Washington, DC, USA

Edward Elgar
Cheltenham, UK • Northampton, MA, USA

Published by
Edward Elgar Publishing Limited
Glensanda House
Montpellier Parade
Cheltenham
Glos GL50 1UA
UK

Edward Elgar Publishing, Inc.
136 West Street
Suite 202
Northampton
Massachusetts 01060
USA

A catalogue record for this book
is available from the British Library

Library of Congress Cataloguing in Publication Data
Tanzi, Vito.
    Policies, institutions and the dark side of economics / Vito Tanzi.
    Includes bibliographical references.
    1. Economic policy—Decision making.   2. Institutional economics.   3. Political corruption.   I. Title.

HD87.T376 2000
338.9 21—dc21

                                           99–044605

ISBN 1 85898 729 6

Typeset by Manton Typesetters, Louth, Lincolnshire, UK.
Printed and bound in Great Britain by Biddles Ltd, www.biddles.co.uk

Contents

Figures and tables

FIGURES

TABLES

Preface

For the last two decades I have had the privilege to serve as the Director of the Fiscal Affairs Department of the International Monetary Fund. This department has the responsibility of following fiscal developments around the world and of advising countries on fiscal reforms. It is thus a very good observatory for studying economic developments and for observing how economic policy in general and fiscal policy in particular are formulated and implemented. Over the years I have frequently been brought into contact with ministers and other high-level policy makers from the 182 countries that are members of the Fund; I have led missions to member countries to advise countries' authorities on policy issues and to discuss policy changes; and have participated in many meetings in which economic issues were discussed. I have also read literally thousands of reports on economic and fiscal developments written by economists in the Fiscal Affairs Department and in other places.

During these years I have been struck by the gap that exists between the economics found in economic textbooks and the one discussed at policy makers' meetings. The former is usually formal and normative and largely ignores practical issues and issues of implementation. The latter concentrates on implementation and, thus, on political–institutional limitations. I have also been struck by the uncertainty of the relation between policy actions and results of those actions. Thus, while in theoretical discussions one assumes that the relationship between two variables is direct and clear, so that, if $y = f(x)$ giving a value to x gives a unique result for y, in practice a change in x may be associated with a wide range of possible outcomes for y. The reason is of course the role of the institutions responsible for the implementation of those policies and the behavior of those working for the institutions. That behavior is often influenced by particular incentives that affect their behavior and that makes them unreliable agents of the policy makers. And, of course, the latter may also have their own personal goals.

This book focuses on policies, on institutions, and on what I have called 'the dark side' of economics. It is not a textbook or a treatise on a specific subject but rather a collection of essays all broadly related to the theme that institutions and personal incentives matter, so that the results of policy actions may be different from those expected from normative or theoretical economics. In some way this book may be seen as a contribution to institutional economics and to public choice, although I should stress that I am not a member of either group and my knowledge of the literature in these two fields is very limited. Only in spirit is the book related to those two fields of economics.

The book consists of 15 chapters, some published, some unpublished, and some substantially revised versions of previously published papers. They have, for the most part, been written in recent years. Only the first chapter was written about 25 years ago. I left it unchanged because, at the time it was written, its message was very unsettling to those who wanted to see the role of government in the economic sphere in strictly normative terms.

The 15 chapters form broadly three parts. The first five chapters can be thought of as of a methodological nature. They essentially indicate different ways of looking at the role of government and at the instruments that it uses. The following seven chapters deal with the dark side of economics. They discuss phenomena such as corruption, tax evasion, money laundering and the underground economy, and show why these phenomena are important and the way they can distort economic policy. The last three chapters are examples of the role that institutions play in economic policy.

Three of the chapters were co-authored: Chapter 5 by Ke-young Chu, Chapter 9 by Hamid Davoodi and Chapter 10 by Partho Shome. I wish to thank all of these colleagues. I would also like to thank Ms Champa Nguyen and Ms Beulah David for their great help with the preparation of the manuscript and Ms Deirdre Shanley for helping me with the references. The International Monetary Fund has provided a perfect environment for learning about the problems discussed in this book and for writing about them. My colleagues in the Fund and especially those in the Fiscal Affairs Department have contributed a lot to my own thinking. However it goes without saying that the views expressed are strictly personal and should not be attributed to the Fund or to my colleagues.

My wife, Maria, suffered many hours of solitude while I was busy, generally at weekends, in the preparation of the various papers. I wish to express my great appreciation and thanks to her and also to my sons, who saw less of me than, I hope, they would have liked.

VITO TANZI
23 May 1999

Acknowledgements

The following chapters were originally published, often in substantially different versions, in the source listed: I would like to express my thanks to the former publishers for their permission to republish the articles. Chapter 2, *Fiscal Decentralisation in Emerging Economies: Governance Issues*, edited by Kiichiro Fukusaku and Luis R. De Mello Jr. (Paris: OECD, 1999) pp. 17–36; Chapter 3, *Public Finance in a Changing World*, edited by Peter Birch Sorensen (London: Macmillan, 1998) pp. 51–69; Chapter 6, *The Economics of Organised Crime*, edited by Gianluca Fiorentini and Sam Peltzman (Cambridge: Cambridge University Press, 1995) pp. 161–80; Chapter 7, International Monetary Fund, *Staff Papers*, vol. 45, no. 4 (December 1998) pp. 559–594; Chapter 8, *Economics of Corruption*, edited by Arvind K. Jain (Boston: Kluwer Academic Publishers, 1998) pp. 111–28; Chapter 9, *The Welfare State, Public Investment and Growth*, edited by H. Shibata and T. Ihori (Tokyo; New York: Springer-Verlag, 1998) pp. 41–60; Chapter 10, International Monetary Fund, *Staff Papers*, vol. 40, no. 4 (December 1993) pp. 807–28; Chapter 11, *Responding to Money Laundering: International Perspectives*, edited by Ernesto V. Savona (Amsterdam: Harwood Academic Publishers, 1997) pp. 91–104; Chapter 14, *Proceedings of the World Bank Annual Conference on Development Economics, 1995* (Washington D.C.: World Bank, 1996) pp. 295–316; Chapter 15, International Monetary Fund, *Staff Papers*, vol. 40, no. 3 (September 1993) pp. 697–707.

1. Toward a positive theory of public sector behavior: an interpretation of some Italian contributions[1]

THEORY OF FISCAL ILLUSION

More than a century ago John Stuart Mill wondered whether 'direct or indirect taxes are the most eligible'. After observing 'the unpopularity of direct taxation' and contrasting it 'with the easy manner in which the public consent to let themselves be fleeced in the prices of commodities', he reached the conclusion that 'an Englishman dislikes, not so much the [tax] payment, as the act of paying'.[2] He called this preference for indirect taxes an 'infirmity of the popular mind'. His final assessment, however, was that 'if our present revenue ... were all raised by direct taxes, an extreme dissatisfaction would certainly arise at having to pay so much'.[3] Thus the implication was that indirect taxes are necessary evils used by the government to make possible the raising of needed revenue.

While Mill's argument related to the choice between 'direct' and 'indirect' taxes, Vilfredo Pareto made essentially the same point vis-à-vis the choice between taxes and public borrowing. While not contesting the Ricardian argument of the equivalence, *for a fully rational individual*, of the burden of extraordinary (that is, once-and-for-all) taxes and public loans, Pareto observed that no taxpayer makes the Ricardian calculations. Therefore, the choice *on the part of the authorities* between loans and taxes is made taking into account the taxpayers' *subjective* perception of their respective burden. Pareto's conclusion is reminiscent of Mill's: 'Deficit financing is one way of inducing the citizens to accept what they would not accept with taxes. For example, if during the war the governments had tried to collect through taxes as much as they collected through loans, it is very likely that they would not have succeeded.'[4]

Hugh Dalton, another Englishman who, in addition to having written one of the classic texts in public finance, had the distinction of having held the office of Chancellor of the Exchequer, sided with the 'plain man' in the conviction 'that the best tax is that which is least felt, that is to say which causes the least inconvenience and *conscious* sacrifice to those who pay it'.[5]

Dalton quoted approvingly an ingenious Cambridge rule to be followed by the authorities in choosing among taxes: 'the rich should pay more taxation than they think, while the poor should think they pay more than they do'.[6]

The basic point that these important writers have raised, a point that incidentally has been ignored by the modern public finance literature, is that individuals are not computers who can assess fully and dispassionately the costs and benefits of taxation, but are human beings with instincts and biases who may behave and react in ways not fully consistent with 'rational' behavior. While for Mill and Dalton this realization did not become the keystone of a full-fledged theory of public sector behavior, for Amilcare Puviani, an Italian writer of the turn of the 20th century and, to a lesser extent, for Vilfredo Pareto, it did.

Puviani made, perhaps, the most important systematic contribution to the theory of the *subjective* burden of taxation. In an unusual and, for a long time, forgotten book, Puviani introduced the concept of 'fiscal illusion'.[7] As shown above, in a very limited sense this concept was already implicit in the writing of others. However, and this is a fundamental difference, while for the others it was mainly related to the attitude of taxpayers toward taxes and was not, thus, in any way an interpretation or a description of the *modus operandi* of governments, in Puviani it became the cornerstone of his interpretation of how governments operate and, thus, implicitly, of a *positive* theory of public sector behavior. Furthermore the concept was extended beyond taxation to relate also to public expenditure.

In Puviani's conception, governments do not aim at maximizing the difference between *objective* benefits derived from public expenditure and *objective* costs of providing that expenditure as, for example, assumed by the (Samuelsonian) modern pure theory of public expenditure.[8] For Puviani, governments aim at maximizing the difference between *subjective*, and often erroneous, evaluations of the benefits of public expenditures and their costs. More importantly, this maximization process is not a static but a dynamic one: governments do not (or, at least, may not) just passively accept and exploit these subjective and erroneous evaluations of costs and benefits *as they are*. On the contrary, they are actively engaged in promoting and/or reinforcing these errors through the use of fiscal illusions'. Therefore fiscal illusions are not just random errors on the part of taxpayers but, often, systematic, government-induced errors.

Fiscal illusions are 'errors ... that the political body uses to reach its objectives' and these errors concern both 'revenues' and 'public expenditures'.[9] These illusions can be positive or negative. The positive ones 'consist in [making taxpayers] see things that do not exist',[10] as, for example, in making them believe that a given public expenditure is actually solving a problem, or making a genuine difference to the public welfare, when in fact it is not. The negative fiscal illusions occur when taxpayers do not see or feel the total burden of a tax actually paid.[11] By promoting or reinforcing these illusions governments try to strengthen what Puviani calls the 'contributive push' which we could simply call taxpayers' compliance.[12] It is obvious that, when these fiscal illusions exist, the financial public sector equilibrium in terms of both level and structure of taxation and expenditure will be different from the one implied by the (modern) pure theory of public expenditure.

There are various ways in which governments create and/or take advantage of fiscal illusions.[13] For example, governments (a) will often rely on taxes that are included, or 'wrapped up', to use Dalton's expression, in the prices of the products since, in this case, the taxpayer is less likely to be aware of the tax that he is paying and will thus not feel the sacrifice; or on taxes which are shifted so that the actual burden falls on taxpayers other than those meeting the legal obligation; (b) will not change the basic tax laws too often since taxpayers become particularly insensitive to taxes which have been levied for a long time ('old taxes are good taxes'); on the other hand, minor amendments aimed at benefiting particular groups will be frequent as they will often go unnoticed; (c) will take advantage of shifts in public opinion which decrease the taxpayers' resistance to new or additional taxes;[14] (d) will avoid relying on just one or two taxes since, up to a certain point, the greater is the number of taxes, the lower is the taxpayers' resistance to the total tax burden;[15] (e) will collect the levy when it is least painful to the taxpayer (for example, with withholding at the source); (f) will often rely on borrowing rather than on higher permanent taxes or even on (once-for-all) extraordinary taxes, as borrowing will not result in an immediate obvious burden; (g) will rely on deficit financing, financed not by borrowing from the public but by the expansion of the monetary base, as this 'inflation tax' will not be an obvious tax to the taxpayers; (h) will introduce taxes, clearly intended to be permanent, as temporary; (i) will introduce new spending programs when the cost of these programs appears low (unemployment compensation during full employment, social security programs which do not require payments until much later, and so on).

PRIMAL TYPES OF STATES

Puviani's theory can help to explain to varying degrees the behavior of actual, as distinguished from abstract, governments. In other words, it can be used to develop a positive theory of public sector behavior. In order to do so, however, Puviani's theory must be combined with other Italian contributions. The Italian public finance literature, though not Puviani himself, has at times identified and discussed three primal types of states:[16] the monopolistic (or predatory), the individualistic (or corporate) and the paternalistic (or tutorial). The importance and the use of public illusions will vary among these.

Monopolistic State

In the monopolistic type, which is the one closest to Puviani's and Pareto's own conception of how governments operate, a ruling class, group or party comes to control the government's apparatus of a country and uses it to maximize the welfare of its members. Here there is little concern for the 'public interest'. Rather, most governmental actions are ultimately aimed at maximizing the welfare of the subset of a population that controls the government apparatus. This might simply imply creating government jobs for those supporting the party in power, or promoting public investments or even public education that benefit those groups or regions that belong to the ruling group.[17]

Fiscal illusions become important instruments used to facilitate these actions. These illusions will be promoted and exploited to the hilt by the monopolistic government in order to achieve its own selfish objectives. It will induce the population to increase the acceptability of public spending, intended to benefit the ruling class, by promoting positive fiscal illusions that exaggerate the benefits that the general public derives from public expenditure. It will aim at increasing the acceptable level of taxation by promoting negative fiscal illusions that hide the true (or objective) burden of taxation.[18] This process will result in structures and levels of taxation and public expenditure that are different from those that would be implied by modern theories of public finance (for example, the voluntary exchange approach) which are based on the premise that taxpayers' decisions are not distorted by fiscal illusions. The public expenditure will mainly benefit the ruling class. The incidence of taxation will mainly fall on the rest of the population. The preferred taxes will be those for which fiscal illusions are easiest (import duties and so on). The budgetary process will be such as to hide the true beneficiaries. Extrabudgetary accounts, hidden expenditures and so on will prevail.

A look around the world indicates that this type of government, that was very prevalent in the past, may not have disappeared. One point that is important to emphasize is that even a predatory government finds it useful to promote its selfish objectives by relying on fiscal illusions, rather than simply on coercion or brute force, as it wants to remain in power, and this will be facilitated by some acceptability for these programs on the part of its citizenry. Thus it may still try to justify its actions in terms of the public interest. Even a monopolistic government's ability to maximize the welfare of its members is often limited by various legal–sociopolitical constraints. Therefore, in the absence of fiscal illusions, the cost of remaining in power would be much higher. It was one of the limitations of Puviani's work to assume universality for the monopolistic type of state in the same way as it is one of the limitations of much of the recent literature on public sector behavior to (implicitly) assume universality for the individualistic state.

Individualistic State

In the individualistic type, which is the one implicitly or explicitly assumed by the voluntary exchange approach as well as by much of the recent public finance literature, 'the individual not only has a voice in determining the role of the state; the state exists only to serve him'.[19] Or, as Musgrave puts it, 'the satisfaction of social wants must be based on the preferences of individual consumers or voters'.[20] In other words, there are no collective wants apart from those of the individual. Here public welfare is the summation of the welfare of all the individuals comprising society at a given point in time.[21] There must not be any difference between the objectives of the taxpayers in terms of structure and level of taxation and public spending and those of the governing body. Therefore, in this conception, there should be no scope for the government's exploitation of fiscal illusions. Not only should the government not promote them, but, rather, it should be actively engaged in educating the citizens so that they can avoid these 'errors' with respect to revenues and expenditure. All decisions involving taxation and public spending should be based on illusion-free, educated, conscious and objective evaluations of the costs and the benefits associated with them.[22] The government will thus favor taxes the burden of which can be easily identified by those who pay them (individual income taxes, sales taxes for which the tax is shown separately from the price of the commodity, and so on). The budgetary process will be all-inconclusive and transparent. Only in this way would the resulting equilibrium be consistent with a truly objective welfare maximization.

Paternalistic State

In the paternalistic type of state the public interest is no longer the summation of the interests of all the citizens, *as they themselves would see it in an illusion-free world*, but it can, and usually does, transcend it. In this case the government body, in the interest of the state – which now, at times, acquires a mystical, Hegelian look – can transcend the interests of its citizens and pursue policies that may not be consistent with an individualistic type of state.[23] In other words, the interest pursued by the governing body may diverge widely from the public interest that would result from the summation of the welfare of all the individuals comprising Society, assuming that such a summation were possible.

In the pursuance of these policies the government will be aided by the creation and exploitation of fiscal illusions. However the key difference is that this will be done, not in the selfish interest of the group of individuals comprising or controlling the government, as was the case with the monopolistic state, but, supposedly, in the interest of 'society', or the 'country', or the 'people', or the 'nation', or the 'proletariat', or some other such abstract concept. In paternalistic states, even though the objectives of the governments are fundamentally different from those in monopolistic states, so that the use of fiscal illusions can be considered as benign, the end result would still be a public sector with structures and levels of taxation and of public spending very different from those of the individualistic state.

CONCLUDING REMARKS

These primal (or polar) types of government are probably never found in their pure form in the real world. To varying degrees all governments exhibit characteristics belonging to all of these types.[24] But, of course, for some countries, at some historical juncture, the monopolistic tendency may prevail; for others again, the paternalistic traits may appear dominant.[25] It is for this reason that one can expect to find most governments, to varying degrees, taking advantage of existing fiscal illusions and, perhaps, even creating or promoting some.[26] And it is for this reason that the modern theory of public finance cannot provide a totally satisfactory explanation of public sector behavior in any country.

The positive theory of public sector behavior presented above is an ambitious one as it claims to explain the broad behavior of the public sector in a universal context; it is not limited geographically or historically. The proposed theory does not invalidate the modern theory of public finance – a theory built on the fundamental contributions of Wicksell, Lindahl, Samuelson and others – which not only assigns a benign or at least neutral role to the state but also rules out fiscal illusions. It does, however, bring about a considerable redimensioning of that theory by arguing that its validity and relevance are limited in time and space as only few countries can make (or at times could have made) the claim of belonging to the set of individualistic types of state.[27] Even if it were argued that the modern theory is just a normative one, it should be realized that its normativeness extends beyond the behavior of public expenditure and taxation as it implicitly comprehends the type of state that a country ought to have. Or, putting it differently, the modern theory of public sector behavior, in a basic sense, is not just an economic theory that prescribes the level and pattern of public expenditure and taxes that countries ought to have, but it is essentially a political theory as it prescribes the type of government that a country ought to have.

To be useful, a theory must be testable. Tests can be quantitative or qualitative. Quantitative tests are generally preferable but are not always possible. Thus, at times, we must be satisfied with qualitative or even impressionistic validations. The theory proposed above is difficult to test because it indicates broad directions rather than precise or specific solutions. Furthermore any practical use of this theory must rely on a classification of governments according to the three primal types outlined above. Such a classification demands expertise not generally found among economists. Rather it requires the cooperation of political scientists or historians who better control the tools necessary for this enterprise. These experts, on the basis of various criteria (such as the voting process, the institutional structure of the governmental apparatus, the existence of checks and balances, and so on) could place governments into one of the three categories discussed above. Once governments have been so classified, the theory can be subjected to various tests of which a few are indicated below.

Tax Structure Development

Various studies have shown that, as countries develop, their tax structure changes. In particular, lower-income countries seem to rely more on foreign trade taxes, while higher-income countries rely more on domestic taxes and, for those with high per capita incomes, on income taxes. Equally, over time, there has been a change in the tax structure of countries away from foreign trade toward domestic and income taxes. Is this structural change explained by the change in the type of government that the countries have? If the hypothesis advanced in note 25 is broadly correct, and countries do in fact move from the monopolistic to the individualistic and, finally, to the paternalistic type of government, then the observed change in the structure of taxation can be explained by the change in the type of government. Monopolistic governments would tend to rely on taxes for which fiscal illusions are prevalent (import duties, inflationary financing and so on) without much concern about the effects of those taxes on the economy. Individualistic governments would prefer taxes which are fully felt by the taxpayers (income taxes, property taxes and sales taxes which are shown separately from the price of the products, and so on). To raise the total tax burden to pursue policies aimed at redistributing income, paternalistic states might reduce the importance of income taxes and increase that of general sales taxes, 'wrapped up' in the prices of products, and of payroll taxes, but they would still show a concern for the negative impact of inefficient taxes on the economy.

Social Rate of Discount

Monopolistic governments, especially if they do not expect to remain in power for long, are likely to emphasize immediate benefits to controlling groups; individualistic governments are more likely to take into account the welfare of future generations. This implies that the implicit social rate of discount on investment is highest for monopolistic states and lowest for paternalistic states. Therefore it would be interesting to see whether paternalistic states do in fact have the highest ratios of public investment to gross national product, GNP (and the lowest ratios of current to capital public expenditures). Alternatively do monopolistic states have the lowest ratios?

Inefficiency

Often inefficiency in the public sector is not accidental but, rather, can be considered as intentional policy aimed at transferring income from the private sector to public sector employees. We do know that, at times, public sector employment is pushed to the point where the marginal product of public employees falls to very low levels, or even to zero, and that this is often done to provide an income for those who get these government jobs. In some countries, some of these employees come to consider government salaries as pensions. One relevant question, then, is: why is not the obvious and cheaper alternative of a straightforward cash transfer not used? One possible explanation is that a monopolistic government could find it very difficult politically to provide a cash transfer for the members of the controlling group; therefore it will use a positive fiscal illusion to achieve the same objective. Public employment will, in other words, be justified on the ground that the additional public sector employees are needed to provide services. Therefore the basic test could be the following: is there evidence of greater inefficiency in countries with monopolistic governments than in others? Strictly speaking, one would expect to find the lowest degree of inefficiency in individualistic governments and, perhaps, the highest in monopolistic governments.

Other tests might relate to (a) the use of subsidies to enterprises vis-à-vis tariffs; (b) the use of earmarking; (c) the use of extrabudgetary accounts and more broadly budgetary processes which hide many of the expenditures; (d) the choice of a retail sales tax or a value-added tax; (e) the use of quasi-fiscal regulations and activities compared to explicit taxes and spending.

The theory proposed above would explain why it has often been difficult for tax experts, who spend much of their times advising governments around the world on tax reform, to have their proposals accepted. One basic reason might simply be that the experts make their recommendations assuming that fiscal illusions are undesirable while, in fact, they may play a significant role in the behavior of the governments of particular countries.

POSTSCRIPT

This chapter was written about two decades ago, when the individualistic view of the state was most dominant, when corruption and institutions did not attract much attention, and when there were no economies in transition. I have refrained from revising it. However I must mention that there has been much thinking in economics that has followed some of the directions anticipated by this chapter. Efficiency in government and corruption have become major areas of research. The public choice school has become popular. 'Predatory' or 'grabbing hands' governments have been the subject of studies by economists such as Mansur Olson, Andrei Shleifer and Robert Vishny, and others. And codes of transparency in fiscal policy are being urged on all countries.

NOTES

1. This paper is partly based on research done in 1974 during a sabbatical year spent in Italy. It was written two decades ago. Except for the postscript at the end, I have not changed it. The Banca d'Italia, through the Ente Einaudi, provided generous financial support.
2. John Stuart Mill, *Principles of Political Economy* (Harmondsworth: Penguin Books, 1970), p. 220.
3. Ibid., p. 221.
4. Letter written by Pareto to Benvenuto Griziotti. Cited in Griziotti's 'Fatti e Teorie delle Finanze in Vilfredo Pareto', *Rivista di Scienza delle Finanze* (1944), 136–40. The citation is on p. 137 (my own translation).
5. Hugh Dalton, *Principles of Public Finance* (New York: Augustus M. Kelley, 1967), p. 33. Italics added.
6. Ibid., p. 34.
7. Amilcare Puviani, *Teoria dell'Illusione Finanziaria* (Milan: ISEDI, 1973). The first edition of this book was published in 1903. For a long time, Puviani's ideas were not extensively discussed in the literature. For example, they attracted a total of six lines in Dennis C. Mueller's comprehensive survey, *Public Choice* (Cambridge: Cambridge University Press, 1979), p. 90. The interested reader can find some description in James M. Buchanan, *Public Finance in Democratic Process* (Chapel FEU: The University of North Carolina Press, 1967). Chapter 10 of that work deals with 'The Fiscal Illusion'. An interesting interpretation of Puviani's work is Franco Volpi's introduction to the 1973 edition of the *Teoria dell'Illusione Finanziaria*. For some uses of this concept, see R.E. Wagner, 'Revenue Structure, Fiscal Illusion, and Budgetary Choice', *Public Choice*, Spring 1976, 25, 45–61; and Vito Tanzi, 'Taxpayers' Preferences and the Future Structure of State and Local Taxation', in Institut International des Finances Publiques, *Issues in Urban Public Finance* (Congrès de New York, 1972, Saarbrücken), pp. 459–66. In recent years Puviani's name has become better known.
8. Perhaps this is an unfair interpretation of that theory since, strictly speaking, that is a

normative rather than a *positive* theory; thus it is only supposed to tell us how governments *should* behave. However, as we shall see below, that implies a specific and hardly
realistic conception of the state.

9.   Puviani, op. cit., p. 5 (my translation).
10. Ibid., p. 7 (my translation).
11. Ibid.
12. Ibid., pp. 7–8.
13. Many, but not all, of the ways outlined in this paragraph are illustrated in Puviani's work
     with historical examples.
14. Thus a report by the surgeon general that cigarette smoking causes cancer will be fol-
     lowed by tax increases on cigarettes. There is some evidence that this, in fact, is what
     happened in the United States. For this and other examples, see Vito Tanzi, op. cit.
     Equally, as argued by Peacock and Wiseman, wars will open an opportunity to perma-
     nently shift upward the level of taxation. See Alan T. Peacock and Jack Wiseman, *The
     Growth of Public Expenditure in the United Kingdom*, National Bureau of Economic
     Research (Princeton: Princeton University Press, 1961).
15. One reason for this is that the 'rates of particular taxes can be lower when revenue is
     raised from several taxes than when it is obtained from a few sources'; see Richard
     Goode, 'Limits to Taxation', in *Finance & Development*, March 1980, 17. However, when
     the number of taxes in existence is large, the number itself, as distinguished from total
     revenue, may come to be seen as a burden. This was undoubtedly the case in Argentina
     where, in 1976, 97 different taxes were used to collect total revenues which were not
     excessive when compared to those of other comparable countries.
16. The most complete treatment of this particular aspect of the Italian literature is found in
     Mauro Fasiani, *Principi di Scienza delle Finanze*, vols I and II (Turin: G. Giappichelli,
     1951).
17. For a discussion along these lines, see Vito Tanzi, 'Redistributing Income Through the
     Budget in Latin America', *Banca Nazionale del Lavoro Quarterly Review*, March 1974,
     no. 108.
18. For some discussions of tax limits that call attention to sociological factors, see Richard
     Goode, 'Limits to Taxation', *Finance & Development*, March 1980, 17; and Vito Tanzi,
     'International Tax Burdens', in Vito Tanzi *et al.*, *Taxation: A Radical Approach* (London:
     Institute of Economic Affairs, 1970).
19. Harold M. Groves, *Financing Government*, 4th edn (New York: Henry Holt and Company,
     1954), p. 6.
20. Richard A. Musgrave, *The Theory of Public Finance* (New York: McGraw-Hill, 1959),
     p. 86.
21. Whether this summation is possible is an interesting question but one not relevant to our
     discussion. See on this K.J. Arrow, *Social Choice and Individual Values* (New York: John
     Wiley & Sons, 1951; rev. edn 1963); and Dennis C. Mueller, *Public Choice* (Cambridge:
     Cambridge University Press, 1979), ch. 10, pp. 184–206.
22. It was presumably in this spirit that Ronald Reagan, when he became Governor of
     California, attempted to abolish the PAYE system for state income taxes. In his view that
     system decreased taxpayers' awareness of the cost of public spending and, by thus creat-
     ing fiscal illusion, led to a larger public sector.
23. The Italian paternalistic view of the state is related to, but is not necessarily the same as,
     that advanced by German proponents of the organic theory of the state 'who postulate the
     existence of group needs or of needs that in some way or another are experienced by the
     "group as a whole"'. See Musgrave, op. cit., pp. 86–7.
24. A government may appear paternalistic with respect to some policies, monopolistic with
     respect to others, and may follow the individualistic model with respect to still others.
25. One can hypothesize that historically governments have shown a tendency to evolve from
     the monopolistic to the paternalistic type and that the individualistic conception of the
     state, now prevalent in the literature, but not in the real world, is just a transitory stage.
26. Conservative writers would argue that the popularity of the social security system in the

United States owes much to the exploitation of fiscal illusions. Perhaps the widespread use of deficit financing around the world can also be attributed to fiscal illusions.

27. The rather awkward way in which income redistribution policies have been dealt with by much of the modern theoretical literature on public sector behavior indicates the difficulties of relying on an individualistic conception of the state. For example, the modern normative theory is based on the benefit-received approach to taxation where taxes are strictly the prices that individuals pay for public services. Therefore, to justify the taxes paid for income redistributive purposes, one has to assume that income redistribution is a public good that taxpayers want to buy. Once one introduces a paternalistic conception of the state, the issue of income distribution is no longer a thorny one. But this concept requires the explicit recognition of fiscal illusion that is inconsistent with the pure theory. See Werner W. Pommerehne, 'Public Choice Approach to Explaining Fiscal Redistribution', XXXIV Congress of the International Institute of Public Finance (Hamburg, 1979).

2. The changing role of the state in the economy: a historical perspective[1]

POSITIVE AND NORMATIVE ROLES OF THE STATE

The French poet, Paul Valéry, was reported to believe that 'if the state is strong, it will crush us; if it is weak, we will perish'.[2] The ideal role must, therefore, be between these two extremes. Governments play many roles, some political, some social and some economic. The focus of this chapter is on the economic role. In the pursuit of this role, the government uses many policy instruments and, by so doing, it allocates resources, redistributes income and influences the level of activity.

At least since Richard Musgrave wrote his influential *Theory of Public Finance* in 1959, public finance economists have found useful the distinction between the positive and the normative roles of the state. The *normative* role determines guidelines, principles or norms for welfare-enhancing public sector intervention in the economy. On the basis of fundamental economic principles, it *attempts to define what the government should do* to correct market imperfections and to complement the market in other ways to promote and maximize social welfare.

Although this is not explicitly recognized by economists, the normative role is affected by the political constitution of a country. In Western, market-oriented democracies, where much modern economic thinking originated, the normative role of the state has been implicitly tied to the individualistic, political process that assumes that there are no goals or needs outside those of the individual citizens or voters. The public interest is thus seen as the summation of the interests of the individual citizens or voters.[3] In a way this explains why many see a close relationship between a market economy and a democratic process. In a market economy, individuals vote with their dollars whereas, in a democratic process, they use their votes to promote their political goals. In playing its role, the state cannot have objectives different from those of its citizens. But one could assume an alternative conception of the state such as, for example, a Hegelian conception of an organic or a totalitarian state that exists independently of individuals living at a given time and that has, thus, an existence of its own. This, however, would not be a popular view, especially with Western-oriented economists.[4]

While the normative role attempts to define what the government *should do* to maximize economic welfare, the *positive* role *describes and analyzes what the government actually does*. In an ideal world, the two roles would merge: the ideal and the actual roles would become the same because the state would be doing exactly what it is expected to do and all the reforms needed to maximize social welfare would have been carried out. In the real world, the two roles tend to diverge and, at times, they diverge a great deal, implying that many needed reforms have not been carried out. The reasons for this divergence are several, ranging from possible differences between the interests of those who govern and those who are governed, to mistakes and misconceptions on the part of the policy makers, to inadequate controls on the part of the policy makers over the policy instruments, and to the residual effects of past decisions.

Even when political leaders would like to achieve welfare-promoting social objectives, their economic training may not be adequate for the task. Some of them come from disciplines other than economics and are thus unsophisticated in economic matters. Some may have simplistic notions of how economies operate or may, in Keynes's terms, be slaves of the theories of defunct economists.[5] And yet there are some who may confuse their own personal interest with the public interest. In the latter case they would pursue policies that help them, their friends, their families or their political allies, but are not optimal for the country. Unfortunately examples of rent seeking or even of corruption on the part of policy makers are far from rare.

The role of the state is promoted by the policy makers: those who make the policy decisions. However there can be wide differences between the expectations based on those policies and the final outcomes. The reasons for these differences may be several. The decisions made 'upstream' by the policy makers must be implemented 'downstream' by the public administration or by other institutions. Principal–agents problems are common, especially when those who must implement the policies have objectives of their own or feel that they or the relevant group to which they belong will be hurt by these policies. Therefore, in the process of implementation, the policies may be changed or distorted and the final results may differ from the anticipated results.[6] This outcome occurs also when the public administration is, incompetent or corrupt. In these circumstances, the public employees, in a way, privatize to their benefit the use of some of the policy instruments.

Because many policies have long-lasting consequences, the role of the state at a given moment is much influenced by *past* policies in addition to being influenced by the theories of defunct economists. Policy decisions made by previous governments continue to determine, to a large extent, the current economic role of the state and constrain the actions of current governments. These past policy decisions often create a role for the state that is different from the one that the current policy makers might prefer. Legal, political or administrative constraints may significantly limit the power that the current government has to change economic policies. This is an important reason why ministers often agree with the need for some reform, but argue that it would be difficult or impossible to implement the reform at this time.

Examples of decisions with long-term consequences are those related to the size of the civil service, to whether enterprises are public or private, to the level of public sector salaries, to pension rights, to tenure in public jobs, to tax incentives and subsidies to particular groups or sectors, and so on.[7] These past decisions create legal or implicit entitlements or other claims that the current government may find difficult or impossible to change, especially in the short run. In some countries the interest on public debt and other hard-to-reduce spending, such as entitlements, account for three-quarters of total spending.[8] The reality is that no government has the freedom to start with a new slate or with a *tabula rasa*, so to speak, unaffected by past commitments.

Current economic policy is thus, to varying degrees, a slave of past governments' decisions, which often created particular policies. Those who are benefiting from these policies will oppose reforms even when these would be in the public interest. This is partly the reason why some economists have argued that authoritarian governments may be freer to pursue policies that are favorable to growth.[9] Current governments are often blamed for economic problems that were created largely by the policies of previous governments. In conclusion, the current economic role of the state must be seen as the outcome of present and past economic policy decisions and cannot be assumed to reflect the role *desired* by the current government.

That current role has been shaped partly or largely by historical developments. For example, in many industrial countries it has been influenced by their experience with the Great Depression, major wars and the threat of communism, all of which forced particular policies on past governments. In many developing countries, the economic role of the state has also been influenced by their experience as colonies of foreign powers. For example, in these countries, enterprises were nationalized partly because, at the time of independence, many large enterprises had been in the hands of individuals from the colonial powers.

Other factors may also be important, including (a) social attitudes, which may be determined by the cultural heritage or religion; (b) the level of economic development which, depending on the sophistication of the market and of private institutions, may call for more or less state intervention; (c) the degree of openness of the economy;[10] (d) technological developments, which may create or destroy natural monopolies or may create or increase the need to regulate certain new activities, such as financial markets, communication or transport; and (e) the quality of the public administration, which may impose limits on the scope of effective governmental intervention.[11]

A priori, it would appear that the less developed a country is, the more it could benefit from a larger government role that would supplement the market and correct its many imperfections. Some of these imperfections are the consequence of informational deficiencies, limited mobility of resources and excessive economic power in local markets on the part of some individuals. However it is also true that generally, though not always, the less developed a country is, the less able its public administration. As markets develop, they become more efficient and, for this reason, they require a less active normative role for the state. At the same time, the ability of the policy makers and of the public administration to deal with market deficiencies (and other problems that, at least in theory, could be solved by the government) can be assumed to rise. Also new markets that need to be regulated come into existence.

Finally, one of the unpleasant realities of economic development is that the very countries that would seem to have the greatest need for an expanded public sector role may be the same ones where the public sector is least prepared to play such a role *efficiently*. In these circumstances, when the policy makers attempt to pursue an ambitious public sector role, as they often do, the results tend to be disappointing.[12]

It is customary for economists and political scientists to assess the role of the state in the economy by measuring the ratio of tax revenue or government spending to gross domestic product (GDP). According to this criterion, the role of the state in the economy is much larger (on average, twice as large) in industrial countries than in developing countries. For example, such a ratio is almost five times as large in Sweden as in China. Knowledgeable observers would recognize that the reality is often different. They would be aware that, in recent decades, the public sectors of many developing countries, through regulatory policies, have played a much larger role than the governments of the industrial countries in allocating investment, credit, foreign exchange and economic resources in general.

In many countries permits or authorizations are necessary to engage in most economic activities.[13] In some cases *many* authorizations from various government agencies are required. As a consequence, in some countries, a large proportion of private enterprise managers' time is spent negotiating with officials.[14] This situation often gives government bureaucrats the power to delay or stop economic decisions on the part of private individuals and enterprises and, thus, it gives them the opportunity to demand payments for giving these permits or authorizations. The state has also played an extensive role in the direct production of goods and services.

EXPANSION OF GOVERNMENT ROLE IN THE 20TH CENTURY

The classical economists, from Adam Smith onward, favored a minimal role for the public sector. They generally preferred a role limited to the provision of essential public works, the maintenance of law and order, and the defense of the country. In their view, the government should guarantee property rights and the sanctity of contracts and should protect the economic and political liberties of individuals. These can be considered as *the core activities of the public sector*. This conservative attitude was partly a reaction to the widespread interference of governments with the working of the market, which had characterized 18th-century Europe. The classical economists considered this interference as damaging to economic activity and as an obstacle to growth. Perhaps as a consequence of this attitude and experience, in the 19th century the economic role of the government tended to be much more limited. For example, in most of the industrial countries, public spending was around 10 per cent of GDP and laissez-faire was the dominant economic philosophy.[15]

The 20th century saw a gradual but large expansion in the role of the state in the economy. Such expansion is particularly evident from data on the growth of public spending as a share of GDP. For the new industrialized countries that share grew, on average, from about 12 per cent in 1913 to about 45 per cent in 1995.[16] Both political and ideological factors contributed to this growth. Here we shall ignore the historical and political factors (such as wars and depressions) and focus on the changes in the prevalent attitude vis-à-vis what the state was expected to do. These changes in attitude were important and created the climate that made possible much of the government activism of recent decades.

Marxist and socialist thinking (which emphasized income equality among individuals) created strong pressures on the governments of the market economies to play a significant role in *redistributing income*. Such a role had not even been contemplated by the classical economists who had focused their attention on the allocative function of the state. The advent of communism in the former Soviet Union, and later in other Eastern European countries, and the attraction that central planning had for many intellectuals in the rest of the world, pushed many countries toward a 'mixed' economy. A mixed economy, of course, meant one with a large government role. Income redistribution came to be seen as a major, legitimate policy objective[17] that called for policies to reduce the income of the rich and to increase the income of the poor. Income taxation, with highly progressive rates, subsidies on basic commodities and welfare payments became common government policies. Such policies had not existed, or had been rare, in the past. The growth of public spending on education and health was also often justified in terms of its impact on income distribution.[18]

Keynesian thinking also created pressures on the government to help sustain the disposable income of individuals during cyclical fluctuations, to stabilize the economy. Public works programs and unemployment compensation, together with the expansion in the public sectors, and taxes with high built-in flexibility, were justified for this reason. Public pension schemes, often with redistributive features, and various forms of assistance to those whose income fell below certain levels were introduced in many countries. Public enterprises were used to maximize public employment. The goal was to build an economy with characteristics that reduced its exposure to fluctuations. Countries with large public sectors were believed to be less subject to business cycles. Finally Keynesian thinking was used to justify an expansion in the economic role of the public sector.

In addition to the impact of socialist and, more generally, Keynesian thinking on the policies pursued by the governments of many countries, technical developments in economics, especially after World War II, provided additional justifications for public sector intervention. For example, the concept of 'public good', which was made popular by influential economists such as Paul Samuelson and Richard Musgrave, justified the government provision of many goods with public goods characteristics, because it implied that without such intervention the market would undersupply such goods. The private sector would not have an incentive to produce public goods because of the difficulty of excluding from their consumption individuals who would not contribute to the cost of their production (the free riders).[19]

Closely related to public goods was the concept of 'externality'. The recognition that the consumption, or the production, of some goods may generate positive or negative externalities not reflected in the price of these goods created a further case of market failure requiring governmental intervention.[20] The government was expected to increase the private cost of producing or consuming goods with undesirable externalities and especially to decrease the cost of goods with desirable externalities. Externalities became often cited and politically exploited justifications for expanding the role of the public sector into health, education, research, transport, training and many other areas. Some authors even argued that welfare payments to the poor could be justified in terms of externalities such as the reduction of crime. The argument made was a familiar one: without governmental intervention, the market would underproduce or overproduce such goods depending on whether the externalities were good or bad. The government role could be played through subsidies to the private sector (given either directly or through tax incentives), through the public production of some goods, as in the case of health or education, or through regulations.[21]

In addition to the ideological factors mentioned earlier, which influenced the behavior of the governments of *all* countries, arguments of particular relevance for *developing* countries were also advanced. The earlier literature on economic development often assumed that governments had abilities lacking in the private sector. For example, one of the arguments used to justify the government's role in direct production activities (through public enterprises) was that managerial skills were lacking in the private sector but, somehow, they were available in the public sector. Another was that, because of their large scale, some activities or projects required amounts of capital, or a degree of expertise, that only the public sector could generate or assemble. Still another was that information essential for the successful conduct of some activities was more available, or was only available, to the public sector. This might be the result of 'rational ignorance' when, for individuals, the cost of getting information exceeds the benefit from it.

In the 1950s and 1960s, and especially in developing countries, it was often assumed that the government was the best judge in deciding which goods were 'essential' or 'necessary' and which were not. Therefore the government's judgement replaced that of the market.[22] Incentive legislation accorded favorable treatment (in taxation, the provision of credit, access to foreign exchange) to investments aimed at producing 'essential' or 'necessary' goods. It penalized the production or even prohibited the use of some resources (credit or foreign exchange) for the provision of 'non-essential' or luxury goods. In many countries high protection was provided for the domestic production of 'necessary' goods.

Paternalistic policies, which replace the preferences of the consumers with those of the policy makers, are still common in many countries as, for example, in industrial policy. The assumption is that the government has more knowledge than the private sector on how the market and the economy operate and what the citizens need most. Thus the government can pursue an industrial policy that picks future winners and provides them with 'temporary' protection or assistance. These infant industries are expected to be the giants of tomorrow.

The 1950s and 1960s, the golden age of public sector intervention, were influenced by some naive political perceptions of how governments operate. For example, it was implicitly, if not explicitly, assumed that:

1. the actions of the public sector were driven by the objective of promoting social welfare: rent seeking on the part of those who formulated the policies was assumed to be insignificant or non-existent. The literature on rent seeking appeared only in the 1970s,[23] and the literature on corruption and governance is mainly a product of the 1990s;
2. the public sector was monolithic and with a clear nerve center where all the important economic decisions were made in a rational and transpar-

ent way. Thus policies could not be inconsistent among them. For example, the policies pursued by the public enterprises or by other decentralized entities (such as local governments, stabilization boards and social security institutions) could not be at odds with those pursued by the central government; and, of course, within the central government, there was consistency in the policies promoted by the various ministries.[24] It is puzzling how little interest there was until the 1990s in issues of fiscal federalism and policy coordination *within* countries.[25]

Policies were assumed to be consistent not just in space but also in time. The political horizon of governments would be long enough to prevent current policies conflicting with future policies. Such conflicts can result either from mistakes or from political considerations (such as winning the next elections), that may lead governments to choose, in the short run, policies that are clearly inconsistent with long-run objectives. Once again the literature on the time inconsistency of economic policy is a product of recent years;[26]

3. policy decisions were reversible. Thus government employees could be dismissed when no longer needed, incentives could be removed when their objectives had been achieved or their implementation time had expired, entitlements could be ended, and so on. Recently governments have had to face the unpleasant reality that it is far easier to increase benefits (such as pensions) than to reduce them, or to hire civil servants than to fire them;

4. the policy makers had full control over the policy instruments. They could rely on honest and efficient public sector employees who would implement efficiently and objectively the policies decided at the top. The literature on corruption, principal–agents problems and rent seeking is relevant here and is once again a product of recent years.

Experience has shown that the romantic or idealized view of the way policy making is made and how it is carried out is, at times, far removed from reality.[27] The reality is that (a) public sectors are not monolithic but are characterized by several, or even many, policy-making centers which may not all be guided by the same concept of the public interest; (b) their policies may not be consistent in space or in time; (c) they may be influenced by rent seeking and by pressure groups; (d) those who make some of the policy decisions may be ignorant of the way the economy really works; (e) principal–agents problems may be prevalent; (f) actions may not be reversible; and (g) bureaucracies may be inefficient or corrupt, or both. They may distort the directives they receive from the policy makers, or use to their own advantage the instruments of economic policy. Intellectual developments in these areas have, in recent years, made many people wary or skeptical about the expanded role of the government and have set the stage for greater reliance on the market. These developments have been a frontal attack on the thinking that in earlier years had led to a large role for the public sector.[28]

The view that the government could be a solution to most problems is no longer as widely accepted as it was two or three decades ago. We now have the reality of several decades of expanded state intervention, so that expectations can be compared with results. The results from this experience have been disappointing in many countries, especially in developing countries. There is now ample evidence that *large* state intervention has not improved the allocation of resources, has not promoted a faster rate of growth, has not brought about a better distribution of income and has not provided a more stable economic environment.

Resources continue to be greatly misallocated, often as a direct result of government policies. Available evidence indicates that Gini coefficients and other measures of income inequality have not improved over time and are not much better in countries with large state intervention than in those with a more limited and more focused role for the public sector. Inflation, unemployment and macroeconomic disequilibria continue to affect many countries and, often, especially those with extensive state intervention. There is also ample evidence that the countries in which the role of the state has been more limited and better focused *have performed better*. The countries of South-east Asia, Chile and New Zealand are often mentioned in this context.

THE RETURN TO THE MARKET

In recent years there has been the beginning of a realization that the growth in governmental intervention in the market had been accompanied by *a dereliction of attention to the core activities of the state*.[29] Given the limited time and resources available to policy makers, as they became distracted and overwhelmed by the many responsibilities they had assumed, they were unable to dedicate to the core activities the resources, time, energy and attention that these activities required. Often the objective of equity was appealed to in order to justify the unproductive or questionable use of public resources. The end result was a deterioration in the quality of the basic services provided by the state. The state was doing more and more but doing it less and less well. This deterioration has had negative implications for the working of the market, which depends greatly on how well the state performs its core activities. The role of the state shifted over the years from one that supports or augments the market to one that competes with and thus replaces the market.

In many countries law and order, the most quintessential of the core activities of the state, suffered, thereby imposing large pecuniary or psychic costs on the population. Crime became a big problem, because the services of the police and of the courts were allowed to deteriorate owing to lack of resources or attention. Attempts were made to explain or justify crime on the basis of social conditions.

Disputes among citizens or between citizens and the state could not be solved expeditiously because, in many countries, access to justice became very expensive and the judicial system was on the verge of collapse. Judicial decisions were much delayed (sometimes for many years) and, when they finally came, they were seen by the relevant parties as capricious or unfair and lost much of their deterrent effect. The implementation of these judicial decisions was also capricious and much delayed. All these factors made access to the law highly unequal for different individuals and, inevitably, legal rights, including those related to property and contracts, became uncertain. The situation was not helped by the fact that the judicial systems of many countries became politicized and were susceptible to corruption.

In many countries obtaining basic documents or permits, such as passports, drivers' licenses or authorization to open shops or to import, may take months and/or the payment of some 'speed money'.[30] Governments often do not enforce contracts, thus creating doubts or uncertainties about property rights and encouraging some in ignoring the terms of contracts. This has destroyed or at least hurt some markets. In some countries the threshold costs of getting access to the justice system are so high as to discourage all but the better-off, thus creating unequal justice. A kind of bureaucratic cholesterol has thus clogged the arteries that energize the market economies.

In health, the provision of basic services, such as vaccinations and preventive services, suffered when the state extended its role into more complex and expensive areas, such as curative services provided in large, urban hospitals. Elementary education (a core activity) suffered when the state extended its role in the far more expensive higher education. The maintenance of the basic physical infrastructure suffered when the state became distracted by large investments and when it gave priority to investment expenditure over expenditure for operation and maintenance.[31]

In recent years there has been a universal rediscovery of the market, or at least a greater appreciation by policy makers and the public of the role that the market can play in the economy. As a consequence there has been a gradual reduction in governmental intervention and greater reliance on the *allocative role* of the market. The role of the government is changing from one that competes with the market to one that augments the market and improves its working. In a growing number of countries public enterprises are being privatized; quantitative restrictions on trade are being reduced or removed and import duties are being lowered, in some cases, lowered to very low levels, making trade more responsive to changes in relative prices; restrictions on the allocation of credit and controls on interest rates are being reduced or removed, restoring to the credit market its important allocative function; and price controls have become less popular and many other constraints on economic activities are being reduced.

All these actions are increasing the role of market forces and, *mutatis mutandis*, are limiting the scope of governmental intervention. Policy makers are slowly realizing that the government should not replace the market in allocating resources, but rather take actions that make it work better.

It is perhaps not a distortion of the truth to say that the governments of many countries, though not of all countries, would now like to see the state play a smaller role in the economy. However these governments are confronted by the legacy of past decisions and by the special interests of many groups that benefit from past decisions. These groups are often powerful enough to prevent, or at least to slow down, reform. As a consequence it may take several years before the role of the state can be brought in line with current thinking. What are the main changes that should take place? A full answer to this question would require far more pages and time than can be used here. However we can suggest a broad sketch of some of these changes, fully realizing that often the devil is in the detail and that some of the points made could benefit by much more nuance than is possible here.

It was mentioned earlier that the classical economists, even those who strongly believed in laissez-faire and in the sovereignty of the market, wanted the state to play a significant role focused on the core activities, such as essential public works, law and order – including the guarantee of property rights and the enforcement of contracts – and defense of the country. In these areas the state has simply not performed well. In some cases, the state has been the main violator of property rights and of contracts.[32] Thus a *reallocation of attention on the part of the policy makers to these core activities* would be highly beneficial to the market.

The process of *privatization of public enterprises* must continue and, in many countries, it must be accelerated. In a market economy there is little reason for the state to be directly involved in production activities. If, through privatization, the state can reduce the public sector wage bill and the subsidies it often pays to the public enterprises, as well as improve the efficiency of the economy, then privatization is a good policy. When interest rates on public sector debt are high and some debt can be repaid with the proceeds from privatization, then, from a fiscal point of view, privatization is an excellent policy.[33] Privatization, accompanied by the opening of the market, which in many sectors introduces competition, and accompanied by rules that prevent monopolies, will usually increase the efficiency of the economy. In time privatization will also reduce corruption, although the process can lead to a situation where corruption becomes a major issue.

The government must stop controlling prices, be they of traded goods, domestic goods or of specialized markets, such as financial and rental markets. Price controls always distort markets and create inefficiencies and rent seeking. The government must also stop subsidizing basic commodities; in several cases these subsidies have reduced the prices of some commodities or services to such an extent as to lead to excess demand and waste (for example, grain subsidies in the Middle East). This is an area where some of the most extreme examples of government-induced misallocation of resources have been reported.

The government must reduce its role in allocating investment and economic activities through incentives and/or regulations. It should focus on improving the efficiency of the market: (a) through the opening of the market to foreign competition; (b) through the elimination of unnecessary or inefficient economic regulations (whether the regulations of the government itself or of private groups, such as labor unions or professional associations);[34] (c) through the better provision and diffusion of information; and (d) through the establishment of efficient regulatory bodies that provide needed information to consumers and establish transparent rules of the game that are known to all and applied objectively to all market participants. The government can promote competitive behavior by leveling the playing field for all market participants by removing monopolies and monopolistic practices and by eliminating obstacles to entry to activities.

It may seem a bit odd that we are advocating the elimination of many existing regulations while calling for the establishment of regulatory bodies to set rules of the game. We do this because the economies of many countries are overburdened with useless and damaging regulations,[35] yet suffer from a dearth of controls or rules over some, especially the new, activities. Governments need to play an important role in regulating particular sectors, such as credit and capital markets, and certain industries, such as communication, transport, health and energy. There is a strong need for establishing the rules of the game for a market economy and to provide needed information for consumers, but there is no need to replace the market in allocative decisions except in extreme cases.

A brief digression on the use of regulations to pursue the objectives of public policy may help clarify the point made above. To varying degrees, regulations may be damaging and useless or useful and essential for a modern economy. A few examples of both are provided here.

1. Some regulations have no other purpose than to give power to the government and the bureaucrats charged with enforcing them. This is the case with the myriad of authorizations often imposed by local governments required to enter in legitimate activities, such as the opening of shops and factories.

2. Some regulations aim at achieving social objectives that could be achieved more efficiently in other ways. One example is rent control that is presumably established to subsidize housing for those with low incomes by implicitly taxing those who own houses.

3. Some regulations have purely social, and somewhat debatable, objectives, such as those that control working hours, minimum wages and length of working week.

4. Some regulations are necessary to allow activities to operate smoothly: for example, traffic regulations.

5. Some regulations aim at dealing with externalities until better and more flexible tools are available. For example, regulations are often used in environmental policies when the use of more efficient tools, such as taxes, is not yet feasible.

6. Finally, and this is the area of greatest interest to us, some regulations have the objective of protecting the public in a market economy, especially when the public is unable to get the information it needs to make rational choices. In a modern economy that produces many products or services of which most consumers have little knowledge there are reasons for an expansion of this type of regulation. When individuals step onto a plane, they want to be sure that it is as airworthy as it can be so that the possibility of the plane crashing is very small. Because plane crashes are rare events and are due to many causes, crashes cannot provide the ex ante information to travelers about the objective probability that the plane might crash. When individuals entrust their savings to a bank, they want to be sure that the bank is following sound investment practices. Because bank failures are rare events, bank failures cannot provide a guide for the depositors.[36] When individuals buy a medicine, they want to be sure that the medicine does not have dangerous side-effects; if it does, they want to be so informed. When they buy a product, such as meat, they want to be sure that it does not carry a disease. When individuals buy shares in a publicly traded company, they want to be sure that the value of the shares has not been manipulated and that the available information on the company is reliable.

    In all the above examples it would not be rational, because of the costs, for individuals to acquire on their own the knowledge to make rational decisions. Besides there is a public good element to that knowledge because, once available, it can be shared at zero cost with others. Thus the government must play a fundamental role in both regulating the activities and providing the necessary information for the public.

The above discussion of regulations to protect individuals raises a more general issue about the role of government in protecting individuals from various risks. In a recent paper, Devarajan and Hammer (1997) have argued that much of the difference in spending between developed and developing countries (a difference mostly explained by transfer payments) may be due to attempts by the governments of developed countries to protect citizens from various forms of risks such as unemployment, loss of income due to old age and sickness, and risks inherent to some economic activities. This raises the question of why markets, even in developed countries, cannot provide the institutions (insurances and so on) that would make it unnecessary for the government to enter this area.

Market failure in dealing with risk is often due to two reasons: *adverse selection* and *moral hazard*. Adverse selection results from asymmetric information between those who buy insurance and those who sell insurance. Normally those who buy it have more information than those who sell it; thus it is difficult to establish the ideal price for each individual. As a consequence markets do not develop fully, and the government is expected to intervene. Moral hazard is a consequence of the fact that insured individuals tend to be less careful than those who are not insured or may even precipitate the event for which they are insured, as with fire insurance.

The role of the government in protecting individuals from risk comes in three forms: government *spending, regulations and guarantees*. In some cases, as in the area of pensions, regulation may be an alternative to spending, for example, as the Chilean pension reform has shown.[37] This approach has been endorsed by the staff of the World Bank and by various economists. In this case the government passes a regulation that individuals must allocate a given share of their income to pensions bought from highly controlled private managers. Thus regulation replaces government spending. However regulations do not seem to work well in the health area where, within a country, the amount of money that individuals spend for health cannot be related to their income. Whether one is rich or poor, given medical procedures cost the same, so that an insurance scheme would generate highly differentiated health care. This is why the government continues to be heavily involved through public spending in the health sector.

Government guarantees have replaced government spending in various areas such as banking and, more and more, infrastructure. Especially in the latter, in recent years, there has been a trend towards privatization, at times accompanied by guarantees for investors provided by the government. In this way governments reduce their current spending and fiscal deficits, but at the cost of exposing themselves to potentially large costs in the future. As the guarantees are not shown as expenditures, they may at times create the illusion that government intervention and spending have fallen more than they have actually done.

The general role of the government in dealing with risks is an extremely difficult area in which major economists, including Arrow, Samuelson, Stiglitz and others, have made important contributions. The extent to which improvements in the private sector plus government regulation will be able to replace government spending remains an important development to watch. It is a development that will largely determine whether public spending as a share of GDP, especially in industrial countries, will fall in the future.

The government should rethink its role in income distribution. Broad and vague policies (such as general subsidies, price controls and higher spending for activities like education and health) that are justified on grounds that they benefit the poor should be questioned. These policies do not necessarily benefit the poor. If the government wants to help redistributing income, it will have to do it through well-focused and selective policies both on the expenditure and on the revenue side of the budget?[38] These policies should be designed so that they do not have significant disincentive effects or high administrative costs.[39]

Finally, in most countries, there is a great need for a reform of the public administration. It is within the public administrations that one finds extreme cases of unproductive spending. At times one is reminded of the Russian joke to the effect that, during central planning, the workers pretended to work and the government pretended to pay them. An efficient public administration must expect *all* workers to give a full day's work and must pay them a reasonable wage. There are too many public institutions that give realism to an observation attributed to Pareto: that in public institutions 20 per cent of the workforce performs 80 per cent of the useful work. The employment policies of governments in past decades, often justified on grounds of income distribution, produced large civil services with too many poorly paid workers. The efficient and core role of the public sector can be best promoted by a small and well-paid civil service that is made fully aware of its responsibilities and is penalized when it does not perform.

CONCLUDING REMARKS

This chapter has discussed the changing role of the state in the economy. It has described the forces that, over much of this century, led to an expansion of that role, and the reaction against that expansion, which started a few years ago and is continuing. That reaction is less the result of ideology than of the realization that not much welfare has been gained by the increased role of the state in recent decades. At the same time, many shortcomings associated with the expanded state role have been identified by scholars; their work, inevitably, has affected the way we now feel about the government's role.

There is the danger that the pendulum might swing too far, from a view that assigned to the state the solution of most problems, to one that maintains that the state is the problem. There is a clear, important role for the state to play. To echo Paul Valéry, if the state is weak we may perish.

At this time many economists and political scientists are thinking about the role of the state in a world where technology is making major strides and where the countries' economies are becoming more integrated. We know that in this world the role of the state will have to be different from what it was in the past, when economies were less developed and less open, technology was less advanced, and information was more difficult to obtain. In this new globalized world, the state will have to play a more significant and intelligent regulatory role; the private sector will have to carry a greater burden in areas that have traditionally been the responsibility of the governments, such as the provision of infrastructure and of services traditionally provided by public utilities, and in areas such as pensions, education and health.

Given the recent technological advances, even the traditional 'natural monopolies' may be exposed to some competition and may no longer provide an obvious justification for government intervention. For several 'natural monopolies' (railroads, power and communication) the part that is a genuine monopoly can be separated from the other activities of the traditional monopolies. For example, the generation and the distribution of electricity can be separated from the carrying of electricity, so that competition can be introduced in the former while monopoly is maintained in the latter. In some countries private investment is now playing a major role in several of these traditional monopolies.

In this brave new world, strict but intelligent public supervision of economic activity and clear rules of the game will be necessary. It remains to be seen whether governments will be able to rise to this new challenge. It also remains to be seen how national governments will behave in a world in which many economic decisions may be pushed down to local governments or up to international organizations.

Globalization and tax competition are likely to reduce the scope for redistributive policies, especially those promoted through progressive taxation. Tax competition will reduce the revenue of *central* governments much more than the revenue of local governments, because the latter generally rely on tax sources, such as property and business taxes, less exposed to tax competition. Globalization will reduce the scope for stabilization and redistributive policies by reducing the resources available to the national governments. At the same time the role of national governments in regulating activities will increase. This will involve a major change in the role of the government, especially that of the national government, in the economy.

This chapter concludes with a final comment on the role of the state in income redistribution and in providing safety nets. This issue was only touched upon in this chapter, which mentioned that: (a) classical economists did not recognize income redistribution as a legitimate governmental function and (b) many inefficient policies were pursued in recent decades under the justification of redistributing income.[40] Under proper conditions, markets are very good at allocating resources. They are not very good at generating a distribution of income that reflects the conscience or the prevalent view of society. Therefore the government cannot abdicate this role even though it is indeed a difficult one and will become more difficult because of globalization and tax competition. It must, instead, pursue this role differently from the way it did in the past. It must learn how to make redistributive policies efficient and well directed. And it must not forget that growth is the best medicine for curing the disease of absolute poverty and for providing productive jobs.

NOTES

1. This chapter was presented at a conference on 'Decentralisation, Inter-governmental Fiscal Relations and Macroeconomic Governance', organized by the Advanced School of Public Administration (ESAF) of the Ministry of Finance of Brazil and the OECD Development Centre, held in Brasilia on 16–17 June, 1997. An earlier and shorter version of the paper was presented in March 1997 at a seminar on 'The Role of the State in a Changing Arab Economic Environment', held at the Arab Fund for Economic and Social Development in Kuwait.
2. Cited in Bardhan (1996), p. 11.
3. Whether such a summation is theoretically feasible is an open question. See on this the seminal work by Arrow (1963) and subsequent related literature.
4. Problems may arise also when the nature of the issue requires paying attention to different generations. This is the case with environment, public debt and public pensions. How should the interests of future generations be taken into account? Different but related issues arise in connection with individuals who are not citizens of the countries in which they live. Should the state reflect only the views of the citizens or, even, of the voters?
5. It is not necessary for political leaders to have advanced economic training themselves; however they need to have the sophistication to choose competent economic advisors and to distinguish between good and bad economic advice.
6. A common example is tax reform, where the actual drafting of the laws (which is supposed just to give concrete content to the decisions made) can bring many surprises. Sometimes the basic intent of the legislation is largely neutralized by some innocent-looking clause. At other times the drafting is fine but the tax administration renders the law ineffective by not making the administrative changes necessary to implement the law effectively. For a discussion of some of these issues, see Tanzi (1994a).
7. The current difficulties that many industrial countries and some developing countries, such as Brazil, are having in reforming pension laws or in scaling down the welfare state are good examples of such decisions.
8. See especially Steuerle and Kawai (1996, Part Two, chs 5–7).
9. Chile, under General Pinochet, China in the past two decades, and some South-east Asian countries are assumed to provide examples of economies that have prospered under authoritarian governments able to push growth-promoting policies.
10. In a recent paper, Dani Rodrik argued that more open economies need and have larger public sectors because they are inherently more unstable. See Rodrik (1996).
11. The normative role of the state requires and assumes that public administrations exhibit ideal Weberian characteristics. See Tanzi (1994b).
12. For example, in poor countries, not only is the public administration less skilled, but the

government's ability to raise taxes is much more limited. In these countries the government's more ambitious role is normally played through a greater use of quasi-fiscal regulations. See Tanzi (1995b). These quasi-fiscal regulations replace taxing and spending and often give rise to problems of governance and corruption.

13. De Soto (1989) reported that 11 basic steps were required in Peru in the 1980s to set up a small firm. It has been reported that in Tanzania it took 28 essential steps to get approval for medium and large investment projects.

14. According to a World Bank study (1995), in Morocco it takes as many as 20 documents to register a business; in Egypt 90 per cent of an entrepreneur's time is spent resolving problems with regulatory agencies; and in Lebanon it takes 18 signatures to clear goods from customs. In Ecuador, at one time, it took no less than 30 documents to apply for a tax incentive. See Tanzi (1969, p. 228) For the time spent by managers negotiating with public officials, see World Bank (1997), p. 43, Fig. 3.2.

15. See Tanzi and Schuknecht (1997).

16. It is likely that there was also a gradual growth in economic regulations, although there are no statistics to back this view.

17. In some ways, it became the dominating objective in many countries.

18. Here one should make a distinction between the rhetoric and the reality of income redistribution. Often the impact of governmental action in redistributing income towards the poor was much more modest than one would assume from the rhetoric. The reason was that social spending was often largely appropriated by the middle classes. See Tanzi (1974) and Alesina (1998).

19. See Samuelson (1954) and Musgrave (1959).

20. Externalities had been recognized for a long time, as for example by Pigou. However it was only in the post-World War II era that they became a major justification for public sector intervention. James Buchanan has often argued that externalities were politicized to justify larger governmental intervention.

21. In more recent years this argument has come under attack, in part as a consequence of the work of Ronald Coase, who received the Nobel Prize for it (see Coase, 1960). Coase argued that in a market economy free arrangements among individuals would internalize the effects of externalities and thus lead to an optimum without the need for governmental intervention. Public choice literature has emphasized that, while externalities create market failures, governmental intervention is often characterized by political failure which results from rent seeking. Thus market failure does not necessarily justify governmental intervention.

22. This was a departure from the individualistic view of the public interest, as mentioned earlier. When the government assigns to itself the right to judge the merit of goods, it is behaving in an authoritarian fashion. The concept of 'merit good' proposed by Musgrave reflects, in some way, the same assumption, although Musgrave would never support an authoritarian government.

23. See Tullock (1967); and Krueger (1974). See also Tullock (1989).

24. For examples of inconsistent or uncoordinated policies within the United States government, see Krueger (1993). An extreme example for the United States is provided by the subsidies given to the production of tobacco at the same time as the government was trying to discourage smoking.

25. For examples of inconsistent policies between the central government and the local governments, see Tanzi (1995a).

26. See Calvo (1978).

27. The extreme version of this romantic view is implicit in the work of Tinbergen (1952) and Johansen (1965). Tinbergen's work was very influential in the 1950s and 1960s.

28. The role of the public sector in stabilizing the economy was also subjected to sharp criticism especially in the 1970s by Robert Lucas, Robert Barro and economists associated with the rational expectation school.

29. The 1997 World Development Report of the World Bank elaborates on this theme.

30. In some countries individuals who act as 'facilitators' or go-betweens have come into existence, adding to the transaction costs of operating in certain areas.

31. In many countries a larger public sector workforce has been bought at the cost of low wages. This in turn is likely to have stimulated corruption on the part of the civil service. For empirical support for this intuitive conclusion, see van Rijckeghem and Weder (1997).
32. For example, rent control laws have violated the property rights of owners of houses. Government arrears in payments have violated the sanctity of contractual obligations.
33. In fact, in many cases, this is the best use of the proceeds from privatization. In the process of privatization, a problem has been present. To set the highest price from the privatization of a public enterprise the government should let the enterprise retain some monopoly power, although this would reduce the efficiency of the economy. A government that is much interested in maximizing present revenue is likely to allow the privatized enterprises to retain some monopoly power.
34. Restrictions to competition through regulations imposed by professional associations are common. They have not received the attention that they deserve. They create rents for those who are already members of these associations and unemployment for those who are not.
35. In many cases this policy discourages the building of new houses and the renting of existing houses and, when maintained over the long run, it ends up taxing some poorer people while subsidizing some richer ones.
36. Whether the government should also provide some guarantees (for example, for bank deposits) is a difficult issue that cannot be addressed here. Issues of moral hazard become relevant in this context.
37. For an analysis of Chile's pension reform, see Holzmann (1997).
38. Some conservative writers, such as James Buchanan, argue that the government should pursue only policies that affect everyone equally. They rule out selective policies and thus active, redistributive policies. See Buchanan (1997).
39. In the past, natural monopolies often played some redistributive or nation-building role by providing some of their services at reduced prices to poorer families and to faraway places. The privatization of the railroad in Argentina, for example, has left some rural and faraway places without the services of the trains. With privatization a decision must be made whether to preserve this role through the use of other policy instruments.
40. Because of their inefficient policies, it can be argued that the limited redistribution that has taken place has been achieved at a very high cost.

BIBLIOGRAPHY

Alesina, Alberto (1998), 'The Political Economy of Macroeconomic Stabilization and Income Inequality: Myths and Reality', in Vito Tanzi and Ke-young Chu (eds), *Income Distribution and High-Quality Growth*, Cambridge, Mass.: MIT Press, pp. 299–326.

Arrow, Kenneth Joseph (1963), *Social Choice and Individual Values*, 2nd edn, New York: Wiley.

Bardhan, Pranab (1996), 'The Nature of Institutional Impediments to Economic Development', Center for International and Development Economics Research, Working Paper No. C96-066, Berkeley: University of California, pp. 1–31.

Buchanan, James (1997), 'The Fiscal Crises in Welfare Democracies with Some Implications for Public Investment', paper presented at the IIPF Congress, Kyoto, Japan (August).

Calvo, Guillermo (1978), 'On the Time Consistence of Optimal Policy in a Monetary Economy', *Econometrica*, 46 (November), 1411–28.

Coase, Ronald (1960), 'The Problem of Social Cost', *Journal of Law and Economics*, 3 (October), 1–44.

de Soto, Hernando (1989), *The Other Path: The Invisible Revolution in the Third World*, New York: Harper & Row.

Devarajan, Shantayanan and Jeffrey S. Hammer (1997), 'Public Expenditure and Risk Reduction', paper presented at the IIPF Congress, Kyoto, Japan (August).

Holzmann, Robert (1997), 'Pension Reform, Financial Market Development and Economic Growth: Preliminary Evidence from Chile', *IMF Staff Papers*, 44(2) (June).

Johansen, Leif (1965), *Public Economics*, Amsterdam: North-Holland.

Krueger, Anne O. (1974), 'The Political Economy of the Rent-Seeking Society', *The American Economic Review*, 64(3) (June), 291–303.

—— (1993), *Economic Policies at Cross Purposes: The United States and Developing Countries*, Washington, DC: The Brookings Institution.

Musgrave, Richard A. (1959), *The Theory of Public Finance: A Study in Public Economy*, New York: MeGraw-Hill.

Rodrik, Dani (1996), 'Why Do More Open Economies Have Bigger Governments?', *Discussion Paper Series*, no. 1386, London: Centre for Economic Policy Research, May.

Samuelson, Paul A. (1954), 'The Pure Theory of Public Expenditure', *Review of Economics and Statistics*, 36 (November), 387–9.

Steuerle, C. Eugene and Masahiro Kawai (eds) (1996), *The New World Fiscal Order: Implications for Industrialized Nations*, Washington, DC: The Urban Institute Press.

Tanzi, Vito, (1969), 'Tax Incentives and Economic Development: The Ecuadorian Experience', *Finanzarchiv*, 28 (March), 226–35.

—— (1974), 'Redistributing Income through the Budget in Latin America', *Banca Nazionale del Lavoro Quarterly Review*, 108 (March), 65–87.

—— (1994a), 'The Political Economy of Fiscal Deficit Reduction', in William Easterly, Carlos Alfredo Rodriguez and Klaus Schmidt-Hebbel (eds), *Public Sector Deficits and Macroeconomic Performance*, New York: Oxford University Press, for the World Bank, pp. 513–24.

—— (1994b), 'Corruption, Governmental Activities and Markets', IMF Working Paper, WP/94/99 (August); published as 'Corruption, Arm's Length Relationships and Markets' in Gianluca Fiorentini and Sam Peltzman (eds), *The Economics of Organised Crime*, Cambridge: Cambridge University Press, 1995, pp. 161–80.

—— (1995a), 'Fiscal Federalism and Decentralization: A Review of Some Efficiency and Macroeconomic Aspects', in Michael Bruno and Boris Pleskovic (eds), *Annual World Bank Conference on Development Economics*, Washington DC: World Bank, pp. 295–316.

—— (1995b), 'Government Role and the Efficiency of Policy Instruments', IMF Working Paper, WP/95/100 (October), and in Peter Birch Sorensen (ed.), *Public Finance in a Changing World*, London and New York: Macmillan, 1998, pp. 51–69.

Tanzi, Vito and Ludger Schuknecht (1997), 'Reconsidering the Fiscal Role of Government: The International Perspective', *The American Economic Review*, 87(2) (May), 164–8.

Tinbergen, Jan (1952), *On the Theory of Economic Policy*, Amsterdam: North-Holland.

Tullock Gordon (1967), 'The Welfare Costs of Tariffs, Monopolies and Theft', *Western Economic Journal* (June), 224–32.

—— (1989), *The Economics of Special Privilege and Rent-Seeking*, Boston: Kluwer Academic Publishers.

Van Rijckeghem, Caroline and Beatrice Weder (1997), 'Corruption and the Rate of

Temptation: Do Low Wages in the Civil Service Cause Corruption?', IMF Working Paper, WP/97/73 (June).

World Bank (1995), *Claiming the Future: Choosing Prosperity in the Middle East and North Africa*, Washington, DC: World Bank.

—— (1997), *World Development Report: The State in a Changing World*, New York: Oxford University Press, for the World Bank.

3. Government role and the efficiency of policy instruments[1]

CURRENT DEBATE ON THE ROLE OF GOVERNMENT

For the past several years, a raging debate has been going on about the role that the public sector should play in the contemporary world. The collapse of the centrally planned economies and the real, or alleged, failures of the welfare state in mixed economies have brought about an in-depth re-evaluation of that role in an environment that is much more pro-market than was the case in recent decades. Perhaps, at no other time has so much attention been paid, by economists, political scientists and policy makers, to what the government should do.

In this largely normative debate, some economists argue in favor of a minimalist state, in which the government should have very limited functions essentially justified by the narrow application of economic arguments related to market failure such as the existence of externalities, public goods, monopolies and informational deficiencies. These economists reveal much faith in the market and little faith in the actions of the government. Others argue that the retreat of the state from many activities, and a more timid role for it, would lead to many problems, such as the growing incidence of crime (and especially of organized crime), the growth of poverty, a progressively less even income distribution, and so forth. They justify a larger government role by having recourse to the Musgravian functions, such as allocation of resources, when the market fails to do so optimally, the redistribution of income, when the market generates a distribution that is not considered fair by society, and the stabilization of economic activities, when the automatic working of the market leads to economic instability accompanied by unemployment, inflation and balance of payments disequilibrium.

In modern and complex societies the objectives pursued by the government have become broader and more difficult to define. For example, it is now better recognized that the private sector may fail to allocate resources optimally not just at a moment in time, but intertemporally, thus justifying public sector intervention vis-à-vis many new areas that involve different periods such as the environment, research and pensions. The distribution of income has also acquired more facets as governmental intervention has been justified not just by the uneven size distribution of income but, with increasing frequency, by income differences which may arise because of gender, age and ethnic, regional and physical characteristics of individuals. Even the stabilization

Table 3.1   The growth of government expenditure, 1870–1990 (percentage of GDP)

	Late 19th century About 1870[1]	Pre-World War I About 1913[1]	Post-World War I About 1920[1]	Pre-World War II About 1937[1]	Post-World War II		
					1960	1980	1990
Austria	—	—	14.7	15.2	35.7	48.1	48.6
Belgium	—	—	—	21.8	30.3	58.6	55.5
Canada	—	—	13.3	18.6	28.6	38.8	45.8
France	12.6	17.0	27.6	29.0	34.6	46.1	49.8
Germany	10.0	14.8	25.0	42.4	32.4	47.9	45.7
Italy	11.9	11.1	22.5	24.5	30.1	41.9	53.2
Japan	8.8	8.3	14.8	25.4	17.5	32.0	31.7
Netherlands	9.1	9.0	13.5	19.0	33.7	55.2	54.0
Norway	3.7	8.3	13.7	—	29.9	37.5	53.8
Spain	—	8.3	9.3	18.4	18.8	32.2	41.8
Sweden	5.7	6.3	8.1	10.4	31.0	60.1	59.1
Switzerland	—	2.7	4.6	6.1	17.2	32.8	30.7
United Kingdom	9.4	12.7	26.2	30.0	32.2	43.0	39.9
United States	3.9	1.8	7.0	8.6	27.0	31.8	33.3
Average	8.3	9.1	15.4	18.3[2]	28.5	43.3	45.9
Australia	—	—	—	—	21.2	31.6	34.5
Ireland	—	—	—	—	28.0	48.9	41.0
New Zealand[3]	—	—	—	—	26.9	38.1	44.0
Average	—	—	—	—	25.4	39.5	39.8
Total average	8.3	9.1	15.4	20.7	27.9	42.6	44.8

Notes:
1. Or nearest available year after 1870, before 1913, after 1920 and before 1937.
2. Average computed without Germany, Japan and Spain (all undergoing war or war preparations at this time).
3. GFS data; data available for '1960' is 1970.

Sources: European Commission, *Tables on General Government Data*, 1995; *OECD Economic Outlook*, 1994 and 1995; Vito Tanzi and Domenico Fanizza, 'Fiscal Deficit and Public Debt in Industrial Countries, 1970–94', WP/95/49, May 1995; B.R. Mitchell, 'International Historical Statistics' (various issues); Acha Hernandez, 'Datos Basicos para la Historia Financiera de España', 1976; Bureau of Census, 'Historical Statistics of the U.S.A.', 1975; IMF, *Government Finance Statistics*; IMF, *World Economic Outlook*. Table reproduced from Vito Tanzi and Ludger Schuknecht, 'The Growth of Government and the Reform of the State', (IMF Working Paper, 1995, IMF WP95/130).

function has become more multidimensional and, now, it may relate to output, employment, price level, balance of payment, public debt, level of public spending and level of taxation.

A quantitative impression of what a minimalist state might imply in terms of the level of public spending is provided by the historical statistics, for the 1870–1913 period, shown in Table 3.1. It will be seen that government expenditure, as a share of GDP, was much lower a century ago than in later years. These low shares of public spending in GDP were not exhibited by primitive societies but by societies that were quite advanced and sophisticated. However, in that period the state did not engage in activities such as higher education, provision of health services, social security and public welfare on a mass scale, unemployment compensation, and many others that are now common.

An impression of the level of expenditure needed by an extended role of the public sector is provided by statistics for recent years, especially for the so-called 'welfare states' among the industrial countries. Table 3.1 provides these statistics. It win be seen that, for some countries, total public spending has exceeded 50 per cent of GDP and has even approached or exceeded 60 per cent of GDP. For the group of countries reported in Table 3.1, public spending, as a share of GDP, grew from an average of around 10 per cent at the beginning of the century to 45 per cent in recent years.[2] These data refer to market-oriented industrial countries. In the centrally planned economies that characterized Eastern Europe, the role of the state was even more extended.

THE 'EFFICIENCY' OF POLICY INSTRUMENTS

The economic discussion on the role of the state has been conducted in terms of market failure, emphasized by those who wished to justify a larger role; or, in terms of government failure, emphasized by those who wished to limit that role (see Stiglitz, 1995). Among the latter, a particularly influential group has been that associated with the public choice school. The components of this group have shown how rent seeking by special interests and other bureaucratic behavior lead to the growth of government expenditure and to the failure of public policy in achieving its stated objectives.[3] (See Mueller, 1989.) In the public sector, principal-agent problems are common and the difficulty of writing precise but not excessively *constraining contracts* or instructions for the behavior of agents acting on behalf of the public sector leads to results that are often at odd with the objectives of the policymakers. In many countries, corruption on the part of some public officials adds to the problem. (See chapter 8 of the book.)

In this chapter, I wish to focus on a different aspect of the role of government, an aspect that is related neither to traditional market failure nor to government failure in the public choice sense. This aspect has been largely ignored in the literature and especially in the public finance literature. It relates to the gap that often exists between government goals and the availability of fiscal instruments necessary to pursue those goals and how governments react to that gap. Because the policy instruments are the vehicles that must implement, or are supposed to implement, the intentions of the policy makers, when these instruments are not available or are not efficient, difficulties may arise.[4] When this gap exists, there are two possibilities: either the policy makers give up the pursuit of some of their objectives or, at least, they modify their objectives to make them consistent with the available instruments; or they continue to pursue the same objectives but they do so through reliance on less efficient instruments.

Unfortunately the second possibility seems to be common, thus resulting in poor economic policy and in a more confused role of the state. The final results from governmental action are, thus, often different from the intended results. In this context the 'efficiency' of a policy instrument is defined à la Tinbergen: an instrument is efficient when a modest change in it brings about a significant change in the policy objective pursued through the use of that instrument. (See Johansen, 1965, pp. 12–14.) It is thus not the usual allocative definition of efficiency.

Economists and political scientists generally associate the scope and the importance of the public sector (or, putting it differently, the role of the government) with the share of public spending or tax revenue in national income. Public finance courses deal with taxing and spending and ignore monetary or foreign trade policy because the latter is not supposed to deal with *fiscal* objectives. Also these courses generally do not discuss regulations.[5] The implicit assumption is that those objectives can only be pursued through tax and public expenditure instruments. The higher the level of taxation or of public spending, the greater the role of the government in the economy is assumed to be. On this assumption the government plays a much larger role in Sweden than in Japan and in industrial countries than in developing countries. Those who wish to impose constitutional limits on the level of taxation ought to be pleased with its level in developing countries.

Developing countries are generally characterized by (a) an income distribution that is less even than in industrial countries;[6] (b) less stable macroeconomic developments, as measured by fluctuations in output, prices or balances of payments outcomes; and (c) more pervasive market failure due to lack of information, prevalence of monopoly or monopolistic practices, and externalities of various kinds.[7]

While the evidence available points to a greater *need* for governmental action in developing countries as compared with industrial countries, it is the latter that exhibit a much larger role for the government when that role is measured by levels of taxation and public spending: on the average, the level of taxation and of public spending, measured as a share of GDP, is at least twice as large in industrial countries as in developing countries. As pointed out above, this difference cannot be explained by a lower need for public sector intervention in developing countries. It is, rather, explained by these countries' difficulties in raising tax revenue. For a variety of reasons, which cannot be discussed here, the developing countries are far less successful at collecting taxes than the industrial countries. Does this mean that the policy makers of the developing countries scale down their policy objectives to reflect this reality? An argument will be made in the next section that, often, governments that cannot raise a desired level of tax revenue do not scale down their role in the economy but, rather, they attempt to pursue that role through non-fiscal instruments. Thus the role of the government is not reduced, but the way in which that role is pursued is changed. These other instruments are largely, but not exclusively, *quasi-fiscal activities and quasi-fiscal regulations*. These are activities not connected with the budget but which can have effects broadly similar to those of fiscal actions.

Quasi-fiscal activities and regulations have also been important in industrial countries when the desire to maintain a larger role for the government has collided with the reality of inadequate tax revenue. In some cases, as for example in Italy for much of the 1970s and part of the 1980s, this led to the creation of quasi-fiscal activities within the financial system which allowed the government to finance more cheaply its public debt. (See Bruni et al., 1989.) In other cases, such as the United States in the 1980s, this led to the use of quasi-fiscal regulations often referred to as unfunded mandates to local governments and to private enterprises. In general one finds that these quasi-fiscal activities tend to be used more by the less advanced industrial countries.

THE IMPORTANCE OF QUASI-FISCAL ACTIVITIES AND REGULATIONS

If a government wanted to encourage an economic activity, it would normally be best if it did it through a subsidy to that activity given through the budget. If a government wanted to discourage an economic activity, it would be best if it did it through a tax. This is the standard Pigouvian way of dealing with both positive and negative externalities. In reality, however, and especially in developing countries, the economic encouragement or discouragement of certain activities is often not done through the budget but through other means, mainly quasi-fiscal activities or quasi-fiscal regulations.[8] These are *fiscal* actions carried through non-fiscal instruments. They are thus *outside* the budget, replacing the spending–taxing function of the budget.

In a well working market economy, regulations should be limited to helping define the rules of the game and to protecting the citizens against particular risks. Thus the government could regulate the merger of firms, to maintain competition; it could require child vaccination, to ensure good health; it could regulate the distribution of pharmaceutical products for the same reason; it could determine traffic rules and require driver's licenses to ensure traffic safety; it could regulate banks and insurance companies to protect their customers against unwarranted behavior by those who run those institutions, and so on. Within limits, these are considered legitimate regulatory activities on the part of the public sector. They would not be considered quasi-fiscal regulations. The function of a driver's license or of traffic regulations cannot be replaced by a tax and a subsidy.

Quasi-fiscal Regulations

Assume, however, that the government wants to help poor families by subsidizing the rental cost of their lodgings.[9] It could do it with an explicit subsidy to the relevant families given through the budget and financed through taxation. Without discussing the merit of this policy, this would be a normal use of the taxing–spending instruments of governments. Now assume further that the tax or other ordinary resources of the government are limited, but that the government still wants to pursue its objective of subsidizing the rental expenditures of poor families. A quasi-fiscal regulation that will broadly promote this objective is rent controls. Rent controls are equivalent to a policy that subsidizes the rentees and taxes the rentors.[10] In other words, rent controls replace the function of the budget and thus reduce the level of taxation and the level of spending while still broadly pursuing the government objectives. The fact that the end result of this governmental action is likely to be less efficient in terms of the objective sought than if it were done through the budget is part of our story, but it does not change the reality that rent controls are substitutes for actions that could be taken through the budget. There are many other examples of quasi-fiscal regulations, from zoning laws to uncompensated and obligatory military service.

Quasi-fiscal Activities through the Foreign Exchange System

Assume that a country exports coffee and imports medicines and that the government wants to subsidize the use of medicines by taxing the coffee producers. A conventional, though not economically efficient governmental policy[11] would be to tax the exporters of coffee, thus raising the level of taxation, and to subsidize the importers of medicines, thus raising the level of public spending. However the government may have difficulties (administratively or politically) in pursuing this course of action. An administratively or politically easier alternative is to use the exchange rate mechanism to promote the same social objective by using appreciated exchange rates for the import of medicines and for the export of coffee.[12] The government compels the coffee exporters to sell to the central bank their foreign exchange earnings for which they receive a smaller amount (in domestic currency) than they would have received if they had been free to sell their foreign exchange in the market. The government then sells this foreign exchange (also at an appreciated rate) to the importers of medicines, who buy their medicines more cheaply (in domestic currency). Once again, taxing (the coffee producers) and subsidizing (the users of medicines) has taken place without an apparent effect on the level of taxation and on the level of public spending. The unwary observer, who used the conventional data on taxing and spending, would conclude that the role of the government in that country is more limited than it actually is.

The above example can be extended to the export of other agricultural products and, especially, to the export of mineral products. In each case the exporters are forced to yield to the government, at an overvalued exchange rate, the foreign exchange that they earn.[13] Thus, de facto, these exporters are being taxed sometimes at very high rates. When the foreign exchange is provided for the importers of particular products, also at an overvalued exchange rate, the net result is similar to that of a budgetary subsidy to the goods that use this exchange rate for imports. Multiple exchange rate regimes are very common (see IMF, 1994). Depending on the coverage of the special rates, the quasi-fiscal taxes and subsidies they entail can be substantial.

Quantitative import restrictions are also often used by many countries. These also provide implicit subsidies to some groups and implicit taxes to others. However it is often difficult to quantify these effects.

Quasi-fiscal Activities through the Financial System

Quasi-fiscal activities are often carried out through the financial system and can take many forms, but they all result in the implicit taxation of some groups (depositors, holders of cash) and in the implicit subsidy of other groups (borrowers, banks with problem loans, government). In no case do they not result in explicit tax revenue or public spending. They thus lead to lower ratios of taxes or public spending in GDP. A comprehensive analysis of this aspect is not possible here.[14] We limit ourselves to a few examples.

In some cases the financial institutions are required to lend to enterprises or to the government at below market interest rates.[15] Or some financial institutions can benefit from preferential rediscounting practices with the central bank and can thus pass on an implicit subsidy to those who borrow from them. Or highly risky borrowers can get the loans at an interest rate that does not reflect the risk. Or some borrowers can borrow at a risk-free rate because the government (or some part of it, such as the central bank) guarantees the loans. In still other cases the government gets subsidized credit by forcing banks to hold uncompensated or undercompensated high reserve requirements at the central bank. In most cases 'controls on international capital flows [are] coupled with controls on domestic financial intermediaries' (Giovannini and De Melo, 1993, p. 953). These controls result in 'financial repression' which is a form of implicit taxation.

We have provided examples of governmental activities that are common especially among developing countries and economies in transition and that result in implicit taxation. This taxation is at times accompanied by implicit subsidies to particular groups, while in other cases it is for the benefit of the government that can thus pursue some of its objectives without raising explicit taxes. Inflationary finance, that is, the direct lending by the central bank to the government, is an example of a quasi-fiscal operation that is mainly an implicit tax (on holders of cash) collected by the government. Up to a certain point, the revenue from this tax increases with the level of inflation.

In the next section, we provide available quantitative estimates of *some* of these activities. These are by no means all the channels through which what are essentially fiscal objectives of the government are pursued through the use of non-fiscal instruments. In some ways, what we have shown is just the tip of the iceberg.

SOME QUANTIFICATION

The previous section provided examples of quasi-fiscal activities and quasi-fiscal regulations that can proxy for the spending and taxing actions of the government. We have argued that these activities and regulations allow the government to play a larger role without having to raise taxes or spend more. We have no way of quantifying all of these quasi-fiscal activities or the quasi-fiscal regulations. If we could, we would attempt to answer the question: by how much would the tax level and the spending level have to rise to replace the implicit taxes and subsidies with conventional or explicit taxes and government spending? Yet some idea of the dimensions involved can be obtained from the analysis of a few specific quasi-fiscal activities. Here we report some available estimates.

Giovannini and De Melo (1993) have estimated the implicit taxes that the governments of various countries obtained from 'controls on international capital flows coupled with controls on domestic financial intermediaries' (p. 953). These controls allow governments to finance themselves at artificially low interest rates. These authors emphasize that their estimates are minimum estimates because they limit their calculations to the interest that the government saves on servicing its debt. They are thus likely to substantially underestimate the true scope of quasi-fiscal 'revenue' from the financial sector.

Table 3.2 reports these estimates for 24 countries. The table shows that revenue from financial repression can be very high both as shares of GDP and

Table 3.2   The size of revenue from financial repression

Country	Sample	Percentage of GDP	Percentage of tax revenue
Algeria	1971–1987	4.30	11.42
Brazil	1983–1987	0.48	1.57
Colombia	1980–1984	0.24	2.11
Costa Rica	1972–1984	2.33	12.76
Greece	1974–1985	2.53	7.76
India	1980–1985	2.86	22.38
Indonesia	1976–1986	0.00	0.00
Jamaica	1980, 1982	1.38	4.74
Jordan	1978–1987	0.60	2.40
Korea	1975–1987	0.25	1.36
Malaysia	1974–1981	0.12	0.31
Mexico	1984–1987	5.77	39.65
Morocco	1977–1985	2.31	8.89
Pakistan	1982–1983	3.23	20.50
Panama	1977–1987	0.69	2.49
Papua New Guinea	1981–1987	0.40	1.90
Philippines	1975–1986	0.45	3.88
Portugal	1978–1986	2.22	6.93
Sri Lanka	1981–1983	3.40	19.24
Thailand	1976–1986	0.38	2.57
Tunisia	1978–1987	1.49	4.79
Turkey	1980–1987	2.20	10.89
Zaire	1974–1986*	0.46	2.48
Zimbabwe	1981–1986	5.50	19.13

Note: The sample for Zaire does not include the years 1981, 1982 and 1983.

Source: Giovannini and De Melo (1993), p. 959.

Table 3.3   Seigniorage revenue in 26 developing countries, 1984

Country	Percentage of GNP	Percentage of government current revenue
Algeria	1.6	n.a.
Argentina	7.4	46.5
Brazil[1]	2.5	9.1
Chile	0.9	2.7
Côte d'Ivoire	0.4	1.5
Egypt	7.5	16.7
Ghana[1]	0.7	6.2
Greece	3.1	8.7
India	1.0	7.6
Indonesia	0.7	6.2
Korea[2]	0.1	1.4
Malaysia[2]	0.1	0.5
Mexico	7.2	41.9
Morocco	1.7	6.8
Nigeria[2]	0.9	5.1
Pakistan[3]	0.5	2.6
Peru[1]	8.7	58.0
Philippines	2.4	22.1
Portugal	5.3	14.6
Sri Lanka[3]	0.8	3.4
Tanzania[4]	3.1	18.6
Thailand[2]	0.2	1.3
Turkey[2]	2.6	13.9
Venezuela	1.5	5.7
Yugoslavia	9.8	132.8
Zaire[3]	3.0	16.1

Notes:
[1]   1985.
[2]   1986.
[3]   1987.
[4]   Seigniorage, 1985.

Source: IMF, *International Financial Statistics*; World Bank, *World Tables 1989–90*: *Socio-economic Time-series Access and Retrieval System, Version 1.0* (Washington, DC: *World Bank*, March 1990). Taken from Fry (1993), p. 11.

as shares of (conventionally measured) tax revenue. For the years reported, these implicit taxes raised more than 5 per cent of GDP in Mexico and in

Zimbabwe and smaller but still large amounts in several other countries. Greece, Portugal and Turkey are the only European countries in the table each 'raising' a little over 2 per cent of GDP from this source. The unweighted average for the whole group is 2 per cent of GDP and 9 per cent of government revenue.[16]

Fry (1993) has estimated, for 26 countries, the seigniorage that the government received from its monopoly over money creation in 1984.[17] This is revenue *additional* to that from financial repression. When this seigniorage leads to inflation, it is a kind of excise tax whose revenue is obtained by multiplying the tax rate (which is the current inflation rate) by the tax base which is the 'geometric average of beginning-of-year and end-of-year values of currency in circulation plus bank reserves' (p. 10). Fry's estimates are shown in Table 3.3. Once again the revenue importance of these implicit taxes is striking. In five countries (Argentina, Egypt, Mexico, Peru and Yugoslavia) this unorthodox revenue source generated more than 7 per cent of GDP and large proportions of tax revenue. Once again these estimates pertain to 1984. Major changes have taken place since then in some of these countries. Chamley (1991) has also attempted to estimate the tax revenue from implicit financial taxation in four African countries (Ghana, Somalia, Zaire and Zambia) for the 1971–86 period. He has used two alternative methods for this calculation.[18] The *average* revenues for the whole period, shown as percentages of GDP, are given in Table 3.4. Once again the importance of this implicit source of revenue is obvious. The yearly estimations, shown in Chamley's article, indicate a great variability of this source. In particular years it provided much higher values than those shown in Table 3.4.

Unfortunately there are no good estimates of the implicit taxes and subsidies associated with multiple exchange rate systems, domestic price controls or quantitative restrictions on trade. The bits of evidence indicate that these taxes or subsidies may be very high. For example, Pinto (1989, p. 329) has estimated that the implicit marginal tax rate on exports by Ghana was 91 per

Table 3.4   Tax revenue from implicit financial taxation in selected countries, 1971–86 averages (percentage of GDP)

Country	Rate of return method	Cash flow method
Ghana	6.8	4.8
Somalia	4.9	4.3
Zaire	7.8	7.2
Zambia	4.3	4.0

Source: Arranged from Table 2 in Chamley (1991), pp. 524–5.

cent. This implicit tax was a consequence of the overvaluation of the exchange rate.

CONCLUDING REMARKS

This chapter has addressed some issues related to the positive role of the government. It has highlighted the fact that governments can pursue their roles in various ways and through various instruments. These instruments extend well beyond the range of taxes and public spending which are the ones that attract most attention, especially from public finance economists. The use of quasi-fiscal activities and quasi-fiscal regulations is common among countries. These are non-fiscal instruments used to achieve or to influence the same objectives as those pursued through taxes and government spending.

While all countries use, to some extent, these other instruments, much greater prevalence of their use is found in developing countries and, to a lesser extent, in poorer industrial countries. Economies in transition also make much use of them. The information available suggests that quantitatively – in terms of the percentage of GDP that would be needed to replace them with explicit taxes and public spending – these other instruments, in developing countries, may be as important as the traditional tax and spending instruments.[19] Because the developing countries have levels of taxation which, as percentages of GDP, are only about half as large as the industrial countries', it can be concluded that, through the use of these quasi-fiscal instruments, the governments of developing countries attempt to play roles which may not be too different from those of the governments of industrial countries. They just do it with different tools. Thus those who favor a minimalist role for the state should not get excited when the tax level of a country is low until they assure themselves that traditional tax sources have not been replaced by less traditional, or hidden, implicit taxes.

We could formulate a general hypothesis, which, admittedly, has not been fully proved in this chapter. With inevitable variance around the mean, due in part to the random presence of more or less conservative governments at given times and in given countries, most governments would like to play broadly similar roles. When the taxes they can raise are not sufficient to finance the desired expenditures, they tend to rely on less orthodox, non-tax instruments. Perhaps a corollary of this general hypothesis is that *governmental goals change more over time than across space.*[20] Demonstration effects might explain the tendency for the governments of various countries (adjusting again for the political coloring of the party in power) to try to promote similar goals and to play similar roles. When these roles change over time, they tend to change for all countries.

Public finance specialists and, perhaps, most other economists believe that fiscal instruments are more efficient than quasi-fiscal instruments in pursuing the role of the state. Economists normally prefer taxes over regulations, and direct, budgetary subsidies over subsidies given through quotas, subsidized credit and so on. In this context, the term 'efficiency' has two distinct meanings: as defined by Tinbergen, and as generally used by economists (that is, having to do with Pareto optimum and the allocation of resources). On both grounds, economists as a group tend to prefer fiscal to other instruments. However in particular cases, such as for inflationary finance, some major economists, such as Phelps (1973) and Dixit (1991), have argued that the economic efficiency of particular instruments can only be judged in the context of a general equilibrium approach. Thus a priori one cannot be sure that taxation is always preferable to inflationary finance. Furthermore the alternative of raising more tax revenue may not be available and the marginal benefit of public spending may be very high. This latter point was made for multiple exchange rates by E.M. Bernstein as far back as 1950, when he wrote:

> The case of multiple [exchange] rates as a tax service ... does not rest on its economic merit. It rests rather on the fact that it is easy to impose ... [and] that it is easy to enforce ... These are not good reasons for preferring one type of taxation to another. They may, however, have the merit, in countries with budgetary difficulties, of being better than no additional taxes. (Bernstein, 1950, pp. 236–7).

Still, today, most economists believe that these alternative revenue sources are very inefficient. Furthermore the particular case for inflationary finance (the case discussed by Phelps and Dixit) is considerably weakened when one takes into account the loss in tax revenue that often accompanies high inflation in the presence of significant collection lags (see on this Tanzi, 1978).

The above discussion leads to some rather uncomfortable conclusions. Current attitudes and thinking show a strong preference for (a) purely fiscal over quasi-fiscal tools for promoting the government's goals, (b) economically efficient over distortionary taxes, and (c) the complete separation of fiscal from monetary policy and the elimination of monetary repression. The preference for this separation is evident from the many papers now available arguing for the complete independence of central banks which would eliminate the quasi-fiscal role played by these institutions[21] and the removal of all impediments to trade and especially those associated with multiple exchange rates and quantitative restrictions.[22]

These preferences will, in time, significantly reduce the instruments and the controls available to the governments to pursue their goals. This is clearly desirable and consistent with a greater dependence on the market. If the governments can scale down their goals to make them consistent with their reduced ability to control, and with the greater role given to the market, the reduction in the use of quasi-fiscal instruments and in the total resources that the governments have controlled through explicit and implicit taxes will lead to a healthier economy. However, if governments cannot moderate their objectives, and/or do not find market-friendly ways of promoting them,[23] then fiscal deficits might become more common than they have been because governments may not reduce, or may even increase, spending in the face of reduced resources. This problem will be of particular relevance to developing countries and to economies in transition:[24] first, because these countries are the ones that have relied the most on quasi-fiscal instruments and, second, because these countries will have greater difficulties in raising needed revenue from efficient tax sources. In these countries the need to moderate the ambitions of governments and to build strong revenue sources from efficient tax systems will be particularly great. Major reforms in taxes and in public spending will be an essential feature of future developments.[25]

NOTES

1. Paper presented at the 51st Congress of the International Institute of Public Finance, Universidade Nova, Lisbon, Portugal, 21 August 1995, and at a seminar at the Ministry of Finance of China, Beijing, 29 August 1995.
2. This increase was due mainly to governmental policies rather than to technical factors often summarized under the term of 'Wagner's Law'.
3. The contribution of the 'New Italian School' through the work of Alberto Alesina, Guido Tabellini and others is also relevant in this context.
4. Of course, the availability of policy instruments depends on the availability of good institutions. Here we focus on the instruments rather than the institutions.
5. Johansen (pp. 22–5) lists the main instruments at the government's disposal, including monetary policy, prohibitions and government's own business activity, but then limits the fiscal policy instruments to payments to the government (taxes) and payments from the government.
6. Gini coefficients are generally much higher in developing countries than in developed countries.
7. In its *World Development Report 1983*, the World Bank attempted to construct 'indices of price distortions' for many developing countries. It is not clear how accurate is the picture provided by this heroic attempt. See p. 60 of that Report.
8. In the environmental area, regulations have often been used in industrial countries. These often have a quasi-fiscal effect. Of course tax incentives and tax expenditures are also used to achieve this objective.
9. This could be considered the subsidization of a merit good.
10. Please note that the burden of the tax is not on the general taxpayers but on those who own the houses that are rented.
11. Please note that, in this sentence, efficiency refers to the allocative concept rather than to the concept as defined earlier.
12. The fiscal or revenue effect of multiple exchange rates has been recognized for a long time. See Bernstein (1950) and Sherwood (1956).
13. Alternatively they may be forced to sell their products domestically at prices which are

well below the world price for those products. This is frequently the case with petroleum, which, in oil-producing countries such as Nigeria, Iran, Venezuela, Russia and other countries, is sold at what appear to be ridiculously low prices. In this case the implicit taxation of the oil sector and the implicit subsidies to oil consumers do not appear in the budget. In these countries the implicit taxes on the producers and the implicit subsidies to the consumer may be very large.

14. See Mackenzie (1994), Mackenzie and Stella (1996), Fry (1993) and Chamley (1991).
15. In particular circumstances, especially when the inflation rate is high and the interest rates are low, the implicit subsidies to those who borrow can be huge. As these subsidies are not shown in the budget, a country can have high inflation even when the formal budget appears to be in balance. This was the case in Brazil in years past.
16. Please note that the table refers to years in the 1970s or the first half of the 1980s. In some of the countries covered the current situation may be very different.
17. Earlier estimations are available in Fischer (1982).
18. The reader is sent to the original article for details.
19. This is also especially true in economies in transition.
20. This may explain, for example, why there is much less variation in taxing and spending for industrial countries at a point in time than there is over time. Please refer again to Table 3.1.
21. A progressively larger number of countries has been introducing legislation that makes the central bank an independent agency.
22. The tendency is also to remove impediments to capital movements.
23. The Chile-initiated experiment of privatizing the pension system is an example of a market-friendly way to promote a governmental objective.
24. In Russia, for example, the central bank had, until recently, directly financed at highly negative interest rates the activities of state enterprises. To some extent the financing compensated the enterprises for the social expenditures they were carrying. (See Tanzi, 1993.) If the enterprises no longer finance these social expenditures, the budget may have to take over some of them.
25. For a discussion of related issues, see Tanzi and Schuknecht (1998).

REFERENCES

Bernstein, E.M. (1950), 'Some Economic Aspects of Multiple Exchange Rates', *IMF Staff Papers*, 2, 224–37.

Bruni, Franco, Alessandro Penati and Angelo Porta (1989), 'Financial Regulation, Implicit Taxes and Fiscal Adjustment in Italy', in Mario Monti (ed.), *Fiscal Policy, Economic Adjustment and Financial Markets*, Washington, DC: IMF, pp. 197–230.

Chamley, Christopher (1991), 'Taxation of Financial Assets in Developing Countries', *The World Bank Economic Review*, 5(3), (September), 513–33.

Dixit, Avinash (1991), 'The Optimal Mix of Inflationary and Commodity Taxation with Collection lags', *IMF Staff Papers*, 38 (September), 643–54.

Fischer, Stanley (1982), 'Seigniorage and the Case for a National Money', *Journal of Political Economy*, 90 (April), 295–313.

Fry, Maxwell J. (1993), 'The Fiscal Abuse of Central Banks', IMF Working Paper, WP/93/58 (July).

Giovannini, Alberto and Martha De Melo (1993), 'Government Revenue from Financial Repression', *The American Economic Review*, 83(4) (September), 953–63.

International Monetary Fund (1994), *Exchange Arrangements and Exchange Restrictions; Annual Report*, Washington, DC: IMF.

Johansen, Leif (1965), *Public Economics*, Amsterdam: North-Holland.

Mackenzie, George A. (1994), 'Hidden Government Deficit', *Finance & Development*, December, 32–5.

Mackenzie, George A. and Peter Stella (1996), *Quasi Fiscal Operations of Public Financial Institutions*, Washington, DC.

Mueller, Dennis (1989), *Public Choice II*, Cambridge: Cambridge University Press.

Musgrave, Richard A. (1959), *The Theory of Public Finance*, New York: McGraw-Hill: A Study in Public Economy.

Phelps, Edmund S. (1973), 'Inflation in the Theory of Public Finance', *Swedish Journal of Economics*, 75 (March), 67–82.

Pinto, Brian (1989), 'Black Market Premia, Exchange Rate Unification and Inflation in Sub-Saharan Africa', *The World Bank Economic Review*, 3(3) (September), 321–38.

Sherwood, Joyce (1956), 'Revenue Features of Multiple Exchange Rate Systems: Some Case Studies', *IMF Staff Papers*, 5, 74–107.

Stiglitz, Joseph (1995) 'Role of Government in the Contemporary World', paper presented at the IMF Conference on Growth and Income Distribution, Washington, 1–2 June.

Tanzi, Vito (1978), 'Inflation, Real Tax Revenue and the Case for Inflationary Finance: Theory with an Application to Argentina', *IMF Staff Papers*, 25(3) (September), 417–51.

—— (1993), 'The Budget Deficit in Transition: A Cautionary Note', *IMF Staff Papers*, 40(3), (September), 697–707.

—— (1994), 'Corruption, Governmental Activities and Markets', IMF Working Paper WP/94/99 (August); published as 'Corruption, Arm's Length Relationships and Markets' in Gianluca Fiorentini and Sam Peltzman (eds), *The Economics of Organised Crime*, Cambridge: Cambridge University Press, 1995, pp. 161–80.

Tanzi, Vito and Ludger Schuknecht (1998), 'The Growth of Government and the Reform of the State in Industrial Countries', in Andrés Solimano (ed.), *Social Inequality, Values, Growth and the State*, Ann Arbor: The University of Michigan Press, pp. 171–207.

Tinbergen, Jan (1952), *On the Theory of Economic Policy*, Amsterdam: North-Holland.

4. Fundamental determinants of inequality and the role of government[1]

INTRODUCTION

Amartya Sen has stressed that inequality has many faces and, depending on the circumstances, some of these faces become particularly important causes for concern and for policy attention. See Sen (1998). Thus the spotlight of public and policy makers' attention must be directed at the aspect of inequality that at a particular time appears most damaging or most offensive to the prevalent conception of justice. This may be extreme poverty, conspicuous wealth or consumption, the status of particular groups, lack of access to particular goods and services, such as education, health or justice, or just an uneven income distribution.

Regardless of the form it takes, inequality is generally determined by the interplay of various factors. Ignoring the often temporary impact of man-made or natural catastrophes on specific individuals or groups, which may produce famines, the main *systemic* factors are social norms or institutions, broad economic changes and the role of government. At given times, each of these factors may come to play the leading role in determining an aspect of inequality or in shaping the income or wealth distribution of a country. In this chapter, we concentrate mostly on income distribution.

In traditional, relatively close and stable societies, the impact of social norms is likely to be a particularly important determinant of inequality or, more broadly, of inequity. In these societies, social norms tend to be relatively stable over time in specific countries even though they may differ among countries. These social norms can have powerful positive or negative effects on inequality. Together with the initial distribution of assets, they determine the extent of inequality. In these societies, the role of government may be relatively limited and stable. Furthermore broad but slow economic changes might not have, for a long time, an easily determinable impact on inequality. There is now little support for the Kuznets's hypothesis that predicted, first, a deterioration and then an improvement in the income distribution over economic development. See Kuznets (1955).

In the more open societies of today, the role of government tends to be larger than in the past, while the social norms become progressively less important as countries develop. At the same time, important economic changes, such as technological developments, globalization, privatization, trade liberalization and other major structural policies, come to play a greater role. The interaction of these factors inevitably affects inequality in general, and income and wealth distribution in particular. However the effects, though significant, are not obvious.

This chapter will discuss some of these issues, starting with social norms and institutions, a topic that has received almost no attention on the part of economists.

WORLD FORCES, SOCIAL NORMS AND INEQUALITY

Economists have paid little attention to the fact that various societal arrangements and attitudes that develop over long periods of time (and that may or may not be codified in laws) may have powerful effects in determining inequities or the distribution of income that exist in given countries. Some of these arrangements may reflect the existence of formal institutions, such as slavery in the past, or legalized discrimination, such as apartheid, in more recent times. Also the existence of labor unions or of professional associations is another kind of formal institution with potential impact on income distribution. Others may reflect customs, religion or cultural traits, for example de facto but non-legalized racial discrimination, the caste system or the status of women in some countries. Some of the discussion will use for convenience a simple scheme provided by Atkinson (1998). See Figure 4.1.

As Figure 4.1 indicates, world or domestic market forces affect the prices and thus the incomes that individuals receive from their economic activities. For most countries that are only a small part of the world economy the influence goes only in one direction: from the world forces to a country's incomes. For these countries the traditional small-country assumption used in trade theory would be realistic. For a few very large countries, and especially for the United States, the influence might go both ways. What happens in the world has an impact on the United States, but what happens in the United States also has an impact on the rest of the world. In such cases there would be another arrow in Figure 4.1 going from 'Incomes from production' to 'World or market forces'.

The incomes derived from domestic economic activities will in turn influence government policy and may bring changes in the social institutions. The changes in these institutions would affect the distribution of income. Thus government policy and the social institutions would determine the distribution of living standards because that distribution does not depend only on the market value of what is produced.

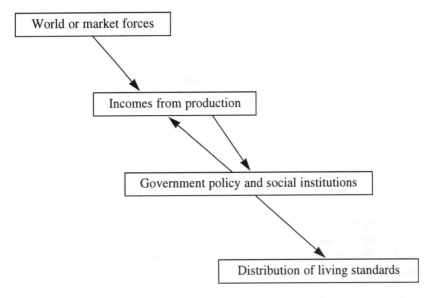

Figure 4.1   Major forces affecting inequality

The market forces include factors such as growth of the rest of the world, the composition of that growth, the world rate of interest, the prices of major commodities, the terms of trade, the growth of world trade, technological developments and so on. These forces will inevitably affect the levels of incomes from production and will have different effects on different groups.

There is now a fast-growing literature that discusses the impact of globalization on the relative wages of skilled and unskilled workers and on income distribution in general, especially, but not only, in industrialized countries. See, inter alia, Rodrik (1997). However, because of institutional arrangements and social norms, the direct impact of globalization and, thus, of market forces on the incomes received by particular groups, say the unskilled, will not result in precise or well-defined values for these incomes. Rather it will result in a potentially wide range of values.[2] The point is that the traditional economic forces of supply and demand will determine a range rather than a single equilibrium value. Within that range existing social arrangements and attitudes will determine values which may differ significantly among countries even when the market forces are the same. In some countries, such as the United States, their culture, attitudes and institutional arrangements may lead to a 'winner takes all' outcome. In others, such as Japan, such an outcome will be much less likely. See Kristoff (1998).

Although the Atkinson discussion relates to the impact of world forces on relative *wages*, in this chapter we generalize it to all *incomes*, including those that, strictly speaking, are not derived from directly productive activities. We need to provide examples of social norms or arrangements that influence the way the social pie eventually gets distributed in a given country. There are many such arrangements but their existence or their relevance varies from country to country.[3] Only a few examples of such arrangements or norms are provided in this chapter. There are undoubtedly many others which can also be equally important.

Take, for example, *rental contracts*, which are common, especially in countries where the ownership of assets is highly concentrated so that those who directly use those assets must rent them. Quite apart from governmental controls on rents that still exist in many countries, tradition continues to play a significant role in these contracts. For example, in parts of Italy, an institution inherited from Roman times called *mezzadria* still determines, today, the way the output of agricultural land is divided between the owner and the tenant, namely one-half each. Thus there is no market-determined, fixed rent paid by the user to the owner of the land.[4] There are many kinds of rental arrangements in countries, especially in developing countries, for the use of land or other assets. These arrangements often depend exclusively on tradition, but tradition has come to play a role that is important in determining in particular the distribution of agricultural income.

Take *labor contracts* which determine labor incomes. In some Asian countries (Korea, Japan) a paternalistic attitude by employers provided an implicit, non-governmental safety net. Employees were hired for life by the enterprises and were retained even during economic slowdowns when their services were not needed. In these countries recessions resulted in large fluctuations in profits and in small fluctuations in the unemployment rate. In Japan and Korea, for example, the unemployment rate was very low and relatively constant over long periods. In Korea, before the recent financial crisis, the unemployment rate was only 2.5 per cent. In these countries the current financial crisis and the sharp recession has so far led to far less increase in the unemployment rate than would have occurred in Western industrial countries and especially in the United States. In fact the unemployment rate in many Western countries which are not in recession is still much higher than the rates now prevailing in Japan and Korea.

The current crisis in South-east Asia and in Japan, which has led to acute economic difficulties for many enterprises, is providing a strong challenge to the paternalistic attitude of employers, with potentially obvious consequences for employment and for income distribution.[5] This crisis may force some relaxation of the life employment norm and force the enterprises to choose between egalitarian values and efficiency or even survival. It may also force the government to expand its role in this area through the introduction of significant, government-financed safety nets. In any case the existence of this paternalistic attitude has had a positive impact on income distribution and its abandonment will, most likely, have a negative impact. These countries had often been praised by economists for having low Gini coefficients.

Institutions and norms about marriage may also play an important role. Customs which influence the size of the dowry, the choice of spouses, the cost of marriages, the age at which people marry, the gifts associated with marriages, and so on are all aspects with significant implications for income and wealth distribution. When the children of the rich marry only the children of the rich, while the children of the poor marry only the children of the poor, as happens in many societies, the income distribution tends to remain unchanged over time and also to be different from that in societies where such matching does not take place and where there is much more freedom in the choice of marriage partners. In societies where marriages are arranged by matchmakers, the latter will make sure that the spouses come from similar backgrounds.[6] Modernization, mobility and globalization can have major impacts on these customs and consequently on inequality.

Customs and rules about inheritance are also important. In traditional societies where real wealth is more important than human capital in determining income, the way in which wealth is passed on between generations is a significant determinant of inequality.[7] How is property divided? In some traditional societies the first son often got the lion's share. In other societies, women are privileged or discriminated against. In any case, rules or customs about inheritance play a role and at times an important one. As long as the standard of living depends significantly on *real* capital that can be inherited, inheritance laws and customs will be important. When *human* capital becomes the most important determinant of income, as it is in advanced societies, then the way in which real capital is passed on between generations becomes less important, although it will remain important as long as real capital is a necessary ingredient for obtaining human capital. And, of course, human capital cannot be passed on in the same way and with the same facility as real capital.

In many societies the heirs inherit, not just real assets, but also particular positions in society. That is, they inherit some 'social capital' along with real assets. This social capital is made up of the family name and the prestige of that name, the family connections, and the family's claims to certain positions. These positions are not just the political ones which, even in some democratic societies, tend to be passed on from father or mother to son or daughter. They extend to many other areas. For example, in some countries the children of pharmacists, notaries, accountants or some other professionals can almost inherit the activity of their parents.[8] Because of restrictions to entry in these activities, they are essentially small monopolies with high market values. Thus high standards of living can be maintained by those who inherit the right to these activities.

These rents, which could be defined as *positional rents*, are very important in determining the distribution of income and privileges in many countries. But the concept of 'positional rents' extends beyond these cases. Even in activities where there is no formal or apparent restriction to entry, the children of well placed individuals often have major advantages in following the footsteps of their parents. The field is often not leveled for children in the real world. 'Positional rents' are also derived from rules on promotion and on hiring that give priority or preference to individuals with certain characteristics (orphans, widows, war veterans, those with certain ethnic or political characteristics, and so on). In Japan promotions are largely based on seniority, while in the United States the element of merit or performance is supposed to play a larger role. They are also connected with customs that determine the 'commissions' that individuals in certain activities (architects, real estate agents, stockbrokers, lawyers) get in relation to particular transactions or activities.[9] They are also important in transmitting some human capital directly through the families. As many studies have shown, the educational background of the families from which students come is of some importance in determining school performance. This implies that even human capital can, to a limited degree, be passed on.

Social norms tend to be stable, especially in traditional societies. As such they have a strong influence in maintaining the existing income and wealth distribution. This may be the reason why some authors have found that, in many countries, Gini coefficients remain relatively unchanged over long periods. (See Bruno *et al.*, 1998.) However, in periods of great internal turmoil such as major wars, severe depressions, foreign occupation, revolutions and so on, social norms tend to break down.[10] They will also change when major economic developments occur. In societies where the government aims specifically at removing implicit privileges for some groups, or at establishing preferences for groups previously discriminated against, norms can have a powerful influence on the distribution of income or wealth. This, for example, has often been stated to have happened in Malaysia over the past two decades. It will happen in South Africa in the years to come.

Even in the absence of explicit governmental decisions to change the existing social norms, globalization and major economic developments are likely to relax or modify the prevailing norms, thus affecting the existing inequalities.[11] Modernization often brings more labor mobility and, inter alia, mobility modifies institutions and norms related to marriages. Individuals who move to a distant area, or even to another country, lose some of the constraints in terms of their choice of spouses. Cross-class marriages become more common. Dowries lose their importance, especially when human capital in the form of high educational levels replaces real capital as the most important factor for the generation of income. For many individuals, human capital rather than real wealth becomes the determining factor in the choice of spouses. In time new and different norms may develop. For example, in time highly educated people may tend to marry highly educated people, thus reducing the social mixing that brings an improvement in the distribution of income. The stratification in the quality of schools may contribute to this development.

Rules or at least customs about inheritance also change with economic development. For example, the objective of keeping all the family wealth in one hand, which justified the custom of leaving the inheritance to the first born, becomes less important. This custom was particularly important when much wealth was held in the form of relatively indivisible assets, such as buildings, single pieces of land such as farms or haciendas, or family-controlled enterprises.

Modernization and mobility progressively reduce the importance of the 'positional rents' that play a large role in traditional societies and that still play some role in modern societies. Some of these rents are lost when the beneficiaries from them move. The family name becomes a less important asset, except for those of very prominent families. The family connections come to have less marketable value, especially when extended families are replaced by nuclear families. A person who moves from the north east of Brazil to São Paulo is not very likely to find his or her family connections worth as much in the new environment as they were in the old one. On the other hand, genuine human capital is much more mobile.[12] Globalization and the changes it brings with it are likely to change the norms of some societies faster than those of other societies where these norms are more deeply imbedded. Therefore the effect of globalization on different countries will not be the same.

Before leaving this section, it may be worthwhile to formalize a little the somewhat implicit structure of our reasoning so far and draw some conclusions. We have implicitly assumed that in traditional societies incomes depend to a large extent on real wealth and on 'positional rents'. Therefore the distribution of income, and inequality in general, are much influenced by the distribution of real wealth and by positional rents. Furthermore real wealth is likely to be a major factor in the distribution of positional rents. At this stage of development, human capital plays a relatively modest role because much of the income goes to real wealth. Thus factors that change the distribution of real capital (such as land reform) and of positional rents (such as social or structural reforms) will have an impact on inequality. In its *fiscal* role, the government may be able to influence the distribution of wealth and income more than the distribution of positional rents, although in both cases its influence is likely to be limited. In its *regulatory* role, the government is more likely to maintain than to modify the distribution of positional rents.

In more advanced societies, human capital and its distribution acquire more importance and the share of total income received by human capital increases dramatically. At the same time traditional or culturally generated positional rents become less important, while market forces, especially those coming from the rest of the world, come to have progressively more powerful effects because of globalization and because they conflict less with the social norms. At this stage the government can change the income inequality or it can reduce other kinds of inequities, mostly through the influence that it has on the generation and the distribution of human capital.[13] Of course the extent to which the government allows market forces to influence economic activity and to determine the allocation of resources will also determine the degree of inequality in society. In some cases governments may replace traditional norms with legislated norms that have the objective of creating new positional rents to favor particular groups. The rent seeking literature of the public choice school has put particular emphasis on this possibility.

Two simple diagrams may clarify the main argument. (See Figures 4.2 and 4.3, which are a stylization of known empirical observations.) Total income is of course the return to total wealth. Total wealth is the summation of real wealth and human capital. The relative importance of real wealth in generating income is very high in poor societies but falls gradually with economic development, while the importance of human capital grows with economic

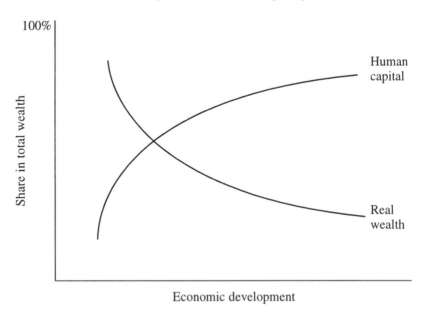

Figure 4.2   Economic development and shares of human and real wealth

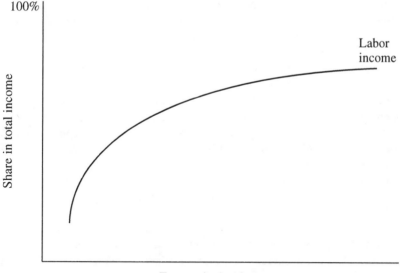

Figure 4.3   Economic development and labor income share

development. The two curves in Figure 4.2 show these trends. At high levels of development the relative importance of real wealth in determining total income becomes low, while that of human capital becomes high. These results are supported by the available statistics of many countries. Another way of making the same point is to show that the share of labor in total income tends to grow with economic development.[14] (See Figure 4.3). The return to labor can be assumed to be largely a return to some form of human capital. Thus the way labor income is shared and the way human capital is divided among the population become much more important than at early stages of development. Of course, while real capital can be highly concentrated – in theory one person could own everything – human capital tends to be much less concentrated, especially in modern societies. As a consequence, in more developed countries, the increased importance of human capital tends to reduce income inequality as compared with less developed societies.

THE TRADITIONAL ROLE OF GOVERNMENT

The role of government in a country is conditioned by the level of economic and institutional development. There is a vicious circle in the sense that, when the government is most needed (because the market needs many corrections, the income or wealth distributions are considered socially or politically unacceptable and the market is unable to insure against particular risks), it is often least capable of carrying through the needed corrective functions in an efficient way. Advanced industrial countries, with efficient markets, tend to have much larger governments, measured by the share of public spending in GDP, than developing countries. The reason is not that the former need more government than the latter but that they can collect more taxes. Being unable to raise taxes, the governments of the poorer countries tend to promote their objectives through less efficient tools, such as regulations and quasi-fiscal activities. In the process the role of government becomes more distorting. (See Chapter 3.) The governments of poor countries would find it much more difficult to promote policies aimed at reducing inequality except perhaps through expropriations and inefficient regulations.

Even a government highly concerned about inequality should promote, first of all, macroeconomic stability which is a necessary requirement for growth. And growth is not only a good provider of jobs, but also a strong provider of public resources necessary to finance social programs that can reduce poverty and inequality. (See Aninat, 1998.) Aninat has argued that stability *and* growth have provided an increasing amount of resources for the Chilean government, allowing it to better pursue its social objectives.

The experience of Brazil, after 1995, has shown that a reduction in the rate of inflation is often an important contributor to the growth of the income of those at the bottom of the income distribution. (See Clements, 1997.)[15] Poor people are much less able than rich people to protect themselves from the effects of inflation. If stability brings both growth and stable prices, its positive effect on the poorer groups can be important. Whether this also reduces overall inequality, that is, whether it leads to lower Gini coefficients, is more debatable. (See Tanzi, 1998.)

However stability can come with a minimal government role or with a more ambitious role. Some authors have argued that the government role, measured through the tax and expenditure levels, can be too low or too high. See Tanzi and Zee (1997) and Alesina (1998a). A level of taxation that is too low will not allow the government to carry out its essential functions. A level that is too high may be too burdensome on the economy and lead to wasteful and unproductive spending. Thus stability should be maintained at a level of government expenditure that best allows the government to pursue its essential or core functions. The more efficient the government in carrying out its functions, the lower the level of public spending needs to be. Thus efficiency should be an important objective for any government.

In the literature on the role of government in income distribution much emphasis has been placed on taxing and spending even though, of course, the regulatory role can also be very important. Through its many regulations and through other policies, such as rent and price control and land reform, the government can have powerful effects on the distribution of income and wealth. However these effects will not always be in the desirable direction.

It is now broadly accepted that the role of taxation in income distribution has been somewhat limited. See Tanzi (1974) and Harberger (1998). Because of the importance of tangible wealth in income distribution in poorer countries, a redistributive role could be pursued through the taxation of land and property. Unfortunately, for political or administrative reasons, countries, especially poorer countries, have rarely been able to tax wealth or property effectively. Thus they have, instead, attempted to tax income rather than wealth. In past years, when high marginal tax rates were imposed, they were often accompanied by so many loopholes and such poor tax administration that their progressivity was mostly neutralized while the high tax rates created many inefficiencies in the economy. The present thinking, based largely on the past experience, is that the major contribution that a tax system can make to an effective government role in reducing inequality, especially in developing countries, is, first, by providing the revenue needed for essential expenditure programs and, second, by avoiding the generation of horizontal inequities that occur when taxpayers with similar incomes end up paying very different effective tax rates. Tax systems with broad bases, limited exemptions and special treatments (tax expenditures) and low rates better satisfy the two objectives.

It should be recognized that the above conclusion is based on past experiences. It is not necessarily a normative conclusion. Thus a country that was able to impose an effectively progressive tax system, and that could do so without creating excessive disincentives, should not refrain from relying on the tax system for redistributive purposes.

Much faith remains in the ability of governments to reduce inequality through the use of public spending. There is some evidence that the industrial countries with high public spending levels have more even income distributions and less extreme inequalities than countries that spend less. However this result may have come at the cost of high unemployment and lower rates of growth. Over the years many bad policies have been justified in the name of income redistribution. Public spending, justified in the name of equity, has at times contributed little to equity and much to macroeconomic instability.

Two major problems that often characterize public spending reduce its potential contribution to equity. First is the *hijacking of expenditure programs by special interest groups*. The public choice literature on this aspect is now very extensive. Political pressures often push spending away from the intended or the desirable targets and redirect it toward the general population or toward less desirable destinations. Thus subsidies may start as well directed and may become general; spending may be diverted toward tertiary or secondary education and away from primary education;[16] too much health expenditure may go for modern hospitals in big cities and not enough for basic health care, especially in poorer areas; too much money may go for new projects and not enough for operation and maintenance expenditure, especially in less developed or poorer areas. It is a common observation that roads in poorer areas are less well maintained than roads in richer areas.[17] This problem has been recognized for a long time. See, for example, Tanzi (1974) and, more recently, Alesina (1998b). The existence of this problem implies that the level of social spending may provide less information about the impact that social spending is having on poorer groups than is commonly believed. Thus simply looking at the share of spending on health and education in GDP or in the total budget may not tell much about the impact of governmental actions on these areas. It is necessary to know who the real beneficiaries are. Thus governments cannot be labeled as for or against equity simply on the basis of how much they spend on so-called 'social expenditure'.

A second problem, and one that has attracted much less attention, is the significant probability that the hijacking will not be done politically, by the recipient of the public services, but administratively, *by the provider of the service*. For certain public functions, and especially for those that are highly labor-intensive, such as education and health, the role of the providers, such as school teachers, school administrators, doctors, nurses and so on, is fundamental. Unlike transfers made in cash, such as pension payments, where much of the actual spending is received by the legal benefactors of the services, for activities such as education and health much of the actual spending goes to the providers (the public employees) in the form of wages and salaries or in other forms. These providers are supposed to produce an output or a service (education, good health) that benefits the users of that output or service. There is a tendency to measure the output on the basis of the cost of the input but the two may be widely different. (See Tanzi, 1974.)

Education and health often absorb a very large share of the public sector's labor force. This labor force may or may not be productive; and through salaries and other expenses it can absorb a large share of total public spending. If this labor force is unproductive, or if additional spending is absorbed mostly by high wages, it is possible that large public spending may generate few real or concrete benefits to the students or the patients.[18] And this may happen even in relatively well-run countries. Aninat (1998) mentions the Chilean experience where a tripling of the real spending for health over a few years did not result in any quantifiable or visible increase in the quantity or the quality of services to those who used the public health system. There have been episodes where large increases in educational spending have not resulted in any objectively measurable increase in educational output. To ensure that this kind of hijacking through inefficiency or job shrinking does not occur, deep and complex administrative and legal reforms are necessary.

In conclusion, the impact of governmental action on inequality cannot be measured only by the level of spending for social categories, although that level is of course important. The input (the spending) is not as relevant for equity as the output. It is the output (what the citizens actually receive) that determines the impact the government is having on human capital and on income distribution. But, of course, without social spending there is no hope that the government will affect the income distribution in a positive way.

THE ROLE OF GOVERNMENT IN ASSETS AND HUMAN CAPITAL DISTRIBUTION

Available statistics indicate that the share of wages and salaries in national income rises with economic development.[19] It is also known that human capital grows with economic development. (See Barro and Sala-i-Martin, 1995.) This implies that, in the determination of inequality, the distribution of real assets must be more important at low levels of development, while the distribution of human capital must become more important at high levels of development. This conclusion has a powerful message for policy.

For poor countries the distribution of real assets (land, buildings, factories) is very important not only in determining incomes but also in providing access to scarce resources. For example, as pointed out by many studies, access to credit often requires collateral in the form of *real* assets. In these countries, families with real assets probably also have more 'social capital' as defined earlier. Furthermore social capital provides the contacts and the connections that make it easier for a person to get important information as well as access to scarce resources such as credit, foreign exchange, positional rents and so on.[20] In these countries there will be clubs or associations of individuals whose common characteristic is real wealth.

In the imperfect and inefficient markets that characterize many developing countries, information does not flow easily and is not as readily available as in advanced countries. Much of it is often obtained through a network of personal contacts. The rich people, that is those who have real assets, are likely to have better contacts and better connections than those who do not have them. At higher levels of development information becomes more easily available and the network created around *human* capital becomes more important than the network created around *real* assets. Also income from employment, which depends on a person's human capital, becomes an important collateral for obtaining credit. The establishment of a market, based more on arm's length relationships and rules of law than on the personal relationship, reduces the importance of personal connections and the value of the 'social capital', as defined above.

In developed countries, human capital thus acquires fundamental importance. It contributes enormously to the generation *and the distribution* of income. The more widespread education and human capital among the population, the less inequality there will be in a society.[21] Also the social capital based on family connections and real assets is progressively replaced by a social capital based on school connections and profession-related contacts. To a large extent, professional associations replace class-based or wealth-based clubs. This points to the fundamental role that the government can play in this area.

We have thus been led to a conclusion that should be hardly novel to modern economists. This is the conclusion that human capital is not only the most fundamental factor for promoting growth, but, *provided that it is broadly spread among the population*, may well be the most important factor for promoting a more equitable and just society.[22] However we should not fall into the trap of believing that the fundamental policy change is simply to allocate more resources in the budget for education and health. Such a policy may well reinforce a pattern common in many countries, including Brazil, where the output of this spending goes largely to the urban middle classes while much of the input (the budgeted money) goes to the public employees who provide the services and who are not poor.

Thus countries need to allocate far more brain power and, possibly though not necessarily, more money to bring the educational and health reforms that will change the character of these programs in a fundamental way *aimed at producing better human capital for as large a share of the population as possible*.[23] This may require reform of curricula, retraining of teachers and doctors, special attention for poorer groups and, of course, major administrative and legal changes. This is a very difficult enterprise which has often failed in the past. The government should also play a larger role in training activities. In modern societies high incomes do not go exclusively to those with high formal education but also to those with high developed skills such as athletes, musicians, computer experts and so on. There is no reason why public educational spending should not cover these areas when they give opportunities to people from the poorest backgrounds. Human capital is a function for formal education, innate ability, health, training and other undefined characteristics. The government cannot do much about the innate abilities of individuals, but, by judiciously using its budget, it can create opportunities for the poor through the role it plays in educating, training and improving the health of the population.

SUMMARY AND CONCLUSIONS

Inequality is much influenced by systemic factors such as social norms and attitudes, broad economic changes and governmental activity. In close and traditional societies, where public sector intervention is limited, social norms are very important. They differ among countries but change little over time within countries, thus generating Gini coefficients that are relatively stable within countries but different among countries. In more open and more developed societies the role of government and the impact of broad economic forces are more important.

This chapter has analyzed some of these aspects, stressing in particular the role of social norms. It has argued that in traditional or poorer societies the interconnection of real wealth with existing norms goes a long way to determining the extent of economic inequality that exists. Social norms and asset distribution also contribute to the existence of 'social capital' and 'positional rents' that are very important in maintaining or even creating inequality.

The opening of markets and the broad economic changes brought about by structural reforms and globalization can have powerful effects on social norms. When these trends lead to economic development, the result will be a progressive replacement of tangible wealth (assets) by human capital as the main determinant of income. Thus, as countries develop, the distribution of human capital becomes progressively more important than the distribution of real assets in determining inequality.

The government can play a significant part in this process because of its role in human capital formation. It must first maintain economic stability and promote economic growth. Both stability and growth are powerful factors in reducing poverty (though not necessarily inequality). Second, it must generate the public revenue needed to support an adequate level of public spending. The more efficient the government is in its spending activity, the lower the tax burden need be.

Past experience indicates that taxation may not be able to do much to reduce inequality directly. Its main role should be the indirect one of financing public spending, unless the government is able to impose efficient, progressive taxes. The imposition of taxes should minimize horizontal inequities among taxpayers as well as welfare costs. Thus public spending to generate human capital should be the essential tool for promoting a more equitable society. However the chapter cautions against two common and major problems. First is the hijacking of the potential benefits from public spending by powerful vested interests. These groups will attempt to redirect spending towards them, thus decreasing the potential benefits on income distribution and equity from that spending. For example, pension expenditure may become too high while spending for primary education may become too small because of the political power of the elderly. Second is the form of hijacking that is undertaken by the providers of the public services. Through higher costs, inefficiency and at times corruption, this form of hijacking can significantly reduce the value of the output without reducing the budgetary costs of the activities, thus reducing the rate at which human capital is created.

The chapter concludes that over the long run the distribution of human capital becomes the most important factor in determining the distribution of income. Governments can do a lot to increase the quantity and the quality of human capital and to make sure that all sectors, and especially individuals at the lower end of the income distribution, have full access to relevant and high quality education as well as to relevant training provided outside formal education. In fact some of the highest incomes in advanced societies such as the United States are received by individuals using human capital but a human capital of a kind not derived from formal education.[24]

This chapter has focused on inequality. However its major concern has been the incomes of the lowest sectors in society. This is clearly the group that merits most attention, although there was a time, not too long ago, when the incomes and the wealth of the richest groups also attracted a lot of attention. Societies still differ, not only in their attitude vis-à-vis the very poor, but also vis-à-vis the very rich.

While I was finalizing the last version of the paper on which this chapter is based, two recent articles attracted my attention. First was an article which gave the news that the lawyers who negotiated the settlement between the states of Florida, Mississippi and Texas, on the one side, and the tobacco industry, on the other, will receive US$8 billion (*sic*) for their efforts. (See Barry Meier, 1998.) Now US$8 billion is more than the GDP of many countries and about the yearly income of 21 million Indians! The payment, which does not seem to be based on any possible relationship to effort, reflects one of the social arrangements described in this chapter.[25] Second, an article in *Forbes* (15 December 1998, p. 8), which reports that Kirk Kerkorian made $660 million in six and a half hours in the stock market selling Chrysler stocks. This is equivalent to the total annual income of about 1.8 million Indians! The same article reports that, in 1997, Bill Gates increased his wealth at the rate of $2.1 million per hour.

It is not obvious whether news of this kind, or the news about heads of American enterprises receiving tens of millions of dollars in annual compensation for their efforts, should be cause for public concern. They do not seem to be in the United States. It is, however, obvious that this kind of compensation is much more acceptable in some societies than in others. And, of course, public attitude towards it has an impact on the income distribution that a country ends up with.

NOTES

1. Revised version of a paper presented at a conference on Asset Distribution, Poverty and Economic Growth: Theory, Empirical Evidence and Policy Implications, organized by the Brazilian Ministry of Land Reform in conjunction with the Economic Development Institute and the Development Research Group of the World Bank, Brasilia, 14–17 July 1998.
2. According to Atkinson (1998), a 'range theory' of wage differentials was implicit in Hicks's work and was developed by Lester (1952).
3. Because they were writing about industrial countries, the social norms that Lester and Atkinson had in mind related to issues of labor organization, existence of unions and so on. In this paper, I bring in norms particularly, but not exclusively, important in developing countries.
4. Incidentally this arrangement is conceptually similar to that for the use of money in Islamic countries, where the payment of a fixed interest is forbidden.
5. For example, in Korea, labor unions have accepted the fact that restructuring by enterprises will require some laying off of workers and have accepted reductions in real wages so that fewer workers need to lose their jobs.
6. The role of professional matchmakers in traditional societies is in fact that of finding spouses from similar backgrounds.
7. In fact recent writing on income distribution in developing countries has highlighted the importance of the initial distribution of assets.
8. In Great Britain the House of Lords is filled with individuals who have inherited their positions. Great Britain may be removing this inherited privilege soon.
9. Even in advanced societies such as the United States these 'positional rents' may be important in particular activities (dentists, doctors, lawyers) where the children of well established professionals have an easier time following the parents' steps.
10. In some sense our hypothesis bears some resemblance to Mancur Olson's hypothesis about the role of special interest groups in the economy. See Olson (1982).
11. One reason why safety nets are required in modern economies is that modernization tends to destroy the traditional safety nets. In Japan and Korea income distribution, as measured by Gini coefficients, had been relatively good (about 0.34) in part because of the traditional safety nets that insured life employment and that required family members to assist other members that ran into difficulties. The current crisis is likely to modify these traditions and especially life employment, thus leading to a worsening of the income distribution and forcing the government to develop more formal, explicit safety nets.
12. However even human capital can lose value in the movement from place to place when specific certifications or residency requirements have created some 'positional rents' for those already established in one place. Think of the many doctors or other professionals who emigrated to Israel from Russia and could not exercise the profession they had been trained to do. Of course an easy explanation of this situation is to assume that, on the average, those who move to other countries have a training that is not as good as the average training of the professionals in the country of destination. However, in some cases, this is a convenient rather than a valid explanation.
13. For example, inequities vis-à-vis women or particular ethnic groups can be reduced by giving them more access to education or even to health services.
14. It is known that the share of labor in national income rises with the growth of income. In very advanced countries the share of capital may again show some increase because of the growing share of national income going to pension funds.
15. See also Guitián (1998) for evidence that price stability brings a better distribution of income.
16. Clements (1997) argues that this has happened in Brazil. Tanzi (1974) made the same point.
17. Some misdirection of spending may reflect regional political power. Some regions may end up with disproportionate shares of spending.
18. It is a known fact that, in some countries, doctors working in public hospitals and thus

receiving a government salary spend most of their energy and often a good share of their working hours in private practices. School teachers may be ill-prepared or often absent.

19. Unfortunately data are available for limited numbers of developing countries. Still they indicate that the share of wages in national income is much higher in industrial countries.

20. Wealth will also provide access to political power and political power often brings higher income.

21. Many economists tend to identify human capital with formal education but, while education is very important, human capital is a much broader concept. In the United States and in other industrial countries some of the highest incomes received by individuals with high human capital are not returns to education.

22. High educational levels were given as the main reason why the countries of South-east Asia that grew fast also had good income distribution.

23. Because primary education benefits a larger share of the population than higher levels of education, it is obvious that primary education should receive the greatest attention.

24. See the incomes received by some professional athletes, entertainers or actors. These individuals often do not have much formal education and come from less privileged groups.

25. Incidentally the $8 billion compensation for the lawyers will make individuals who are already well-to-do very rich, while it will make poorer the final contributors to that payment, the smokers, who tend to be low-income individuals. The implications for income distribution are obvious.

REFERENCES

Alesina, Alberto (1998a), 'Too Large and Too Small Governments', paper presented at the Conference on Economic Policy and Equity, IMF, 8–9 June.

—— (1998b), 'The Political Economy of Macroeconomic Stabilization and Income Inequality: Myths and Reality', in Vito Tanzi and Ke-young Chu (eds), *Income Distribution and High-Quality* Growth, Cambridge, Mass.: MIT Press, pp. 299–326.

Aninat, Eduardo (1998), 'Addressing Equity Issues in Policymaking: Principles and Lessons from the Chilean Experience', paper presented at the Conference on Economic Policy and Equity, IMF, 8–9 June.

Atkinson, A.B. (1998), 'Equity Issues in a Globalizing World: The Experience of the OECD Countries', paper presented at the Conference on Economic Policy and Equity, IMF, 8–9 June.

Barro, Robert J. and Xavier Sala-i-Martin (1995), *Economic Growth*, New York: McGraw-Hill.

Bruno, Michael, Martin Ravallion and Lyn Squire (1998), 'Equity and Growth in Developing Countries: Old and New Perspectives on the Policy Issues, in Vito Tanzi and Ke-young Chu (eds), *Income Distribution and High Quality Growth*, Cambridge, Mass.: MIT Press, 117–46.

Clements, Benedict (1997), 'Income Distribution and Social Expenditure in Brazil', IMF Working Paper 97/120 (September).

Forbes (1998), 'The 400 Richest People in America', 12 October, pp. 8, 37.

Guitián, Manuel (1998), 'Monetary Policy: Equity Issues in IMF Policy Advice', in Vito Tanzi and Ke-young Chu (eds), *Income Distribution and High Quality Growth*, Cambridge, Mass.: MIT Press, pp. 333–50.

Harberger, Arnold (1998), 'Monetary and Fiscal Policy for Equitable Growth', in Vito Tanzi and Ke-young Chu (eds), *Income Distribution and High Quality Growth*, Cambridge, Mass.: MIT Press, 203–41.

Kristoff, Nicholas D. (1998), 'Japan is Torn Between Efficiency and Egalitarian Values', *New York Times*, 26 October.

Kuznets, Simon (1955), 'Economic Growth and Income Inequality', *American Economic Review*, 45, 1–28.

Lester, R.A. (1952), 'A Range Theory of Wage Differentials', *Industrial and Labor Review*, 11(3), 55–74.

Meier, Barry (1998), 'Lawyers in Early Tobacco Suits get $8 Billion', *New York Times*, 12 December, pp. A1 and A15.

Olson, Mancur (1982), *The Rise and Decline of Nations: Economic Growth, Stagflation and Social Rigidities*, New Haven: Yale University Press.

Rodrik, Dani (1997), *Has Globalization Gone Too Far?*, Washington: Institute for International Economics.

Sen, Amartya (1998), 'Economic Policy and Equity: An Overview', paper presented at the Conference on Economic Policy and Equity, IMF, 8–9 June.

Tanzi, Vito (1974), 'Redistributing Income through the Budget in Latin America', *Banca Nazionale del Lavoro Quarterly Review*, 108 (March), 65–87.

—— (1998), 'Macroeconomic Adjustment with Major Structural Reforms: Implications for Employment and Income Distribution', in Vito Tanzi and Ke-young Chu (eds) *Income Distribution and High Quality Growth*, Cambridge, Mass.: MIT Press, pp. 351–74.

Tanzi, Vito and Howell H. Zee (1997), 'Fiscal Policy and Long-run Growth', *IMF Staff Papers*, 44(2) (June), 179–209.

5. Modernization, ethics and public policy

INTRODUCTION

Ethical behavior has been a vital ingredient, for both traditional and modern societies, in limiting and resolving conflicts between individuals and between individuals and groups. Compassion – a particular form of ethics – has been a crucial factor for both types of societies in protecting the poorer groups given the unequal distribution of endowments.

The conflicts of interests between individuals and between individuals and the groups to which they belong are more transparent in traditional societies than in large modern societies. In dealing with these conflicts, traditional societies rely on personal interactions and on informal codes of behavior. Thus, in small traditional societies, compassion induces the more fortunate members to help the less fortunate ones who are often personal acquaintances or even family members.[1] In contrast, large modern societies need to rely on formal arrangements, often through government intervention, to provide safety nets.

In this chapter we argue that, in a modern society, the growth of formal institutions and the increase in the social and geographic distance between benefactors and beneficiaries reduce the individual's willingness to help others voluntarily.[2] If redistribution reflects some coercion, it can have efficiency costs. The greater the degree of coercion, the greater are likely to be these costs. We argue that educational programs that promote more ethical behavior and greater compassion will have positive efficiency implications. These result from the effects of greater ethical behavior on the work efforts of those at both the giving and the receiving ends of income transfers. These efficiency gains could be substantial, considering the efficiency losses resulting from higher government taxation to finance redistribution and, of course, fraud and criminal activities. Therefore public policy needs to take these implications into account.

Discussions of taxation and of tax incentives for charitable contributions and redistribution implicitly assume a given ethical behavior. However, the possibility of *changing* ethical standards through public policy, for example through education, should not be disregarded, although cynics might argue that such a change is impossible. The current discussion of the returns to education tends to stress the effect of education on labor productivity, but ignores the kind of externality discussed in this chapter.[3] The appropriate mix of human capital and physical capital is a crucial economic policy issue. We argue that the appropriate mix of professional education and ethical education should also be a crucial economic policy issue.[4]

The chapter is organized as follows. The second section discusses the economic implications of ethical behavior in traditional societies and the need for a certain form of ethical behavior arising from modernization. The third section discusses the implications of ethics for efficiency, equity and public policy in modern societies, while a fourth section concludes the chapter.

MODERNIZATION AND CHANGES IN ETHICS

In small traditional societies, especially those with extended families living in small communities, social cohesion and daily contacts among their members facilitate and stimulate voluntary income redistribution within the group, although they may play no role in redistribution across spatially separated groups.[5] Formal institutions are often not needed in these societies. Modernization and urbanization tend to undermine social cohesion. By alienating individuals from their environment and by thus tearing the social fabric of traditional societies, modernization and urbanization increase the need for a formal redistributive role of the government. In fact, in modern societies, this redistributive role has been the leading factor in bringing about an increase in the size of the public sector.

Economic Implications of Ethics and Compassion

Ethical behavior includes various elements with diverse economic implications. First, there are *passive* elements which induce individuals to avoid actions harmful to others and to behave in accordance with what they consider to be socially acceptable norms. For example, one instinctively observes written and unwritten social regulations because they conform to one's ethical code of conduct and not because the non-observance of those regulations may be costly in terms of penalties, criticisms and so on. Ethics affects the attitudes of individuals toward tax laws, anti-pollution regulations, traffic regulations, and so forth. In a sense, even courtesy can be considered a form of ethics. Different individuals facing the same legal system and the same social norms may behave differently because of their own different ethical backgrounds.[6] A higher ethical behavior is likely to reduce the cost of regulations and to improve the efficiency of markets.[7]

Second, there are *active* elements that affect ones behavior toward others, including family members, friends and acquaintances, and other members of society. These elements motivate some individuals to help others or to promote the public interest, even at the cost of their own pecuniary interests. Compassion is such an element. Compassion reinforces bequest motives and induces individuals to make charitable contributions and to support and vote for programs aimed at helping those in less fortunate economic conditions.

What we call 'passive and active ethics' might be compared with the negative and positive injunctions in the Bible. The negative injunctions include 'thou shalt not kill' and 'thou shalt not betray'; the positive injunctions include 'defend the fatherless' and 'plead for the widow.' Ethicists have referred to the passive ethics as 'decency' and the active ethics as 'nobility'.[8]

A mix of passive and active ethical elements can thus influence the economic behavior of citizens. For example, it is conceivable that these elements affect individuals' work ethics. One might work harder to satisfy one's own ethical norm and, at the same time, to save more for heirs. Both elements might shape one's view on a social security system. A social security system often has both an element of insurance and one of income redistribution. By supporting such a system we provide an insurance for our own future and that of our relatives; but we also support a program that redistributes income toward the poor, since these programs are often weighted in favor of those with low incomes.[9] Both passive and active ethical elements would influence an individual's attitudes toward such a system.

One could argue that, in its pure form, compassion or charity should not be motivated by self-interest. Whether purely altruistic compassion exists has been debated. In this chapter we take an agnostic view of the ultimate motives for compassion. Thus compassion can be motivated either by self-interest or by altruism.[10] We distinguish, however, between income transfers motivated by compassion and those induced by tax incentives and other external factors. One may also distinguish between what we call 'personal compassion' and 'institutional compassion'. The former is generally the compassion toward individuals one personally interacts with: the compassion that results in direct assistance to them. The latter is compassion toward those in need, without direct personal contacts, expressed through the support for public and private social institutions. Thus one makes contributions to charitable institutions, bears the burden of higher taxes (to finance social programs) and votes for, or tolerates, a progressive tax system essentially to help unknown individuals.[11]

The two types of compassion can coexist in societies but tend to coincide in small traditional societies. One can have both types of compassion, and the behavior of different individuals can reflect different mixes of them. For example, one may help the poor in a spontaneous act of charity while giving political support for redistributive policies. Alternatively one could help a poor family in the neighborhood, while opposing redistributive policies.

Ethics may be a useful, if not a necessary, condition for reducing market failures. The efficiency of the competitive equilibrium, based on the pursuit of 'self-interest' by individuals, cannot be claimed in the absence of a clear ethical foundation that guides the individuals' pursuit of their self-interest. Thus Adam Smith's individuals, who are assumed to promote the public interest while pursuing their own gains, also seek the approval of an 'impartial spectator'. Without such a foundation, the cost of maintaining fair rules of competition to allow the market to function properly can be prohibitively high.[12]

Adam Smith's individuals, however ethical they are, cannot prevent market failures or uneven income distribution. Thus Smith considered it necessary for the government to play a corrective role by providing public goods and by helping the poor obtain basic education.[13] Direct government intervention is not the only way to provide public goods and to achieve equitable income distribution.[14] Societies have often resorted to active elements of ethics to strengthen their provision of public goods and to ensure more equitable distribution of income. For example, wartime patriotism and heroism have been important means of complementing taxation in financing the government provision of national defense.[15] In important respects, their contributions have even transcended the financial aspects of national defense. Compassion has helped society to achieve a more equitable income distribution. Note that, in this sense, the economic agents in Smith's model of competition are only passively, not actively, ethical.[16]

While high marginal tax rates may reduce work effort, ethical behavior may promote it. The efficiency costs of income redistribution are likely to depend on how it is achieved. When income transfers are voluntary, the negative effect on the work efforts of those at the giving end should be small or insignificant. And if they are voluntary and direct, the bureaucratic costs may also be very low. Involuntary income transfers are more likely to have negative effects on the work effort of the taxpayers. Regardless of motivation, however, income transfers can have negative effects on the work efforts of those at the receiving end who are capable of working. The so-called 'poverty trap', whereby potentially active individuals are induced to remain unemployed by the benefit they receive, is an expression of this possibility. Enhanced ethical behavior among these beneficiaries could reduce these negative effects of income transfers.[17]

Ethical Behavior and Income Transfers in Traditional Societies

A representative traditional society is assumed to be a small and somewhat isolated village. The members of this society neither pay taxes to, nor receive benefits from, the government. The village includes a small number of extended families. In this society, compassion implies, inter alia, helping less fortunate members of the family or of the community. The principal form is personal compassion, although it does not necessarily mean that the redistributive force is pure altruism. There may be an element of insurance in the sense of 'If I help you when you need my help, I would expect that you will help me should I need your help'.[18] A difference from a formal insurance is that the implicit obligation is not legally binding.

Take, for example, the Mbuti, a Pygmy group in Central Africa. They live in small bands of seven to 30 households. They regard the whole band to be a grand family without political centralization, legal system or social classes. The members of the band conduct productive activities both individually and collectively. The members are free to remain or leave the band; therefore their contribution to the communal production is voluntary. Another example is the nomadic Bushmen of the Kalahari Desert in Africa. A Bushman band may number between 25 and 60 people, related to each other by blood or marriage ties. Whereas band members produce in accordance with their skills, the output is shared. For example, food and water are divided according to seniority'.[19]

The Plains Indians in North America provide another example. Great Plains Indians could best maintain their status by lavish generosity to the poor. In the Oglala society it was a custom for a new member to look after the poor, especially the widows and the orphans. A Blackfoot man wishing to become a leader competed with others by helping the poor even at the cost of his own impoverishment.[20]

The informal social security arrangements in many traditional fishing villages of Asia, Latin America and Sub-Saharan Africa are also good examples of these informal redistributive arrangements. Whereas fulfilling the rights of the villages resembles a tax system, income transfers take place through informal arrangements, but are not entirely altruistically motivated.[21]

Note some of the common features of these societies. First, there is a communal character of production, allocation and distribution, which has strong equity implications. These arrangements are informal and to a large extent voluntary. Skillful producers, who are at the giving end of income transfers, join the communal arrangements voluntarily. The second feature is that one's compassion or generosity toward the poor is often strongly motivated by a desire to gain a higher social status or greater recognition. Thus what we call personal compassion in these cases is voluntary.

While income transfer schemes in a traditional society have a characteristic of a social compact, their informal and largely voluntary nature reduces, if not eliminates, efficiency losses. There could even be efficiency gains; one could not rule out the possibility that a highly compassionate individual might work harder to earn additional income to help others.

The smallness of the above societies makes the social consequences of individual actions more transparent and diminishes the need for coordination of individual acts. It also reduces the bureaucratic costs of redistribution, which can be very high in modern societies, and the possibility of abuse by benefit recipients. This tends to reduce the need for the regulatory and redistributive role of a central authority or a government.[22]

Modernization and its Implications

Modernization and the growth in the size and complexity of a society reduce or even eliminate the daily personal contacts among its members. Modernization brings with it the disintegration of the social cohesion that characterizes a small traditional village. In modern societies, the rich and the poor are likely to be socially and spatially segregated. However, while the value of compassion remains undiminished, the size and the anonymity of the members increase the need for a formal redistributive role of the government.

The increase in the need for intermediation of income transfers creates demand for a new type of compassion. It is the kind of compassion that would induce the members of society to create institutions for income transfers. This kind of compassion seems to be stronger in some societies (such as Sweden) and weaker in others (such as the United States) and it affects the size of public sectors. The traditional form of compassion remains important for income transfers within small boundaries of personal contacts. It becomes increasingly inadequate, however, as the size of the society grows. In a modern and highly urbanized society income transfers require the capacity of its members, particularly the higher-income net taxpayers, to perceive the needs of largely invisible and unknown individuals and to support social plans for helping them. In a democratic political system the role of the median taxpayer becomes of great importance while individuals vote on social institutions (for example, tax systems and social programs) aimed at improving equity and at helping those at the lower end of the income distribution.[23]

The deterioration in social cohesion is not necessarily a recent phenomenon. Smith observed, in a somewhat different context, that the growth of cities resulted in a breakdown of the mechanism of the 'impartial spectator'. Thus, in a great city, the 'man of low condition' may be 'sunk in obscurity and darkness'.[24] Smith pointed out the possibility that urbanization and the breakdown of moral standards would promote antisocial behavior of the poor. Sociologists have often called attention to the fact that individuals who behave in a socially accepted manner in their own traditional societies may develop antisocial behavior when they migrate to large cities where they feel totally alienated and no longer constrained by strict traditional norms of behavior.[25] Especially in these situations, the new type of compassion is required on the part of the wealthy: the compassion that enables them to empathize with the vulnerable they rarely meet and that enables them to extend 'the kindness of strangers'.[26]

Institutionalized income transfers have obvious negative efficiency implications even in a democratic political system, where individuals vote on public institutions aimed at improving equity, because the majority voting rule does not ensure purely *voluntary* income transfers between income groups. In establishing public institutions, the majority voters impose their decisions on the minority voters who may not be in agreement with those decisions. Thus, for the latter group, income transfers are involuntary even when the decision is democratically made. Furthermore institutionalized income transfers often require substantial administrative resources which may introduce a large wedge between what the taxpayers give and what the beneficiaries receive. Additionally there may be abuses by recipients who are capable of working but fake their true condition. For example, when invalidity requirements for pensions have been introduced, there has often been an explosion in the number of 'invalids'.[27]

Institutional compassion in a contemporary society, however, does not have only negative efficiency implications. The sheer size of the society enhances the value of coordination of individual acts.[28] This coordination helps locate and identify the potential beneficiaries of social programs. Uncoordinated individual acts, although well-intended, are unlikely to result in sufficient and efficient income transfers for all members of society in need. Thus the government has a unique role to play: it is the role of ensuring equitable income transfers between groups and between ages and maintaining a 'safety net' for all in times of distress, as for example when unemployment soars. A sufficient and secure redistribution of income toward all those in need cannot be achieved without the intervention of the state.

To some extent the advancement of communication has helped reduce the distance between the rich and the poor. The newspapers and television programs can describe the life of the poor. In that sense the modern society is becoming smaller. However the personal contacts between the poor and the rich are still severely limited.

ETHICS AND PUBLIC POLICY IN A MODERN SOCIETY

Ethical Issues in Public Policy

Social decision making can create ethical dilemmas. The use of majority voting rules is a case in point. When the cost of obtaining a unanimous decision is too high, efficiency considerations rule out unanimity as the optimal decision-making rule.[29] Majority rules, however, result in the domination of the majority voters over the minority voters?[30] Only in extreme cases it may be practical or possible to compensate the losers in a majority decision. Compassion may limit *the tyranny of the majority*. In the absence of compassion, a majority voting rule in a society where the poor are a minority will not adopt social programs aimed at the poor group unless this is done for selfish reasons (say, to reduce crime committed by people in need). The majority voting rule does not even rule out the possibility of regressive redistribution of income aimed at maximizing the welfare of the non-poor: the opposite of a Rawlsian state of equity.[31]

This case illustrates a possible conflict between efficiency and ethics in social decision making without unanimity. The case also indicates the importance of compassion in resolving conflicts. In this connection it is worthwhile to note that the truly democratic tradition has stressed the importance of respecting the interest of minority voters, as a countervailing force, to mitigate the possible adverse implications of majority voting.[32]

Another type of ethical dilemma arises in the frequent cases when a government has to decide on a policy measure whose benefit is large in aggregate, but small for each of a large number of individual beneficiaries, whereas the cost is small in aggregate, but large for a small number of individuals. In this case the majority voting rule, in theory, should ensure the adoption of the measure with possible compensation for the losers. The dilemma is similar to the one discussed above – the dominance of the majority voters over the intentions of the minority.[33] In practice, voters may often reject the adoption of the measure. Given the small individual benefits, many of the potential gainers may abstain from voting, whereas a large portion of the minority voters would lobby and vote against the measure. Thus a determined and well-organized minority may prevent the adoption of policies that are beneficial to the society.

Social decisions driven by ethical considerations could at times even be counterproductive. For example, the proliferation of social programs designed to help the poor could undermine work efforts and/or increase macroeconomic imbalances, thus actually hurting the poor. Low wages imposed on public sector employees could demoralize them, increase corruption, or induce an exodus of the most qualified, thus reducing the quantity and/or the quality of public services. In these cases the bureaucratic (or transfer) costs of redistribution may become very high. But, again, heightened compassion and ethical standards could reduce the need for government-sponsored redistributive policies and could strengthen work efforts and reduce corruption among civil servants.

Ethics, Compassion, Efficiency and Equity in a Modern Society

We can highlight the implications of ethics and compassion for individual behavior in a simple utilitarian analytical framework. Let us assume a consumer–worker–philanthropist, called hereafter a consumer, who derives utility from consumption, charitable contributions and leisure.[34] He allocates his available time between work and leisure, derives income at a given wage rate, pays income tax and allocates the disposable income between consumption and charitable contributions. For simplicity, we eliminate saving. The income tax is calculated at a flat rate on the taxable income, but the latter excludes the amount of charitable contributions. To maximize his utility, the consumer would have to satisfy two familiar conditions: (a) the marginal rate of substitution between consumption and leisure should be equal to their relative price, which in this case is equal to the post-tax wage rate; (b) the marginal rate of substitution between consumption and charitable contributions should be equal to their relative price, which in this case is equal to the disposable component of the wage rate, that is, one minus the tax rate.

In this setting, what would be the implications of an enhancement of work ethics or personal compassion? Characterizing an enhancement of work ethics as a reduction in the marginal utility of leisure, in a conventional case, one would expect that an enhancement of ethics would induce the consumer to allocate more time for work, thus increasing income, tax payment and charitable contributions. This result may be contrasted with an increase in the tax rate, which would raise the price of consumption, thus inducing both substitution and income effects. The former effect would induce the consumer to substitute leisure and charitable contributions for consumption, but the latter effect may work either way, thus leaving us unclear as to what would be the net effects. With strong substitution effects, however, it would not be unreasonable to expect a tax increase to result in less work, income and consumption, but possibly more charitable contributions. An enhancement of compassion, which may be characterized as an increase in the marginal utility of charitable contributions, is likely to induce the consumer to increase charitable contributions, to reduce consumption and even to increase work efforts to achieve these goals.[35] It is noteworthy that an enhancement of work ethics and an increase in compassion strengthen work efforts, while an increase in the tax rate weaken them, although all promote charitable contributions.

We now turn to aggregate implications, assuming a group of identical well-to-do individuals and a group of poor individuals. In Figure 5.1(a), an Edgeworth diagram shows the utility-maximizing consumption and charitable contribution for the well-to-do at e_1 on the assumption of no government intervention. The share of the well-to-do of the aggregate income RO is Rd_0, and the share of the poor is d_0O. The well-to-do give away e_1d_1 ($= d_1d_0$) to the

(a) Choices

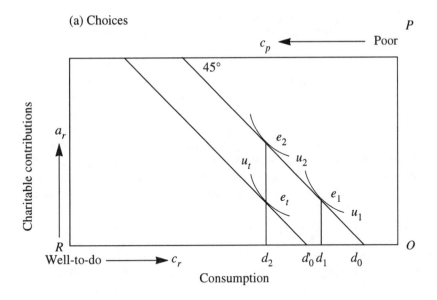

(b) Utility possibilities

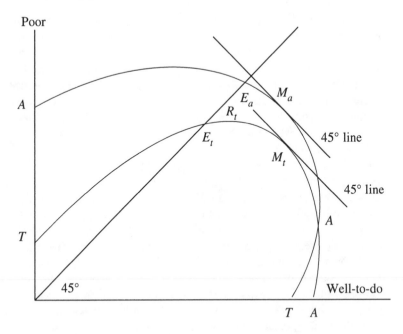

Figure 5.1   Taxation, charity and utility possibilities

poor and consume Rd_1. The poor, since they do not make charitable contributions, consume d_0O from their own income and the income transfer d_1d_0 from the well-to-do.

What would happen if the government attempted to redistribute income by taxing away a part of the income from the well-to-do to provide income supplements for the poor?[36] If aggregate income were to remain the same, the government could transfer $d_1'd_0$ from the well-to-do to the poor to raise the poor's consumption to d_2O, to be financed from the poor's own income d_0O, government income transfers d'_1d_0, and private income transfers e_td_2 ($=d_2d'_0$) from the well-to-do, who would have the new utility maximization at e_t.[37] In this case, although not shown explicitly in the diagram, the taxation can have adverse effects on the work efforts of the well-to-do, resulting in a reduction in the aggregate income.

Alternatively an enhancement of compassion could result in the new utility-maximizing consumption and charitable contributions for the well-to-do at e_2 and increase consumption of the poor to d_2O, but without a reduction in aggregate income. In Figure 5.1(a), on the assumption that tax payments do not give utility, the indifference curve u_2 dominates u_t, although it does not dominate u_1.[38]

The efficiency implications of compassion may be illustrated in a utility-possibility frontier that can be derived from Figure 5.1(a). Figure 5.1(b) compares two hypothetical stylized utility possibility frontiers that can be derived from Figure 5.1(a), one for the situation in which income transfers are achieved through taxation and the other for the situation in which they are achieved through direct voluntary transfers from the well-to-do to the poor. Locus TT represents the utility possibility frontier, reflecting the effect of redistribution through taxation; locus AA represents the utility-possibility frontier, reflecting the effect of redistribution through direct transfers. The two loci are normalized for easy comparison; the maximum utilities for the well-to-do in both situations are the same.

On the TT locus, the point A represents the utilities the poor and the well-to-do derive from their respective incomes in the absence of redistribution. A greater redistribution of income away from the well-to-do to the poor is assumed to have increasingly negative effects on the well-to-do's work effort. At an extreme where the entire income of the well-to-do is taxed, they are assumed to stop working; thus the poor derives the entire utility only from the outcome of his work. On the TT locus, point M_t represents the distribution of income between the poor and the well-to-do that maximizes the social welfare, which is assumed to be the sum of the utilities. Point R_t represents the distribution that maximizes the utility of the poor. Point E_t represents the distribution that equalizes the utilities for the poor and the well-to-do.

The implications of the dominant role of voluntary direct income transfers in redistribution can be shown by comparing locus *AA* with locus *TT*. The efficiency loss is smaller in the former, and the complete equalization of the utilities of the poor and the well-to-do can be achieved at a higher welfare level for the society. Other things being equal, an elevation of the aggregate level of compassion would tend to cause a shift of the *TT* locus toward the *AA* locus. This shift may be called an efficiency gain resulting from the elevation of compassion.

Implications for the Role of Government

Many of the optimum properties of competitive markets in theoretical models are predicated on the ethical foundation of the members of the society. However the ethical standards of market participants are far from ideal, and the functioning of the real-world markets far from perfect. Heightened ethical standards would improve the efficiency of markets. The discussions in the previous sections indicate how ethical behavior, in particular the active kinds such as compassion, can even be effective in the satisfactory resolution of the basic flaws of competitive markets: their failure to provide public goods and to achieve an acceptable degree of distributive equity

Root causes of these fundamental problems in a competitive economy are conflicts of individual interests and divergence between individual (private) and social (public) interests. The traditional solution to these problems in modern societies has been the imposition of regulations, public provision of goods, and public tax and expenditure programs for redistribution. These interventions, however, pose difficult, and often impossible, dilemmas discussed earlier in this section. Therefore it may be worthwhile for the government to use more of its resources to promote both passive and active ethical standards of the members of the society. The government can be a paternalistic promoter of ethics.[39] Does this recommendation imply a larger role of the government? Not necessarily. An increase in government expenditure for promoting ethical behavior may be more than offset, in the long run, by a decrease in government expenditure for regulating private economic activities. Thus, in the terminology of health economics, an effective *preventive* ethics education program may reduce *curative* public expenditures on criminal justice and costly litigation and those arising from social disturbances. Moreover ethics education does not have to be expanded at the cost of professional education; the entire educational programs, in particular the humanities program, could be restructured to focus more on ethics. Crucial questions in this regard are how effective are the programs designed to promote ethical behavior and, more fundamentally, how feasible is it to change the ethical standards of human beings? It is obvious, however, that most of the conflicts discussed in this chapter cannot be resolved satisfactorily without the help of ethics.

Whereas this proposal may sound idealistic or radical (or even alarming for some), societies, through various public and private means, have been engaged in a wide range of ethics promotion. The feasibility and desirability of changing human beings have been widely recognized. The widespread emphasis of college admissions offices on the applicants' records of philanthropic activities, such as community services, as a factor for evaluating their candidates is aimed at making high school students more compassionate. For example, Swarthmore College stresses that the factors of interest to it include 'strength of character, promise of growth, initiative, seriousness of purpose, distinction in personal and extra-curricular interests, and a sense of social responsibility'. Bryn Mawr College is interested in 'candidates of character and ability.'[40] As mentioned earlier in this chapter, some business schools offer courses addressing ethical issues. For example, Harvard Business School requires its MBA students to take 'Leadership, Values and Decision Making', aimed at helping students 'to develop an ethical framework to use as a guide in decision making'. Stanford Business School offers an elective 'Ethical Dilemmas in Management', which explores 'the role of values and ethics in American and international business, and the impact of values and ethics on the decisions of managers'.[41]

While guarding against moral indoctrination, ethicists, philosophers, psychologists and economists support moral education of various forms. Noting that moral education that promotes a definite moral perspective 'tends to be toward indoctrination and the denial of moral autonomy', Robert Hall has argued that there is 'a middle way which neither indoctrinates young people into one set of moral rules nor gives them the impression that decision making is all a matter of personal opinion'.[42] Arguing that there is a universal sequence of moral development, Lawrence Kohlberg has stressed that it is possible to stimulate moral development by using what he called 'the developmental approach', which 'tries to move students' thinking in a direction that is natural for the student rather than moving the student in the direction of accepting the teachers' moral assumptions'.[43] George Sher and William J. Bennett have even advocated 'directive moral education', in which students are explicitly encouraged to accept and to behave in accordance with specific principles.[44] More recently Robert Coles has emphasized 'moral intelligence' and explored how parents and school teachers may give shape to the values of children as expressed in their behavior and encourage them to uphold in daily life one or another set of beliefs.[45] He notes the 'disparity between character and intellect' and the inadequacy of emphasizing the importance of intellectual development, but not moral development.[46]

Public education programs in any society include some schooling in ethical behavior. A primary duty of effective public officials is considered to be education – by setting an example. Great public figures (Thomas Jefferson, Abraham Lincoln, Mahatma Gandhi and Albert Schweitzer) have been, and will continue to remain, in an important way, great ethics educators. Religions and churches in many societies have been prominent institutions of ethical education. In many countries the state supports religious educational institutions.

What more can be done? *The government can devote a larger share of its expenditure to ethics promotion. A substantial expansion of ethical education of children at schools beginning at an early age, persistently followed through later years, may prove to be effective.* The state could more actively support religious schools regardless of their denomination. As pointed out earlier in the chapter, this may not be excessively costly. It is noteworthy that the effectiveness of government social programs will increase political support for the programs. An ineffective government social program would not induce even a truly compassionate person to support the taxation to finance it.

A major argument against a substantial expansion of ethical education at public institutions is that such an expansion could infringe freedom and civil liberty. It is easy to see that formulating ethical education programs could be a controversial issue. On the one hand, one may question whether it is morally right for the government to attempt to reform the citizens and to impose certain ethical standards. One should also consider the possibility of abuses of educational programs by political authorities. Supporting religious schools could be politically controversial in some countries. We are fully aware that this proposal is politically unacceptable to many in the United States. On the other hand, however, it is not unusual in other countries, such as Canada, for the government to support religious school. Societies have been attempting to reform their members in many ways, and it may not be difficult for the members of a society to reach an agreement on what should be lasting ethical qualities for the members of a society.

It is undeniable that excessive substitution of ethics for self-interest may be counterproductive. As Arrow has pointed out, 'ethically motivated behavior may even have a negative value to others'.[47] We believe, however, that ethics can play a much wider role than Arrow has suggested, that is, where market fails.

The importance of ethics in the sound functioning of an economy becomes clearer when one considers a society with widespread corruption, crimes and other illegal activities including manifestations in high places. In these societies the key issue is not lack of active ethics; it is a lack of even passive ethics. Certain parts of government and society can become predatory, bringing about, not only inefficiencies, but also breakdowns of a market system. To some extent this seems to have happened in Russia and in some other transition economies. While research has pointed out that 'discretionary government regulations' are a key factor underlying corruption, it must also be recognized that, for a given degree of discretionary regulations, different ethical standards of those who enforce regulations can make a difference. Moreover, without the ethical conduct of governmental officials, particularly at the top, it would be difficult for a government to formulate and implement regulatory reforms that do not give rise to ample opportunities for corruption.

Ethics and International Transfers

Globalization is bringing about new issues concerning ethics and economics. The age of international aggression and colonialism is gone, but what are the transnational implications of ethics? The communication revolution has shrunk the world, enabling the members of rich societies to learn about the plights of the impoverished people far away from their communities. Peter Singer, among others, argued that affluent people are morally obligated to contribute part of their time and income toward alleviating hunger.[48] In a similar vein, some have claimed that the earth is like a spaceship whose passengers each have an equal claim to its scarce resources. While the global implications of our thesis are beyond the scope of this chapter, we should note that a heightened degree of compassion over the world would reduce the need for a global *public* transfer scheme, which would give rise to familiar problems regarding disincentive effects.

We should also note that authors are not in agreement on the feasibility of massive international aid. Garrett Hardin has rejected the spaceship simile and pointed out that, rather than being likened to a spaceship, which operates with one captain, the world should be compared to an ocean with several lifeboats with unequal stocks of food. He argues that the spaceship ethics, and the sharing it requires, lead to 'the tragedy of the commons'.[49] Hardin's analysis does not make a distinction between voluntary and forced sharing or between private and institutional compassion.

CONCLUDING OBSERVATIONS

Ethical behavior has substantial efficiency and equity implications. Enhanced ethics in general imply greater work efforts by those both at the giving and at the receiving ends of income transfers. Compassion has important implications for efficiency and redistribution. Institutional compassion and personal compassion have different implications for the work efforts of those at the giving end of income transfers. The former type of compassion implies greater efficiency losses arising from income transfers.

Ethics may be the only means of resolving many policy conflicts and dilemmas. Traditional economic analysis of these conflicts tends to limit itself to possible trade-offs with given ethical standards. Many of the traditional economic policy instruments are powerless to resolve them. Public policy instruments might prove to be more effective when they are aimed at improving ethical standards. Such an improvement may reduce, or even resolve, policy conflicts and have substantial efficiency implications. Economics should pay more attention to these implications.

In this chapter, we have suggested that more public resources be devoted to ethics education, perhaps beginning with primary schooling or even earlier. The social rate of return to such expenditures could be high. Decentralization of income transfers and enhancing compassion can also be a very productive means of achieving efficient redistribution.

NOTES

1. The concept of family is generally much more extended in a traditional society.
2. In traditional societies the poor and the rich tend to live in the same areas. In modern societies they tend to live in different areas, thus reducing the possibility of contacts among them.
3. In the so-called 'modern growth literature', the spillovers from educational spending are emphasized (see, for example, Romer, 1989). However the issue discussed in this chapter is not dealt with.
4. Some business schools (such as Harvard Business School and Stanford Business School) are offering courses examining ethical aspects of business decisions. Some colleges (such as Yale College) offer an interdisciplinary major in Economics, Ethics and Political Science.
5. Groups can be relatively isolated from each other even when the physical distances are not great.
6. For example, the theoretical literature on tax evasion has emphasized that the propensity to evade tax is influenced by (a) the probability of being caught and (b) the penalty that would accompany detection. But that literature does not explain why, given (a) and (b), the propensity to evade varies from country to country or from individual to individual in a country.
7. It is also likely to affect the composition of public spending since some expenditures (for police, prisons, the judiciary system and so on) will be reduced while others (redistributive ones) will be increased.
8. See Philip Hallie, 'From Cruelty to Goodness', Institute of Society, Ethics and the Life Sciences, 360 Broadway, Hastings-on-Hudson, New York, reprinted in Christina Sommers and Fred Sommers (eds), *Vice & Virtue in Everyday Life: Introductory Readings in Ethics* (Harcourt Brace Jovanovich, Fort Worth, Texas, 1993), pp. 9–24.
9. In fact it is this redistributive aspect that largely justifies the governmental role. Without it, private pensions might satisfy the insurance requirement.
10. Moral philosophers have pointed out that ultimately only self-interest can account for obeying moral rules, although the pursuit of self-interest may have either sociological (Thomas Hobbes) or psychological (Adam Smith) roots. For example, either we obey moral rules because it promotes our long-term interest through social harmony (Hobbes) or we pursue psychological satisfaction by seeking praiseworthiness of an 'impartial spectator' who knows our motives (Smith). See Hobbes (1946) and Smith (1976). In many

religions moral behavior increases the chance of access to heaven and thus promotes an ultimate form of self-interest. In the Catholic tradition, donating one's wealth to the poor was one of the best ways to get to heaven.

11. Some charitable institutions attempt to transform institutional into personal compassion, for example, by providing pictures of those who are benefited. Presumably this increases the propensity to give.

12. Kenneth Arrow has noted, for example, how virtues (such as truth, trust and loyalty) significantly facilitate the process of exchange. He has also noted that virtue is not usually paid for at market rates (see Arrow, 1974).

13. For example, Smith stressed the importance of public provision of basic education for the poor. He states: 'The education of the common people requires, perhaps, in a civilized and commercial society, the attention of the public more than that of people of some rank and fortune' (see Smith, 1937, pp. 236–7).

14. In many societies religious orders have played and continue to play an important role.

15. Patriotism has been called upon to induce citizens to buy government bonds during war years.

16. We have to admit that we are now making a normative judgement on the optimality of a state of distributive equity. We rule out the possibility, pointed out by Friedman, that the state of income distribution we observe might reflect the tastes and preferences of the members of the society, that is, the possibility that it reflects a desired result rather than an accidental outcome (Friedman, 1962). We are making a judgement that the present state of income distribution in many societies is hardly 'equitable' in accordance, for example, with the criterion of 'non-envy', as defined by Foley (1967). Therefore we maintain that a more equitable distribution of income is a worthwhile goal for a society to achieve provided that it does not result in excessive bureaucratic costs and in a lower rate of growth by reducing savings and incentives. Income redistribution, on the other hand, enhances the nutrition, health and education of the poor and thus both ensures labor supply and raises labor quality (see Tanzi and Chu, 1989; and Blejer and Chu, 1990).

17. There are reasons to believe that informal transfers between individuals would have less adverse effects on the work efforts of the beneficiaries than in institutionalized transfers through the government. The so-called 'stigma effects' often prevent potential beneficiaries from abusing government income transfers; personal income transfers would be more difficult to abuse.

18. Lawrence Kohlberg has observed a transcultural three-level, six-stage moral development: pre-conventional, conventional, and post-conventional. In the pre-conventional, second stage of moral development, human beings recognize the importance of fairness, reciprocity and equal sharing, but interpret these in a pragmatic way as a matter of 'You scratch my back and I'll scratch yours'. See Kohlberg (1993).

19. John Middleton *Peoples of Africa* (New York: Arco Publishing Company, 1978).

20. R.H. Lowie, *Indians of the Plains* (The University of Nebraska Press, 1954).

21. See, for example, J. Platteau (1994).

22. We recognize that a social chain of charitable giving can arise from egoistic cooperative behaviors, as explained by Kenneth Boulding (1973). It is undeniable, however, that even egoistic cooperation is not feasible without an ethical foundation, particularly in comparison with plausible alternative situations, in which unethical, antisocial and even predatory behavior of individuals triggers destructive social processes.

23. In a democratic society it is conceivable for a poorer majority to initiate social legislation for income transfers from a wealthier minority to them; such legislation, however, has nothing to do with ethics. This aspect has been emphasized by James Buchanan and his followers.

24. Smith (1937), p. 747.

25. A classic Italian movie illustrated this possibility. See Visconti, *Rocco and His Brothers.*

26. Williams (1955).

27. These abuses on the part of the recipients of benefits are similar to tax evasion and may be as important quantitatively, but they have not received as much attention (see Smith,

1986). The literature on the underground economy has often called attention to the 'unemployed' who are very busy working in underground activities (see Tanzi, 1982).

28. At times social programs miss needy individuals who, for particular reasons, may not fit the eligibility requirements.

29. See, for example, Wicksell (1958). Wicksell therefore suggested that the only way for a democratic society to achieve a collective decision making without prohibitive cost is through approximate unanimity.

30. For this reason these rules are often accompanied by limitations (constitutional or otherwise).

31. The political influence of the middle-income and upper-income groups may be the main reason underlying the use of generalized subsidies (for example generalized food subsidies), which are not aimed at the poor, in many countries.

32. See Kennedy (1956). In this treatise, Kennedy analyzes the moral courage of parliamentary leaders who on behalf of principle confront 'the passion of colleagues, constituents and a majority of the general public'. See its foreword by Allan Nevin.

33. Governments and voters seem to be more inclined to raise spending than to raise the taxes needed to pay for it.

34. The reader will note that this formulation of a utility function is in line with Kenneth Arrow's second hypothesis about the utilitarian implications of giving. The assumed utility function includes charitable contribution, rather than others' income or well-being. The consumer derives a utility from actively giving to others. For a discussion of the three hypotheses, see Arrow (1974), pp. 343–62.

35. Actually, an optimizing model including a Constant Elasticity of Substitution (CES) production function yields the following effects. First, an enhancement of work ethics would induce one to work more to use additional earnings for more consumption and charitable contributions. Second, greater compassion would induce one to work more, but one would spend more for charity than on one's own consumption. Third, an increase in the tax rate would induce one to work less, but to spend more for charity and to consume less.

36. For simplicity, we assume that charitable contributions are not tax-deductible.

37. Note that, in this model, the well-to-do's utility depends on charitable contributions, but not on the utility of the poor. Some authors have analyzed voluntary income transfers resulting from the well-to-do's maximizing an objective function including both their own and others' utilities. See Mueller (1989).

38. A full analysis would have to include the effect on utilities deriving from leisure, but we do not consider them for simplicity.

39. For a discussion of a paternalistic state, see Chapter 1.

40. Both quotations are from their bulletins (1993).

41. See the Internet home pages of Harvard Business School and Stanford Business School.

42. Hall (1978).

43. Kohlberg (1993).

44. Sher and Bennett (1982).

45. See Coles (1997).

46. The last chapter, 'Letter to Parents and Teachers', of his *The Moral Intelligence of Children* highlights the disparity between character and intellect by reporting on a conversation with his student 'Marian'. His point is to stress the importance of teachers and parents noting that children are 'on the lookout for moral direction'.

47. Arrow (1974).

48. Singer (1972).

49. Hardin (1974).

REFERENCES

Arrow, Kenneth (1974), 'Gifts and Exchanges', *Philosophy and Public Affairs*, summer, 1(4), pp. 343–62; reprinted in Edmund S. Phelps (ed.), *Altruism, Morality and Economic Theory*, New York: Russell Sage Foundation, 1975, pp. 13–28.

Blejer, Mario I. and Ke-young Chu (1990), 'Fiscal Policy, Labor Markets, and the Poor', IMF Working Paper, WP/90/02 (July).

Boulding, Kenneth (1973), *The Economy of Love and Fear: A Preface to Grants Economies*, Belmont, Calif.: Wadsworth Publishing Company.

Coles, Robert (1997), *The Moral Intelligence of Children*, New York: Random House.

Foley, D. (1967), 'Resource Allocation and the Public Sector', Yale Economic Essay.

Friedman, Milton (1962), 'The Size Distribution of Income', in Milton Friedman, *Price Theory: A Provisional Text*, Chicago: Aldine; reprinted from 'Choice, Chance and the Personal Distribution of Income' rev. edn, *The Journal of Political Economy*, LXI (4) (August).

Hall, Robert (1978), 'Moral Education Today: Progress, Prospects and Problems of a Field Come of Age', *The Humanist* (November/December), 12.

Hardin, Garrett (1974), 'Lifeboat Ethics: The Case Against Helping the Poor', *Psychology Today*, September; reprinted in Christina Sommers and Fred Sommers (eds), *Vice & Virtue in Everyday Life*, Fort Worth, Texas: Harcourt Brace Jovanovich, 1993, pp. 853–76.

Hobbes, Thomas (1946), *Leviathan or The Matter, Forme & Power of a Commonwealth, Ecclesiastical and Civil*, Oxford: Basil Blackwell, originally published in 1651, ch. 14.

Kennedy, John F. (1956), *Profiles in Courage*, a Cardinal edn, New York: Pocket Books.

Kohlberg, Lawrence (1956), 'The Child as a Moral Philosopher', from 'Indoctrination v. Relativity in Value Education', in Lawrence Kohlberg, *The Philosophy of Moral Development*, vol. 1, San Francisco: Harper & Row; reprinted in Christina Sommers and Fred Sommers (eds), *Vice & Virtue in Everyday Life*, Fort Worth, Texas: Harcourt Brace Jovanovich, 1993, pp. 557–82.

Lowie, R.H. (1954), *Indians of the Plains*, Lincoln, Nebraska: The University of Nebraska Press.

Middleton, John (1978), *Peoples of Africa*, New York: Arco Publishing Company.

Mueller, D.C. (1989), *Public Choice II*, Cambridge: Cambridge University Press, pp. 446–8. *Peoples of Africa*, New York: Arco Publishing Company, 1978.

Platteau, L. (1994), 'Traditional Systems of Social Security and Hunger Insurance: Some Lessons from the Evidence Pertaining to Third World Village Societies', in E. Ahmad, J. Drèze, J. Hills and Amartya Sen (eds), *Social Security and Social Welfare in Developing Countries*, Oxford: Oxford University Press, pp. 112–170.

Romer, Paul (1989), 'Human Capital and Growth Theory and Evidence', NBER Working Paper No.31735.

Sher, George and William J. Bennett (1982), 'Moral Education and Indoctrination', The Journal of Philosophy (November), 665–7; reprinted in Christina Sommers and Fred Sommers (eds), *Vice & Virtue in Everyday Life*, Fort Worth, Texas: Harcourt Brace Jovanovich, 1993, pp. 582–97.

Singer, Peter (1972), 'Famine, Affluence and Morality', *Philosophy and Public Affairs*, 1(3) (Spring); reprinted in Christina Sommers and Fred Sommers (eds), *Vice & Virtue in Everyday Life*, Fort Worth, Texas: Harcourt Brace.

Smith, Adam (1937), *The Wealth of Nations*, New York: The Modern Library; originally published in 1776.

—— (1976) *The Theory of Moral Sentiments*, London: Oxford University Press; originally published in 1759, Part III, chs 2–3.

Smith S. (1986), *Britain's Shadow Economy*, Oxford: Oxford University Press, ch. 8.

Tanzi, Vito (ed.) (1982), *The Underground Economy in the United States and Abroad*, Lexington, Mass.: D.C. Heath.

Tanzi, Vito and Ke-young Chu (1989), 'Fiscal Policy for Stable and Equitable Growth in Latin America', in *La Herencia de Raúl Prebisch y los Problemas dee Desarrollo de América Latina*, a volume in the proceedings of the Prebisch Foundation Seminar held in Santa Fe, Argentina, June.

Visconti, L., *Rocco and His Brothers*, film.

Wicksell, Knut (1958), 'A New Principle of Just Taxation', in R.A. Musgrave and A.T. Peacock (eds), *Classics in the Theory of Public Finance*, London: Macmillan, pp. 72–118.

Williams, Tennessee (1955), 'A Streetcar Named Desire', in *New Voices in the American Theater*, New York: The Modern Library, p. 109.

6. Corruption, governmental activities and markets

INTRODUCTION

On 8 May 1993, the day when the author of this chapter sat down to start drafting its first version, *The Washington Post* carried a front page story about a division of the US National Institute of Health in Bethesda 'in which some female employees were promised promotions and raises if they agreed to have sex with their male managers' (Jennings, 1993, p. 1). On the same day, an article in *The New York Times* reported that in China, in the process of privatization of land, 'individuals seem to be expropriating the state's property at bargain prices' (Dunn, 1993, p. 3). The article went on to state that 'today's real estate boom raises troubling questions about land that is allocated not [so much] by prices but by *guanxi*' (ibid.).[1] *Guanxi* is the Chinese word for 'connections'. The article cited a Chinese businessman to the effect that 'if you have *guanxi*, it is the time to make big money'. Thus, according to this article, in today's China 'connections' have great economic value and smart people can capitalize on them to earn large 'incomes'. On 8 May 1993 French newspapers were still carrying stories about the suicide of former Prime Minister Pierre Bérégovoy, attributed in part to his despondency as a result of the accusation that he had received an interest-free loan from a friend. And Italian newspapers were providing further details about private entrepreneurs who had paid large bribes to well-placed politicians in order to get lucrative contracts with the Italian public sector. On 10 August 1994, when the final version was completed, front page news in *The New York Times* and *The Washington Post* reported on the accusation that gifts given to a high US government official might have resulted in favorable decisions vis-à-vis certain business activities.

What is the unifying thread in all of these stories? Essentially it is the accusation that the 'arm's length principle' was not applied to economic decisions. This principle requires that personal relationships should play no part in economic decisions involving more than one party. Equality of treatment for all economic agents is essential for a well-functioning market economy. In the examples cited above, economic decisions – in land markets, in labor markets, in financial markets, in the market for government contracts and in government decisions concerning private sector's activities – were allegedly not guided by the arm's length principle.

GOVERNMENT AND MARKETS

Economic theory tells us that, if markets were perfect, there would be no need for the government to play an economic role. Furthermore, almost by definition, these markets would be guided by the extreme version of arm's length-relationships among market participants implied by pure or perfect competition. Decisions concerning the selling and buying of goods, the hiring, retaining and compensating of workers, the lending and borrowing of money, the timing, size and location of investment projects, and so forth, would be determined by economic considerations and profit opportunities alone. Personal relationships among the parties would play no part.

However markets are not perfect; the existence of public goods, of externalities in production and consumption, of informational deficiencies and of monopolistic practices, justifies and requires that the state play an economic, corrective role.[2] The work of Lindahl, Wicksell, Musgrave, Samuelson and others has been influential in determining the optimal *theoretical*, or normative, role of the state. A fundamental but unstated assumption in the theoretical work on the role of the public sector is that public sector officials (both policy makers and civil servants) know what they are doing and are neutral and impersonal in their pursuit of the social welfare.[3] When these officials make mistakes, they are honest mistakes. This assumption, though of fundamental importance, is hidden in the pure theory of public expenditure.[4]

The theoretical work on how the public sector should pursue its corrective role owes a great deal to Max Weber's *ideal*, or normative, type of rational–legal bureaucracy. As Robin Theobald has put it, Weber's bureaucrats would operate 'according to rational procedures and universalistic principles in which there is no place for personalism, cronyism, and, most of all, the confusion of public with private interests'.[5] This bureaucracy 'is run by hierarchically ordered corps of officials who are recruited and promoted according to objective criteria such as educational qualifications and professional experience; who are paid a regular salary which is graded according to rank and qualifications; and who are allocated fixed jurisdictional areas governed by clearly laid down rules and procedures' (Theobald, 1990, p. 56). Weber was aware that 'Bureaucracy, thus understood, is fully developed ... only in the modern state, and in the private economy only in the most advanced institutions of capitalism' (Weber, 1978, p. 56). In other words he was fully aware that he was presenting an ideal type of bureaucracy rather than describing reality.[6]

The extent to which the real world approximates the Lindahl–Samuelson–Weber ideal is, of course, an open question. The Italian *Scienza delle Finanze*, which had a lot of influence on James Buchanan's work and, through him, on the development of public choice, would have been very skeptical on various grounds about the realism and, indeed, about the usefulness of the normative theory of public expenditure.

In the real world the economic role of the state is exercised through the use of various instruments, such as (a) public spending for government consumption and transfers; (b) taxation and borrowing; (c) various forms of regulation; (d) lending activities; and (e) occasionally, less orthodox governmental actions such as expropriation, conscription, nationalization, privatization, exhortation, and so forth. Depending on the level of development of a country and on its sophistication, some of these instruments are used more than others. For example, poorer countries are less able to raise large shares of their national incomes in taxes; as a consequence they tend to abuse the instruments listed under (c), (d), and (e).[7]

The behavior of real world bureaucracies (and policy makers) may depart significantly from the Weber ideal for several reasons. Some of these reasons have provided the basis for the public choice literature.[8] In this chapter the focus is on the economic role of 'corruption'. An important conclusion will be that, the more real-life bureaucracies diverge from Weber's ideal, the less control will the government have over its policy instruments and the less correction it will be able to bring, through its actions, to the imperfections of the market. In other words the less legitimate and justified will be the corrective role of the government.

The divergence between the optimum of the Samuelson solution and the real outcome of the public sector's action may be due either to policy makers pursuing policies that are not consistent with the achievement of the social welfare function or to bureaucrats distorting, in various ways, the signals that they get from the policy makers. The issue of corruption obviously concerns both. There is thus administrative and political corruption (see Rose-Ackermann, 1978). This chapter deals mostly with administrative rather than political corruption. In other words, it focuses on the activities of individuals who, in their positions as public officials, control various activities or decisions. It does not focus on the corruption associated with particular political systems. The issues discussed transcend the political configuration of the country; they are not limited to whether a country has democratic or authoritarian institutions. *Political* corruption, however, is likely to be more influenced by a country's political system.

ARM'S-LENGTH RELATIONSHIPS AND CULTURAL FACTORS

On 25 January 1992 *The Economist* reviewed a paper by Prakash Reddy, an Indian social anthropologist who, reversing the common pattern of Western scholars going to study developing countries' social behavior, obtained a research grant to study a village in Denmark. He spent a few months in this village, Hvilsager, and registered his impressions of the relations among its inhabitants.[9] These impressions formed the basis of Reddy's paper reviewed by *The Economist*. Professor Reddy had been amazed to observe that the villagers hardly knew one another. They rarely exchanged visits and had few other social contacts. They had little information on what other villagers, including their neighbors, were doing and apparently little interest in finding out. Even the relationships between parents and children were not very close. When the children reached adulthood they moved out and, after that, they visited their parents only occasionally.

Professor Reddy contrasted this behavior with that prevailing in a typical Indian village of comparable size. In the latter, daily house visits would be common. Everyone would be interested, and getting involved, in the business of the others. Family contacts would be very frequent and the members of the extended families would support one another in many ways. Relations with neighbors would also be close.

This story has implications for the concept of arm's length and, in turn, for the role of corruption. Arm's-length relationships in economic exchanges would be much more likely to prevail in the Danish village than in the Indian village. In the latter, the concept of arm's length would seem strange and alien. It would even seem immoral. The idea that, economically speaking, one should treat relatives and friends in the same way as strangers would appear bizarre. Relatives and friends would simply expect preferential treatment whether they were dealing with individuals in the private or in the public sphere.

If a government were established in each of the two villages, with a bureaucracy charged with carrying out its functions through the instruments described earlier, it would be far easier for the Danish bureaucrats to approximate in their behavior Weber's ideal than for the Indian bureaucrats. In the Indian village the attempt to create an impersonal bureaucracy that would operate 'according to ... principles in which there is no place for personalism, cronyism, etc.' would conflict with the accepted social norm that family and friends come first. In this society the government employee, just like any other individual, would be expected to help relatives and friends with special treatment or favors even if, occasionally, this behavior might require bending, or even breaking, administrative rules and departing from 'universalistic principles'. The person who refused to provide this help would be seen as breaking the prevailing moral code and would be ostracized.

Once civil servants begin to make distinctions among the people they deal with according to the degree of family relationship or friendship, they have abandoned the arm's length principle. It would consequently be a small step to begin to expect some compensation from more distant members of the community for performing for them tasks that should be the duty of the civil servants to perform or for treating them in the same favorable way as others. Without such compensation those who required particular permits or legal documents or other services might have to wait a long time to get them.[10] Thus 'speed or oil money' may be required to accelerate the process, and payments of various kinds ('bribes') to get a positive response in cases where the bureaucrat has the power of refusal.

The Indian and Danish villages described above represent polar or extreme cases of the way individuals may interact within a community. Whether Professor Reddy's description of them is or is not accurate, they provide convenient polar cases. Most societies probably fall somewhere between these two extremes, with North European and Anglo-Saxon countries probably closer to the Danish village model and many other countries closer to the Indian village model. The Anglo-Saxon concept of 'privacy' is probably just a manifestation of arm's-length relationships.[11] Many developing countries would probably be closer to the model represented by the Indian village. Some industrial countries, such as Italy and possibly Japan, would also come closer to the latter than the former. Sadly the very features that make a country a less cold and indifferent place are the same that increase the difficulty of enforcing arm's-length rules so essential for modern efficient markets and governments.

In this connection, the concept of 'social capital' introduced by Coleman (1990) is of relevance.[12] Coleman criticized the economic theory of perfect competition in a market since it accepts the 'fiction ... that society consists of a set of independent individuals, each of whom acts to achieve goals that are independently arrived at, and that the functioning of the social system consists of the combination of these actions of independent individuals' (p. 300). He maintains that 'individuals do not act independently, goals are not independently arrived at, and interests are not wholly selfish' (p. 301), and that 'personal relations and networks of relations' are important to achieve personal goals. He considers these relations and networks as a capital asset for the individual, a kind of social capital. This social capital is not tangible and is not completely fungible but is 'productive, making possible the achievement of certain ends that would not be attainable by the individual in its absence' (p. 302). The concept of social capital can be adapted to our discussion to reach conclusions that are not necessarily those intended by Coleman.

In our interpretation social capital is an asset to the individual who possesses it. It is in essence the summation of all the 'I owe you's' that the individual has accumulated vis-à-vis others. Some of these may come from his family background, some from connections developed in school or at work, some from past favors done, and so forth. But, of course, the social capital of an individual does not represent a one-way street in obligations. While the individual can use this capital to ask others to do things for him, others can draw from *their* social capital to ask him to perform tasks or do things for them. One could, thus, distinguish a *gross* from a *net* concept of social capital. The obligations that others have toward the individual might be largely balanced by the obligations that he has toward them. The existence of social capital links individuals in a network of obligations that both increases their opportunities and reduces their individual freedom. It puts strong pressures on individuals to accommodate the needs of friends and relatives and creates a presumption that they will in turn accommodate the individuals' needs.

In some societies (those closer to the polar case of the Indian village) the *gross* social capital of individuals, as we have defined it, will be particularly large. The examples of the *guanxi* in China and the relations in the Indian village all reflect the existence of social capital. The net social capital of individuals is likely to be unevenly distributed. This net social capital will play a large role in determining the distribution of income within countries. The existence of social capital is likely to interfere with arm's-length relationships and, in particular circumstances, to lead to corruption.

ON CORRUPTION

Not long ago the word 'corruption' was infrequently used in professional works, although the problem reflected by its existence is obviously a very old one.[13] The word did not appear often in newspapers and it was rarely mentioned by economists, even though sociologists, political scientists and a few economists did pay some attention to it. Very few economists spent much time assessing its economic significance.[14] Recent newspaper articles indicate that this phenomenon is far more widespread and universal than previously thought. Evidence of it is everywhere, in developing countries and, with growing frequency, in industrial countries. A perusal of recent daily newspapers would show that this problem has attracted a lot of attention in Brazil, France, Germany, Greece, India, Italy, Japan, Korea, Russia, Spain and many other places.[15] Prominent political figures, including presidents of countries and ministers, have been accused of corruption and, as a consequence, some have resigned or have been forced out of office.

Corruption comes in many shapes and forms. It is very difficult to define and at times it is even more difficult to identify. Several definitions have appeared in the literature, but none seems to be fully satisfactory.[16] Here we shall simply define it as the intentional non-compliance with an arm's-length relationship, aimed at deriving some advantage, for oneself or for related individuals, from this behavior. In the Danish village described by Professor Reddy, if corruption existed, it would reflect the isolated acts of particular individuals who would try to take advantage of their positions for personal gain. In other words it would reflect clearly unwarranted and antisocial behavior not induced by social pressures or prevailing social norms. In this case its identification might be easier since the victims of this corruption would be more likely to report the perpetrators. Its punishment would also be easier since it would conform to generally accepted social norms. However, in societies with close social or interpersonal relationships, its frequency is likely to be greater, its identification much more difficult, and its punishment more problematic. This implies that the models of criminal or illegal behavior of the type pioneered by Becker (1968) and by Allingham and Sandmo (1972) will be of limited applicability since some of the requirements of those models (knowledge of probability of getting caught and knowledge of the penalty) would not be satisfied.

The term 'corruption' comes from the Latin verb to break, *rumpere*. It thus implies that something is broken. This something might be a moral or social code of conduct or, more often, an administrative rule.[17] If it is the latter, a requirement must be that the rule that is broken is precise and transparent. Another is that the official who breaks it derives some recognizable benefit for himself, his family, his friends, his tribe or party, or some other relevant group. Additionally the benefit derived must be seen as a direct quid pro quo from the specific act of 'corruption'. This simple description reveals potential difficulties.

First, there must be evidence that a precise rule is broken. This requires that all the rules must be precisely stated, thus leaving no doubts about their meaning and no discretion to the public officials. But what about cases where the rules are not precise or where the bureaucrats are specifically given some discretion? For example, in many countries legislation related to the granting of tax incentives or import licenses has often left a lot of discretion in the hands of the officials who must make the decisions to grant them. They must decide whether an investment or an import is 'essential' or 'necessary' to the country. These officials are often the sole arbiters of what those terms mean. Thus, in a way, they are in a position of monopoly, since they can grant or deny these permits and these permits cannot be obtained from other sources. Or, taking a different example, what about the selection of a tax return for an audit, or the selection of an enterprise for an on site tax inspection when there are no precise rules for making these choices; or the hiring of a new employee when there are no precise objective and honest tests for the selection?

Over the years there has been a lot of controversy among economists over whether economic policy should be guided by precise rules or should have an element of discretion.[18] It evident that the greater the element of discretion, the greater is the possibility that it might be used to someone's (rather than the public's) advantage. Thus the possibility of corruption would seem to create a presumption in favor of precise and rigid rules.[19] But, of course, the creation of such rules can itself reflect an attempt on the part of some officials to benefit in large measure from that creation. Some rules may be created just to give some government officials the power to benefit from their application. Often it is precisely the excess of rules that creates a fertile ground for corruption. Furthermore the lack of discretion can make the rules too rigid and create obstacles to the proper functioning of the economy or the particular organization. At times workers who have wanted to embarrass an organization have complied rigidly with the existing rules, bringing the organization to a standstill.[20]

Second, when social relations tend to be close and personal, it may be difficult to establish a direct link between an act that could be assumed to reflect corruption and a particular payment for it. An employee who uses his official position to favor an acquaintance – say by helping him or her get a valuable license, a government contract or a government job – may be compensated with an immediate or explicit payment (clearly a bribe). Alternatively he may be compensated, at a much later time, with a generous gift to his daughter when she gets married, or with a good job offer for his son when he completes his studies. In other words there may not be any direct, explicit and immediate compensation for the favor. The payment may be delayed in time and, when made, it may appear completely unconnected with the favor received.[21] In many cases the 'corrupted' and the 'corruptor' may never even have discussed the payment. It would simply be understood that a favor today creates a presumption or even an obligation for a reciprocal favor later. In other words it contributes to the growth of the giver's 'social capital'. In some societies a shadow market for favors develops with demand and supply and with implicit prices. This market, which often does not use money but trades in what could be considered the equivalent of 'IOUs', could lend itself to economic analysis. Implicit prices for favors are established and possibly even discount rates for future favors. A kind of honor system guarantees that favors received today will be repaid tomorrow. In this market it becomes very difficult to separate genuine favors from favors that are close to being bribes and is thus difficult to clearly identify bribes and punish those who receive or pay them.

This takes us to the third and final difficulty. In societies where family or other kinds of relationships are very strong, and especially where existing moral or social codes require that one helps family and friends, the expectation that the public employee will routinely apply arm's-length principles in his relations with friends and relatives is unrealistic. In these societies the Weberian type of ideal bureaucracy will prove very difficult to install. Century-old and widely accepted social norms will often prove more powerful as guides to behavior than new and often imported rules based on arm's length, impersonal and universalistic principles. When this reality is ignored, disappointment is likely to follow. This explains why some reforms imposed by foreign powers or promoted by foreign advisors, which may implicitly require or assume arm's-length relationship, often do not survive the test of time.

In these societies the cost of the corrective role of the government in the market is likely to rise. Economic relationships within the private sector will also be affected, thus rendering more difficult the establishment of a well-functioning market economy.[22] To argue that the personal relationships that come to be established between public sector employees and individuals who deal with them reflect a 'corrupt' society may be correct in a legalistic sense but it misses the point that these relationships simply reflect different social and moral norms.

The instruments that make corruption possible are many. Important examples include (a) regulations (such as the issuance of licenses of various kinds; zoning and other sorts of regulations which may have great economic value; and permits of various kinds); (b) fines for alleged or actual violations of existing legal norms; (c) control over procurement contracts; (d) control over public investment contracts (roads, airports, bridges) which can benefit some areas over others, and some contractors over others; (e) programs related to the provision of tax incentives, subsidized credit or overvalued foreign exchange; (f) controls over hiring and promotions; (g) controls over the assignment of entitlements and other benefits (pensions for disability, scholarships or subsidies); (h) controls over access to underpriced public services (electricity, telephone, water); and (i) tax administration decisions (auditing, determination of presumptive income, and so on).

These examples are far from exhaustive. The greater the use of these instruments by a country, the greater will be the potential for corruption. Control over these instruments can give government employees great power which, given the right social environment, the right incentive systems and weak and uncertain penalties, may allow them to extract large rents for themselves or for their families and friends. Gary Becker's analysis of crime, or Allingham and Sandmo's analysis of tax evasion, can be applied to the analysis of corruption when it occurs in an environment more like that of the Danish village than that of the Indian village. In the latter case, the difficulty of identifying many acts of corruption, of proving that a bribe has actually been paid, and of inducing society to apply significant penalties to these acts is likely to reduce the relevance of that analysis.

ECONOMIC CONSEQUENCES OF CORRUPTION

When civil servants appropriate, for their own use, the instruments that the government has at its disposal to influence the economy and to correct the shortcomings of the private market, they reduce the power of the state and its ability to play the intended and presumably corrective role. In a way this represents a privatization of the state, where its power is not shifted to the market, as privatization normally implies, but to government officials and bureaucrats. This will inevitably damage the functioning of the market.

Assuming that government policies had been or would have been guided by the traditional criteria that justify governmental action,[23] corruption distorts the end result in several ways. It distorts the allocative role, first, by favoring taxpayers who, because of the special treatment they receive from tax inspectors, are able to reduce their tax liability. If the statutory tax system has been designed to be neutral, corruption will not only reduce the revenue collected by the government but it will also destroy the tax system's neutrality by giving a competitive advantage to some producers over their competitors. The loser will be the proper functioning of the market.

Secondly, it distorts the allocative role through the arbitrary (that is, non-arm's-length) application of rules and regulations, thus giving preferences to some individuals over others. This may be particularly important in the allocation of import permits, subsidized credit, zoning permits and permits related to various economic activities. If, for example, these instruments had been developed to assist genuine 'infant industries', but end up assisting others, the corrective role of the governments would be distorted and once again the functioning of the market would be damaged.

The allocation of public work, or procurement, contracts to enterprises which win the competition, not because they can do the job at the least cost, but because of their connections and the bribes they pay,[24] has the same effect, as does the arbitrary hiring and promotion of individuals who would not have been selected or promoted on the basis of fair and objective criteria. The selection of these individuals will damage the economy, not only by lowering the quality of the decisions made by them and by increasing the frequency of mistakes, but also by discouraging more able but less well-connected individuals from pursuing particular careers if they feel that the decks are stacked against them. In societies where the best jobs are seen to be in the public sector and where these jobs go disproportionately to those with special connections,[25] the incentive to work hard in school and to get a good education for those without these connections will be reduced, thus lowering the growth potential of the economy. The market for labor is obviously distorted.

Some individuals will try to get jobs, not in the areas in which they might use their particular ability for productive use, but in areas which provide more scope for higher rents. Rent-seeking activities will be stimulated by corruption. The official wage will not play a significant role in attracting individuals to particular jobs if it diverges much from the total earnings that a particular position allows. In a South Asian country, for example, over the years the proportion of individuals taking the exam to become income tax inspectors has increased sharply in spite of the low wages that these jobs pay. At the same time, the proportion of those taking exams for better paid foreign service jobs has fallen. The reason seems to be that those who take these exams have sensed that the low-paying positions as tax inspectors can generate substantial extra earnings. There have even been reports that at times, in particular countries, some jobs with clear potential to earn high rents have either been sold or have been auctioned by those with the power to assign them.[26]

Baumol (1990) and, independently, Murphy *et al.* (1991) have argued that in any society the few individuals with significant managerial skills, and thus with the greatest potential to contribute to growth, will gravitate towards activities likely to generate the highest rate of returns *regardless of whether these are productive or rent-seeking activities*. If corruption allows some of them to gain more by pursuing rent seeking than more productive activities, they will pursue the former. The loser will be the performance of the economy.

Corruption distorts the *redistributive role* of the government in myriad ways. If the well connected get the best jobs, the most profitable government contracts, the subsidized credit, the foreign exchange at the overvalued rates and so forth, and if they are able to reduce their tax payments by bribing officials, it will be less likely that the activity of the government will improve the distribution of income and will make the economic system more equitable.[27]

Finally, in all its ramifications, corruption is likely to have negative implications for the *stabilization role* of the government, if that role requires, as is often the case, a reduction of the fiscal deficit. This will occur because corruption will most likely raise the cost of running the government, while it will reduce government revenue. For example, the allocation of disability pensions to people who are not disabled, of unemployment benefits to people who are not unemployed, of government contracts to people who pay a bribe on the contracts and thus raise their costs; the increase in unproductive capital spending often promoted by those who get 'commission' for capital projects; and the many other ways in which corruption distorts spending decisions must very likely raise total government spending in relation to the benefits that the economy receives from that spending.[28] By the same token, government revenue falls when some of the potential tax payments to the government are diverted or are never collected. In some developing countries the *effective* tax burden (that is, the ratio of all tax-related payments by taxpayers to national income) may be significantly higher than the *official* tax burden because some payments end up in the pockets of the tax inspectors.

There is a corrosive quality to the effect of corruption. Given the fertile ground created by close interpersonal relations, there is a learning-by-doing aspect that almost guarantees that, in a country where regulations are widespread and public sector intervention is large, corruption will grow over time. The civil servants who begin to bend the rules for close friends and relatives will in time begin to break them, thus exploiting their monopoly positions. The belief that 'everyone does it' is likely to lead to a situation where, if not everyone, many will do it. As with tax evasion, imitation will prove to be a powerful force.

Governments that come to power with a strong idealistic or even a revolutionary agenda may be able for a while to rely on that idealism or revolutionary fervor to contain the spread of corruption. However, as that idealism or fervor begins to dissipate, behavior associated with corruption will appear and eventually spread. This is likely to have happened to the centrally planned economies. For a while they did not seem to be affected by corruption more than other countries. However, with the passing of time, the revolutionary spirit abated and corruption spread. The fact that the role of the government in the economy was overwhelming provided a fertile ground for the spread of corruption. By the time these regimes collapsed, the effect of corruption was felt through most economic activities.

POLICY IMPLICATIONS

Several factors are likely to determine the extent to which corruption will play a significant role in a country: (a) the role of the state and the range of instruments it uses to pursue that role; (b) the social characteristics of the society, that is the extent to which arm's-length relationships prevail in social and economic relations; (c) the nature of the political system; and (d) the penalty system for acts of corruption that are uncovered.

In some countries corruption is prevalently an activity of the political leaders, in others an activity of the civil servants; in still others it is an activity of both. In a truly democratic system, with checks and balances exercised through fair elections, through the parliamentary process and through a vigorous free press, the extent of corruption among the political leaders will generally be checked or, at least, it will eventually be discovered and, one hopes, controlled. Corruption will exist, but it will rarely reach the extreme level reached in some authoritarian governments (see Harsch, 1993).[29] Therefore if, as has been argued in a recent bestseller, the inevitable course of history is to transform authoritarian governments into democratic governments, because of this change, the future should experience less corruption than the past or even the present (see Fukuyama, 1992). But let us consider the other factors that determine corruption, focusing mainly on the role of the state and on the social characteristics of the countries' citizens.

Especially in societies where arms-length relationships are unlikely to be enforceable (because of the close and continuous contacts among closely-knit groups of citizens who tend to personalize most relations), the larger the role of the state, the greater the probability that its instruments will be used by public officials and civil servants to favor particular groups in addition to themselves. When this happens the cost of government rises and its ability to correct the shortcomings of the market falls. In other words the effective control that the government has over the economy is reduced.[30] In this situation the best policy to reduce corruption will be a reduction of the opportunities to engage in it by scaling down the government's role in the economy. Both the demand for and the supply of corruptive practices can be contained by a sharp reduction of that role in all its aspects: spending and taxing activities and, especially, in economic regulations. It is no accident that in centrally planned economies, where regulation of economic activity was most widespread, corruption seemed to be a far more common occurrence than in many other countries and to affect not just the bureaucracy but the whole machinery of government. In his Pulitzer Prize-winning account of the last years of the Soviet Empire, David Remnick writes: 'The Communist Party apparatus was the most gigantic mafia the world has ever known' and 'the Party's corruption under Brezhnev was not a matter of exception' (1994, p. 183). 'But in the Soviet Union no economic transaction was untainted. It was as if the entire Soviet Union were ruled by a gigantic mob family; virtually all economic relations were, in some form, mafia relations' (ibid., p. 185).[31]

Unfortunately, in countries that had been centrally planned, the process of reducing the role of the state in the economy (by freeing prices, privatizing state enterprises and so on) may itself produce enormous opportunities for corruption during the transition when the institutions necessary to limit it have not been developed, while the habits developed in the previous period may not have changed.[32]

When corruption characterizes modern states in the Weberian sense, it can be reduced by increasing penalties on those who engage in it, by increasing the transparency of the rules, regulations and laws, and by strengthening audits, checks and other controls on the civil servants. In this environment the

analysis suggested by Becker will be relevant. However, when it characterizes more traditional societies, this option, while still worth pursuing, is not
likely to give by itself very positive and, especially, permanent results. History is full of examples of campaigns against corruption (and against tax
evasion) that started with great fanfare but that, over the long run, did not
accomplish much. By the same token, one should not officially sanction
corruption by, for example, reducing the wages of the civil servants on the
assumption that they are getting payments under the table. In an African
country, for example, a few years ago, the government reduced to zero, for
six months, the wages of customs officials, on the assumption that 'they
could take care of themselves'.[33] Unrealistically low wages always invite
corruption and at times lead society to condone acts of corruption. This is the
reason why repression of public sector wages, if carried too far, is never a
good policy.

Because it is social intimacy that creates the environment that promotes
corruption, a policy that has been effective in some cases (for example in tax
administration) in reducing corruption is that of forced and periodic geographical mobility for civil servants, in order to remove them from the region
where they have their closest social or family relations and to prevent the
formation of new relations. Some forms of social relations take time to
develop so that, for a while, after a government official has moved to a new
region or to a new function, they will not play a large role in the contacts
between the bureaucrats and the citizens who depend on them. Thus periodic
mobility, especially in a large country, could be an effective policy to reduce
bureaucratic corruption. It is no accident that in large countries, such as the
United States, corruption is more a problem for local governments where
bureaucrats and citizens often know each other and where arm's-length relationships are less likely to prevail. In general one can speculate that, the
larger a country and the more mobile its population, the less of a problem
corruption will be.

CONCLUDING REMARKS

Economists have developed elaborate and elegant theories about the workings of markets and the role of the public sector's action in those markets. A
normative role has been assigned to the government, aimed at correcting for
market failure. Public choice economists have in recent years stressed that,
in addition to market failure, one could also have political failure when
political action or the action of civil servants is influenced by objectives
other than the need to correct market failures and to promote the public
interest.

Over the past decade economists have begun to pay some attention to phenomena that were largely ignored in earlier periods, such as underground economic activities, tax evasion, money laundering and corruption. These represent the dark side of the economy. All these activities have major implications for the functioning of markets. When these activities are present, markets do not operate efficiently. Acts of corruption by public sector officials often play a role in promoting or sustaining underground economic activities and in facilitating tax evasion and the laundering of dirty money. These acts are facilitated or even stimulated by close interpersonal relations that characterize some societies. They are also facilitated by the many instruments that governments use to promote their often very active role in the economy.

Given the existence of close interpersonal relations in a society, and given that a government is pursuing a very active role in the economy through various policy instruments that lend themselves to be used by some public sector employees for personal gain, corruption is likely to grow with the passing of time. The passage of time will submit public sector employees to growing pressures from friends, acquaintances, relatives or simply those who want to buy favors from them; and the passage of time will teach some government officials (those who are more likely to abuse their power) how to take advantage of the situation.[34] This may explain why corruption grew over the years in centrally planned economies and in some of the economies which tried to promote a welfare state.

NOTES

1. It has been reported that the process of price deregulation is creating opportunities for corruption. See Wong (1992).
2. An economic role for the state may also be justified by concerns for equity and stabilization. See Musgrave (1959) and Stiglitz (1989).
3. Without this assumption, one could not defend a corrective role for the state. The definition of the social welfare, or the public interest, raises difficult theoretical and practical questions ignored here. For the classic treatment of the theoretical difficulties, see Arrow (1951). See also the discussion of a social welfare function in Mueller (1989), pp. 384–407.
4. See Samuelson (1954) and Musgrave (1938). See also Mueller (1989), pp. 144–7.
5. See Theobald (1990), p. 47. Max Weber's fundamental work is in *Economy and Society* (1978 edition), in two volumes. For a discussion of the characteristics of a modern bureaucracy, see especially vol. 2, ch. XI, pp. 956–1005.
6. See also Weber (1947).
7. For this reason, the fact that developing countries have much lower tax levels than industrial countries does not imply that the government plays a smaller role in them.
8. Mueller (1989) is probably the best source on that literature. Issues such as voting rules, multi-party systems, rent-seeking activities and so forth are the essence of the public choice literature.
9. The title of the English manuscript is 'Danes are Like That'. The published version is in Danish.

10. For example, tips or bribes may become necessary to get a telephone installation, to get quickly the results of blood tests, to get admission to schools or hospitals, to clear goods speedily through customs, to get import licenses; in some countries, even to get train and plane tickets, and so forth. David Remnick reports that in the Soviet Union even the access to morgues or coffins by dead bodies required the payment of bribes. See Remnick (1994), pp. 184–5.

11. Interestingly enough the word 'privacy' is very difficult to translate into other languages. Translations generally do not render the precise English meaning.

12. The interpretation given in this chapter to that concept is not the same as that given by Coleman. Here we emphasize the social capital as it concerns the individual rather than society.

13. Writing more than two thousand years ago, Kautilya (prime minister of a state in northern India) wrote in the *Arthashastra* (New Delhi: Penguin Books, 1991) that 'just as it is impossible not to taste honey or poison that one may find at the tip of one's tongue, so it is impossible for one dealing with government funds not to taste, at least a little bit, of the King's wealth'. The quotation is on p. 281.

14. There is, of course, some economic literature on it, but much less than one would have expected from the importance of the phenomenon.

15. In countries without a free press, of course, newspapers may have been prevented from reporting on it.

16. See, for example, the various definitions given in Theobald (1990), p. 2 or in Klitgaard (1988), pp. 21–4. A famous definition is the one given by the Indian Penal Code and reported in Goode (1984), pp. 310–11. According to that code, a person is guilty of corruption who 'being or expecting to be a public servant, accepts, or obtains, or agrees to accept, or attempts to obtain from any person, for himself or for any other person, any gratification whatsoever, other than legal remuneration, as a motive or reward for doing or forbearing to do any official act or for showing or forbearing to show, in the exercise of his official functions, favor or disfavor to any person or for rendering or attempting to render, any service or disservice to any person'.

17. This already points to the difficulty faced when the behavior expected from the moral or social code conflicts with that from the administrative rule. Saying that the administrative rule should always prevail opens up a lot of other difficulties not discussed here.

18. This controversy has usually related to major macroeconomic decisions such as the growth of the money supply, the size of the fiscal deficit, and so forth. However, in recent years, the public administration literature has also shown a distinct preference for rule-based administrations.

19. Perhaps this explains why some countries apply strict objective criteria for promotions (years of service, specific educational achievements and so on) while others rely on the judgement of the supervisors as to the performance of their subordinates. In general Anglo-Saxon countries seem to prefer the latter option while countries such as Japan, France and Italy seem to prefer a system based on more objective criteria, such as seniority, education and so on.

20. Some writers have argued that corruption can contribute to growth when existing regulations are too rigid and too stifling. Presumably corruption is the equivalent of introducing discretion in the application of the regulations. The same argument has been made about the contribution of the underground economy to growth. By getting around the many government-imposed restrictions, underground activities are supposed to give the economy a dynamism that it would otherwise not have. See various papers in Tanzi (1982).

21. It has also been reported that in some Asian countries members of parliament or other public sector employees are at times given envelopes with cash from businessmen, not for any specific immediate favors but for possible future favors (Pye, 1985).

22. It is worthwhile to consider why arm's-length relationships are not fully operative in Japan or why the privatization of state enterprises is proving so difficult in previously planned economies. The role of personal relationships is clearly important.

23. This is, of course, a big assumption which is unlikely to reflect reality in many cases. The corrective role of the state relates to the allocation of resources, the redistribution of

income and the stabilization of the economy.

24. For the public works budget a key question is whether it is only its allocation that is affected or its size. It is possible that more spending is allocated to investment projects because they allow for the transfer of large amounts through bribes. There is a strong suspicion in some countries that capital spending is often inflated by kickbacks. (See Tanzi, 1991, ch. 3.) It is now evident that a substantial share of Italy's public investment budget, which had been one of the highest among the OECD countries, was de facto a transfer payment to political parties and to individuals. To capitalize on this aspect in 1993, the Ciampi government tried to reduce the budgetary allocations for capital spending by asking the various ministries to renegotiate public works contracts so as to remove the inflating effects of bribes.

25. In Italy these individuals are often referred to as 'pacchi raccomandati', that is registered packages, which always reach their destination. A recent book has documented the extent to which nepotism has been prevalent in the Italian public life of recent years. (See Locatelli and Martini, 1991.) The English translation of the title of the book is *My Father Sends Me*.

26. For example, Remnick (1994, p. 184) reports that in the Soviet Union 'even high Party positions were for sale. The magazine *Smena* ('Change') reported that the position of regional Party secretary cost a bribe of $150,000, and an Order of Lenin ... cost anywhere from $165,000 to $750,000.'

27. This may explain why some countries have at times introduced quotas for the less privileged.

28. In other words corruption is likely to increase the capital output ratio or the total cost of providing government services. It should probably enter as a variable in production functions especially when its impact is changing over time.

29. See also Klitgaard (1990) and Remnick (1994).

30. In a powerful book, MacMullen (1988) has argued that the Roman Empire declined because, as a result of widespread corruption, the government lost control over its instruments of policy.

31. Campbell (1991) has reported that 'In the USSR at the end of the eighties about 18 million households had telephones, while there were 15 million households on the waiting list for them. The people who finally get a telephone installed tend to be those with special political influence or those who can offer bribes' (p. 71). See also the chapter by Grossman on the USSR in Tanzi (1982).

32. The *South China Morning News* (26 October 1993, p. 1) has reported the Chinese government announcement of an active corruption crackdown 'to halt the collection of illicit payments from among the mainland's staggering 1.11 million categories of government fees'.

33. Sandbrook reported a speech by President Mobuto Sese Seko to Zairian civil servants, in which he stated: 'if you want to steal, steal a little in a nice way' (see Sandbrook, 1986, p. 95).

34. Quoting once again Remnicks book: 'That was one of the most degrading facts of Soviet life: it was impossible to be honest' (1994, p. 185).

REFERENCES

Allingham, M.E. and A. Sandmo (1972), 'Income Tax Evasion: A Theoretical Analysis', *Journal of Public Economics*, 1(3–4) (November), 323–38.

Arrow, Kenneth (1963), *Social Choice and Individual Values*, 2nd edn, New York: Wiley.

Baumol, William (1990), 'Entrepreneurship: Productive, Unproductive and Destructive', *Journal of Political Economy*, 98(5), 893–921.

Becker, Gary (1968), 'Crime and Punishment: An Economic Approach', *Journal of Political Economy*, 76(2), 169–217.

Campbell, Robert (1991), *The Socialist Economies in Transition*, Bloomington: Indiana University Press.

Coleman, James Samuel (1990), *Foundations of Social Theory*, Cambridge, Mass. Belknap Press.

Dunn, Sheryl Wu (1993), 'China Sells Off Public Land to the Well-Connected', *New York Times*, 8 May.

Fukuyama, Francis (1992), *The End of History and the Last Man*, New York: The Free Press.

Goode, Richard (1984), *Government Finance in Developing Countries*, (Washington: The Brookings Institution.

Harsch, Ernest (1993), 'Accumulators and Democrats: Challenging State Corruption in Africa', *The Journal of Modern African Studies*, 31(1), 31–48.

Jennings, Veronica T. (1993), 'Sex Drove Promotions at N.I.H. Unit, Report Says', *The Washington Post*, 8 May, p. 1.

Kautilya (1991) *Arthashastra*, New Delhi: Penguin Books.

Klitgaard, Robert (1988), *Controlling Corruption*, Berkeley: University of California Press.

—— (1990), *Tropical Gangsters*, New York: Basic Books.

Locatelli, Goffredo and Daniele Martini (1991), *Mi Manda Papá*, Milan: Longanesi & Co.

MacMullen, Ramsay (1988), *Corruption and the Decline of Rome*, New Haven: Yale University Press.

Mueller, Dennis C. (1989), *Public Choice II*, rev. edn, Cambridge: Cambridge University Press.

Murphy, Kevin M., Andrei Shleifer and Robert, Vishny (1991), 'The Allocation of Talent. Implication for Growth', *Quarterly Journal of Economics*, (May), 503–30.

Musgrave, Richard A. (1938), 'The Voluntary Exchange Theory of Public Economy', *Quarterly Journal of Economies*, 53(2) (February), 213–37.

—— (1959), *The Theory of Public Finance: A Study in Public Economy*, New York: McGraw-Hill.

Pye, Lucian W. (1985), *Asian Power and Politics: Dimensions of Authority*, Cambridge, Mass.: Belknap Press.

Remnick, David (1994), *Lenin's Tomb: The Last Days of the Soviet Empire*, New York: Vintage Books.

Rose-Ackerman, Susan (1978), *Corruption: A Study in Political Economy*, New York: Academic Press.

Samuelson, Paul (1954), 'The Pure Theory of Public Expenditure', *Review of Economics and Statistics*, 36 (November).

Sandbrook, R. (1986), *The Politics of Africa's Economic Stagnation*, Cambridge: Cambridge University Press.

Stiglitz, Joseph E. (1989), *The Economic Role of the State*, Oxford: Basil Blackwell.

Tanzi, Vito (ed.) (1982), *The Underground Economy in the United States and Abroad*, Lexington, Mass.: D.C. Heath.

—— (1991), *Public Finance in Developing Countries*, Aldershot: Edward Elgar.

Theobald, Robin (1990), *Corruption, Development and Underdevelopment*, Durham, North Carolina: Duke University Press.

Weber, Max (1947), *The Theory of Social and Economic Organization*, London: The Free Press of Glencoe.

—— (1978), *Economy and Society*, two vols, Berkeley: University of California Press.

Wong, Kar-Yiu (1992), 'Inflation, Corruption and Income Distribution: The Recent Price Reform in China', *Journal of Macroeconomics*, 14(1) (Winter), 105–23.

7.   Corruption around the world

THE GROWTH OF CORRUPTION

In recent years, and especially in the decade of the 1990s, a phenomenon broadly referred to as corruption has attracted a great deal of attention. In countries developed and developing, large or small, market-oriented or otherwise, because of accusations of corruption, governments have fallen, prominent politicians (including presidents of countries and prime ministers) have lost their official positions and, in some cases, whole political classes have been replaced. See, for examples, Johnston (1997).

Corruption is not a new phenomenon. Two thousand years ago, Kautilya, the prime minister of an Indian king, had already written a book, *Arthashastra*, discussing it. Seven centuries ago, Dante placed bribers in the deepest parts of Hell, reflecting the medieval distaste for corrupt behavior. Shakespeare gave corruption a prominent role in some of his plays. And the American Constitution made bribery one of two explicitly mentioned crimes which could lead to the impeachment of a US president.[1] However the degree of attention currently paid to corruption is unprecedented and nothing short of extraordinary. For example, in its end-of-year editorial on 31 December 1995, the *Financial Times* characterized 1995 as the year of corruption. The following two years could have earned the same title.

The degree of attention now paid to corruption leads naturally to the question of why. Why so much attention now? Is it because there is more corruption than in the past? Or is it because more attention is being paid to a phenomenon that had always existed but had been largely, though not completely, ignored? The answer is not obvious, and there are no reliable statistics that would make possible a definitive answer.

Several arguments can be advanced that suggest that corruption is simply attracting more attention now than in the past. First, the end of the Cold War has stopped the political hypocrisy that had made the decision makers in some industrial countries ignore the political corruption that existed in particular countries, such as Zaire. As long as the latter were in the right political camp, there was a tendency to overlook obvious cases of high-level corruption.

Second, perhaps because of lack of information, or reluctance to talk about it by those familiar with these countries, there was also a tendency not to focus on corruption in the centrally planned economy.[2] It is now widely known that centrally planned economies, such as the Soviet Union, or those imitating them through highly regimented economic activities, such as Nicaragua and Tanzania, experienced a great many corrupt practices. However these practices were either ignored or not widely reported at the time. Donor countries also tended to play down this problem in countries which they assisted financially, even in the face of misuse or misappropriation of foreign aid.

Third, the increase in recent years in the number of countries with democratic governments and free and active media has created an environment in which discussion of corruption is no longer a taboo. In some countries, such as Russia, the media have responded with a vengeance to this newly acquired freedom.[3]

Fourth, in all its ramifications, globalization has brought into frequent contact individuals from countries with little corruption and those from countries where corruption is endemic. These contacts have increased the international attention paid to corruption.

Fifth, there has been a growing role played by non-governmental organizations, such as Transparency International, in publicizing the problems of corruption and in trying to create anti-corruption movements in many countries. Recently the international financial institutions and other international organizations have also been playing a growing role in the anti-corruption movement. In addition empirical studies of corruption have contributed to a greater awareness of this problem.

Sixth, the greater reliance on the market in economic decisions has created an environment in which the pursuit of efficiency has acquired greater importance and where distortions attributed to corruption attract more attention.

Finally, the role played by the United States, especially through its influence in some international institutions, has been important. American policy makers have argued that American exporters have lost out in foreign deals because they have not been allowed by law to pay bribes to foreign officials. For American companies the payment of bribes to foreign officials is a criminal act and the bribes paid cannot be deducted as costs for tax purposes.[4] This had not been the case in other OECD countries, although recently, under the sponsorship of the OECD, the situation started to change.

A case can also be made that the increased attention now paid to corruption reflects the growth of that phenomenon in recent decades, a growth that culminated in a peak in corruption activities in the 1990s. Let me briefly consider a few arguments that support this hypothesis. Recent studies have shown the extent to which the role of the government in the economy has grown in recent decades and especially since 1960.[5] The environment that prevailed in these years brought about (a) a large increase in the level of taxation in many countries, (b) a large increase in the level of public spending, and (c) probably, though this is not statistically ascertainable, a large increase in regulations and controls on economic activities on the part of governments. In recent decades, in a significant number of countries, most economic operations have needed various kinds of permits or authorizations on the part of public offices.

I would hypothesize that the impact that high taxes, a high level of spending and new regulations have on acts of corruption is not immediate but, rather, it is a function of time and of established norms of behavior.[6] In a country with traditionally well-functioning and honest bureaucracies, *the short-term impact* of a larger government role on public officials will be limited. For some time public officials will not be asked to perform corrupt acts and will reject bribery attempts. In countries without such a tradition, the more invasive role of government, played through higher taxes, higher public spending and more widespread regulations, would have a more immediate impact on the behavior of civil servants and on corruption. This would be particularly so if fiscal policy suffered from lack of transparency in policy making, in fiscal reporting and in the assignment of responsibilities to public institutions. (See Kopits and Craig, 1998).

However, with the passing of time, and with increasing frequency, some government officials will be approached by bribers and asked to bend rules or even to break laws to obtain a government benefit or to avoid a government-imposed cost. Some will respond and will get compensation from the bribers for their actions. Others may start emulating them. The process is likely to be cumulative in time and resemble the spreading of a contagious disease. Acts of corruption that might have appeared shocking earlier will begin to look less shocking, and they may even begin to be tolerated. The government may respond to this situation, not by punishing the officials who bend or break the rules, but by reducing wages on the assumption that officials are getting extra compensation.[7] It is easy to see where this process could lead if not checked.

Two other factors may have had an impact on corruption in recent years: the growth of international trade and business and the economic changes that have taken place in many countries and especially in the economies in transition. The growth of international trade and business has created many situations where the payment of bribes (often euphemistically called 'commissions') may be highly beneficial to the companies that pay them as it gives them access to profitable contracts over competitors. Large bribes have been reported to have been paid to get foreign contracts or to get privileged access to markets or to particular benefits such as tax incentives. The *Le Monde* of 17 March 1995 reported that the bribes paid abroad by French companies in 1994 had been estimated at FF10 billion in a confidential government report. *World Business* of 4 March 1996 reported that the bribes paid abroad by

German companies had been estimated to exceed US$3 billion per year.[8] It is clear that these were not the only countries in which companies had paid bribes to foreign officials. Some experts have estimated that as much as 15 per cent of the total money spent for weapons acquisition may be 'commissions' which fill somebody's pockets. Here, again, contagion is important. When the economic operators of some countries begin to pay bribes, they put pressure on those from other countries to do the same. The cost of not doing so is lost contracts, as Kantor argued.

Among the economic changes that have taken place in recent years, privatization is the one that has been most closely linked with corruption. There is no question that public or state enterprises have been a major source of corruption and especially of political corruption because, occasionally, they have been used to finance the activities of political parties and to provide jobs for the clienteles of particular political groups. This was clearly the case in Italy, before Tangentopoli (a huge corruption scandal),[9] and in many Latin American countries. Privatization of non-natural monopolies is a necessary step in reducing this form of corruption because it eliminates an instrument often used especially in political corruption. Unfortunately, the process of privatizing public or state enterprises has itself created situations whereby some individuals (ministers, high political officials) have the discretion to make the basic decisions while others (managers and other insiders) have information not available to outsiders so that they can use the process to benefit themselves. These problems have been observed and reported in all regions of the world, but the abuses appear to have been particularly significant in the transition economies.[10] In the latter, terms such as asset stripping and *nomenklatura* privatization have been used to describe the abuses associated with the transfer of state enterprises to private ownership. In these countries some individuals have become enormously rich because of these abuses. This, in turn, has made many citizens suspicious, or highly skeptical, about the virtues of a market economy.

Thus several arguments lead to the conclusion that the current interest in corruption may reflect an increase in the scope of the phenomenon over the years and not just a greater awareness of an age-old problem.

THE DEFINITION OF CORRUPTION

Corruption has been defined in many different ways, each lacking in some aspect. A few years ago, the question of definition absorbed a large proportion of the time spent on discussions of corruption at conferences and meetings. However, like an elephant, even though it may be difficult to describe, it is generally not difficult to recognize when observed. In most cases, though not all, different observers would agree on whether a particular behavior connotes corruption. Unfortunately the behavior is often difficult to observe directly because, typically, acts of corruption do not take place in broad daylight.

The most popular and simplest definition of corruption is *the abuse of public power for private benefit*. This is the definition used by the World Bank.[11] From this definition it should not be concluded that corruption cannot exist within private sector activities. Especially in large private enterprises, this phenomenon clearly exists, as for example in procurement or even in hiring. It also exists in private activities regulated by the government.[12] In several cases of corruption the abuse of public power is not necessarily for one's private benefit but it can be for the benefit of one's party, class, tribe, friends, family, and so on. In fact in many countries some of the proceeds of corruption go to finance the political parties.

Not all acts of corruption result in the payment of bribes. For example, a public employee who claims to be sick but goes on vacation is abusing his public position for personal use. Thus he is engaging in an act of corruption even though no bribe is paid. Similarly the president of a country who has an airport built in his small home town is also engaging in an act of corruption that does not involve the payment of a bribe.[13]

It is important to distinguish bribes from gifts. In many instances, bribes can be disguised as gifts. A bribe implies reciprocity, while a gift should not.[14] However, even though the distinction is fundamental, it is at times difficult to make.[15] At what point does a gift become a bribe? Does the distinction depend on the size of the gift? What about cultural differences that can explain different sizes of gifts? What if a large gift is not made to the person who provides the favor but to a relative of that person? Does the distinction depend on whether the gift is made in broad daylight, for everyone to see, or privately? In any case, this indicates that the identification of a bribe may not always be simple.

Acts of corruption can be classified into different categories. Some of these categories are mentioned below without our specifically commenting on them or even defining them. Thus corruption can be:

- bureaucratic (or 'petty') or political – corruption by the bureaucracy or by the political leadership;
- cost-reducing (to the briber) or benefit-enhancing;
- briber-initiated or bribee-initiated;
- coercive or collusive;
- centralized or decentralized;
- predictable or arbitrary;
- involving cash payments or not.

Undoubtedly other classifications could be added to this list.

FACTORS THAT PROMOTE CORRUPTION: DIRECT FACTORS

Corruption is generally connected with the activities of the state and especially with the monopoly and discretionary power of the state. Therefore, as Gary Becker, Nobel Laureate in economics, pointed out in one of his *Business Week* columns, if we abolish the state, we abolish corruption. But, of course, a civilized society cannot function without a state and in modern, advanced societies, the state must have many functions. The Becker argument collides with the reality that some of the least corrupt countries in the world, such as Canada, Denmark, Finland, the Netherlands and Sweden, have some of the largest public sectors, measured as shares of tax revenue or public spending in gross domestic product. Thus the solution to the problem of corruption may not be as simple as just reducing the size of the state. Rather the way the state operates and carries out its functions is far more important than the size of public sector activity.[16] Particular aspects of governmental activities create a fertile ground for corruption. Let us look at this issue in more detail.

Regulations and Authorizations

In many countries, and especially in developing countries, the role of the state is often carried out through the use of many rules or regulations. In these countries licenses, permits and authorizations of various sorts are required to engage, or to continue to be engaged, in many activities. Opening a shop and keeping it open, borrowing money, investing, driving a car, owning a car, building a house, engaging in foreign trade, obtaining foreign exchange, getting a passport, going abroad and so on require specific documents or authorizations. Often several government offices must authorize the activity and several public servants must be contacted.

The existence of these regulations and authorizations gives a kind of monopoly power to the officials who must authorize or inspect the activities. These officials may refuse the authorizations or may simply sit on a decision for months. Thus they can use their public power to extract bribes from those who need the authorizations or permits. In India, for example, the expression 'licence raj' referred to the individual who sold permits to engage in many forms of economic activities. In some countries some individuals become middlemen or facilitators for obtaining these permits. The fact that in some cases the regulations are non-transparent or are not even publicly available and that an authorization can be obtained only from a specific office or individual – that is, there is no competition in the granting of these authorizations – gives the bureaucrats a great deal of power and a good opportunity to extract bribes.[17]

The existence of these regulations requires frequent contacts between citizens and bureaucrats. They also require enormous amount of time spent by the citizens in acquiring permits and in dealing with public officials. Surveys from different countries and especially from developing and transition countries indicate that very large proportions of the time of the managers of enterprises, and especially of small enterprises, is spent dealing with bureaucracies. This time which is taken away from managing the enterprises can be reduced through the payment of bribes.

Taxation

Taxes based on clear laws and not requiring contacts between taxpayers and tax inspectors are much less likely to lead to acts of corruption. However corruption is likely to be a major problem in tax and customs administrations when:

1. the laws are difficult to understand and can be interpreted differently so that taxpayers need assistance in complying with them;
2. the payment of taxes requires frequent contacts between taxpayers and tax administrators;
3. the wages of the tax administrators are low;
4. acts of corruption on the part of the tax administrators are ignored, not easily discovered or, when discovered, are penalized only mildly;
5. the administrative procedures (for example, the criteria for the selection of taxpayers for audits) lack transparency and are not closely monitored within the tax or customs administrations;
6. tax administrators have discretion over important decisions, such as those related to the provision of tax incentives, determination of tax liabilities, selection of audits, litigations, and so on; and
7. more broadly, when the controls of the state (the principal) over the agents charged with carrying out its functions are weak.[18]

In some countries (Peru and Uganda), at one time, corruption became so endemic in the tax administration that the government decided to close down the existing administrations and to replace them with new ones. In several countries customs administrations have been very corrupt, leading to the jailing of the director of customs and in several cases leading to the replacement of the domestic customs with the services of foreign companies engaged in pre-shipment inspections.

Reports from a number of countries indicate that the number of applicants for poorly paid jobs in administering taxes or in customs has been unusually large, pointing to the possibility that applicants know that these jobs create opportunities for extra incomes.[19]

Spending Decisions

Corruption can also affect public expenditure. Corruption related to the provision by the government of goods at below market prices is discussed below; other aspects of public expenditure are discussed here.

Investment projects

These have lent themselves to frequent acts of high-level corruption. Because of the discretion that some high level public officials have over decisions regarding public investment projects, this type of public spending can become much distorted, both in size and in composition, by corruption.[20] Public projects have, at times, been carried out specifically to provide opportunities for some individuals or some political groups to get 'commissions' from those who are chosen to execute the projects. This has reduced the productivity of this expenditure and has resulted in projects which would not have been justified on objective criteria of investment selection such as cost–benefit analysis.

Procurement spending

The purchase of goods and services on the part of the government is another area affected by corruption. To reduce corruption possibilities, some countries have developed complex and costly procedures that may have reduced corruption at the cost of sharply increasing the prices at which some goods are purchased.[21]

Extra-budgetary accounts

These are common in many countries. Some of them have legitimacy and are set up for specific purposes (pension funds, road funds and so on). Others are set up to reduce the political and administrative controls that are more likely to accompany spending that goes through the budget. In some countries the money received from foreign aid or from the sale of natural resources such as oil and tin is channeled towards special accounts that tend to be less transparent and less controlled than the money channeled through the budget. Some of this money may go into illegitimate uses or pockets.[22]

In all these areas, lack of transparency and of effective institutional controls is the main factor leading to corruption.

Provision for Goods and Services at below Market Prices

In most countries the government engages in the provision of goods, services and resources at below market prices. This may be related to (a) foreign exchange, (b) credit, (c) electricity, (d) water, (e) public housing, (f) some rationed goods; (g) access to educational and health facilities, (h) access to public land; and so on. Even access to some forms of pensions, such as those for disability, fall into this category because the individuals who get them have paid less in contributions to the pension funds over time than the pension they get once their disability status is approved. In some countries disability pensions have been a fertile ground for corruption. In particular countries some individuals benefited enormously when they were able to get access to large amounts of credit or foreign exchange at below market prices.

In some cases, because of limited supply, rationing or queuing becomes unavoidable. Excess demand is created and decisions have to be made to apportion the limited supply. These decisions are often made by public employees. Those who want these goods (the users) would be willing to pay a bribe to get access (or a higher access) to what the government is providing. It is thus not surprising that, in all the areas mentioned above, cases of corruption have been reported.

Figure 7.1 presents the general case. The price for the good or service as defined above is measured on the vertical axis. The demand is measured on the horizontal axis. *OA* represents the supply of the good or service available. *DD'* is the demand schedule. The equilibrium price would be *AP*, at which the quantity demanded would be *OA*. However the price is set by the government at AP'. At that price there is an excess demand equal to AA'. This excess demand brings rationing and offers of bribes by the users or demand for bribes by those who administer these programs.

Other Discretionary Decisions

Besides the areas mentioned above, in many countries some public officials find themselves in positions where they have discretion over important decisions. Especially in these situations corruption and often high-level or political corruption can play a major role. The most important of these areas are listed below.

1. provisions of tax incentives against income taxes, value added taxes and foreign trade taxes which may be worth millions of dollars, in terms of

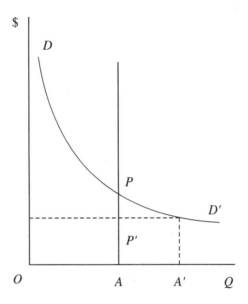

Figure 7.1   Rationing and bribes

the present value of reduced future liabilities, to those who benefit from them;[23]

2. decisions as to the particular use of private land (zoning laws) that determine whether the same piece of land can be used only for agriculture, and thus have low market value, or for high-rise buildings, and thus be very expensive,

3. decisions as to the use of government-owned land, as for example, for logging purposes, which may also be worth a lot to the recipients. Major cases of corruption related to permissions to cut trees from publicly owned forests, or to exploit lands for their mineral wealth, have been reported in several countries;

4. decisions that authorize major foreign investments, often undertaken in connection with domestic interests, frequently providing the privileged investors with some monopoly power;

5. decisions related to the sale of public sector assets, including the right to extract natural resources;

6. decisions on the privatization of state-owned enterprises and on the conditions attached to that process, such as the degree of regulation of the industry;

7. decisions providing particular export, import or domestic activities with monopoly power.

Decisions such as those described above are often worth a lot to individuals or enterprises. It is natural that attempts will be made by some of them to get favorable decisions, in some cases by paying bribes and, in other cases, by simply exploiting close personal relations with public officials. The bribes may be paid to public officials whose salaries may be very low and whose 'temptation price' may be far less than the value of the potential benefit that a favorable decision will provide for those requesting them.

Financing of Parties

Some time before tangentopoli exploded in Italy, Minister Martelli, an important member of the socialist party, in a speech in Bari candidly admitted that the Italian political parties had on their payrolls a small army of employees. The salaries for these employees had to be paid. He implied that the necessary money had to come from somewhere. Martelli had put his finger on a major problem for democracies: the need to finance the activities, including the electoral campaigns, of the political parties.[24] When public money is not available for the activities of the political parties, enormous pressures will build up to generate funds. The recent controversy concerning political donations in the United States is an example of this problem. As Susan Rose-Ackerman (1997) has put it: 'Democracy gives citizens a role in determining their political leaders. Corrupt elected officials can be voted out of office. But democracy is not necessarily a cure for corruption.'

FACTORS THAT PROMOTE CORRUPTION: INDIRECT FACTORS

Besides the factors that promote corruption directly, discussed in the previous section, other factors can contribute to corruption indirectly. Some of these are discussed briefly in this section.

Quality of the bureaucracy

The quality of the bureaucracy varies greatly among countries. In some, public sector jobs give a lot of prestige and status; in others, much less. Many factors contribute to that quality. Many years ago Max Weber (1947), the outstanding German sociologist, described what should be the characteristics of an *ideal* bureaucracy. He was aware that most bureaucracies are not ideal. Tradition and the effect that it has on the pride that individuals have in working for the government may explain why, *ceteris paribus*, some bureaucracies are much more efficient and much less vulnerable to corruption than others.[25] Rauch and Evans (1997) have gathered information on the degree to which civil servants' recruitment and promotions are merit-based for 35 developing countries. Their results indicate that the less recruitment and promotion are based on merit, the higher the extent of corruption.

Absence of politically motivated hiring, patronage and nepotism, and clear rules on promotions and hiring, in addition to some of the factors discussed separately below, all contribute to the quality of a bureaucracy. The incentive structure plus tradition go a long way to explaining why some bureaucracies are much less corrupt than others.[26]

Level of Public Sector Wages

Over the years many observers have speculated that the wages paid to civil servants are important in determining the degree of corruption. For example, Assar Lindbeck (1998) attributes the low corruption in Sweden in the 20th century partly to the fact that, at the turn of the century, high-level administrators earned 12–15 times the salary of an average industrial worker. One can speculate that there may be corruption due to greed and corruption due to need. In Figure 7.2 CC' represents the trade-off between the level of corruption and the level of wages. The higher the wage level, the lower is corruption.

Assume the OR represents a level of wage consistent with the minimum required by the family of a public employee for a decent living. It can be assumed that OA is corruption due to greed while corruption beyond OA would be due to need. The figure implies also that, regardless of the wage level, some public officials will be corrupt perhaps because of their own psychological or moral make-up, or because some of the bribes offered may be too large to resist.

The relationship between wage level and corruption index has been tested empirically in a recent paper by van Rijckeghem and Weder (1997). See also Ul Haque and Sahay (1996). Using cross-sectional data, they have supported the common intuition by finding a statistically significant relationship between corruption and wage levels, similar to that shown by the CC' curve in Figure 7.2. They have speculated that, while an increase in the wage level would reduce corruption, a very large increase would be necessary to reduce it to minimal levels. In other words, the fight against corruption, pursued exclusively on the basis of wage increase, can be very costly to the budget of a country and can achieve only part of the objective.

In recent years several countries have attempted to reduce corruption in particularly sensitive areas, such as customs and tax administration, by increasing the level of salaries for the public employees in these areas (Argentina, Peru and others).[27] These countries have also increased salary differentials to be able to retain and attract more able, productive and honest individuals. Over the years Singapore has pursued a wage policy aimed at reducing the

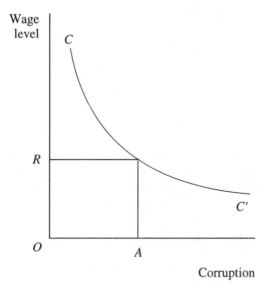

Figure 7.2   Wage level and corruption

temptation for public officials to engage in acts of corruption. Reportedly the salaries of ministers and other high-level officials in Singapore are among the highest in the world.[28]

There has been some speculation in the theoretical economic literature that high wages may reduce the number of corrupt acts, while they may lead to demands for higher bribes on the part of those who continue to be corrupt. The reason is that high wages raise the opportunity cost of losing one's job while they do not eliminate the greed on the part of some officials. Thus, while the number of corrupt acts is reduced, the total amount of corruption money paid may not necessarily fall.

Penalty Systems

Following Gary Becker's (1968) classic analysis of crime prevention, given the probability that the perpetrator of a crime would be caught, the penalty imposed plays an important role in determining the probability that criminal or illegal acts would take place.[29] In theory, *ceteris paribus*, corruption could be reduced by increasing the penalties on those who get caught. This analysis implies that the penalty structure existing in a country is an important factor in determining the extent of corruption in that country. But, once again, at least theoretically, higher penalties may reduce the *number* of acts of corruption, but they may lead to demands for higher bribes on the corrupt acts that still take place.

In the real world relatively few people are punished for acts of corruption, in spite of the extent of the phenomenon. Furthermore, with the exception of a few countries, there seems to be a wide gap between the penalties specified in the laws and regulations and the penalties that are effectively imposed.[30] Generally, effective penalties tend to be more lenient than the statutory ones. The administrative procedures followed before a public employee is punished for acts of corruption are slow and cumbersome. Often legal, political or administrative impediments prevent the full or quick application of the penalties. Due process and the need to provide incontrovertible evidence are major hurdles. The potential accusers are often reluctant to come forward and to spend the time and effort to go through the full process required to punish someone. Also, when corruption is widespread, the costs to the accusers in terms of social capital, such as lost friends, can be high.[31] Furthermore the judges who will impose the penalties may themselves be accessible to corruption or may have political biases, so that they may be bought by the accused or may put obstacles in the way of the proceedings. All these factors limit the role that penalties actually play in many countries, especially when corruption is partly politically motivated. This attitude brings a toleration for small acts of corruption that can in time encourage bigger acts.[32]

Institutional Controls

The other important ingredient in Gary Becker's analysis is the probability that those who commit crimes would be caught. This leads to the role of institutional controls. The existence of these controls reflects to a large extent the attitude of the political body toward this problem. Generally the most effective controls are those that exist *inside institutions*. This is really the first line of defense. Honest and effective supervisors, good auditing offices and clear rules on ethical behavior should be able to discourage or discover corrupt activities. Good and transparent procedures should make it easier for these offices to exercise their controls. Supervisors should be able to monitor the activities of their subordinates. These characteristics vary from country to country. In some these checks are almost non-existent, so that corruption is mostly discovered by chance or through the reporting by outsiders, including the media.

Several countries, including Singapore, Hong Kong, Uganda and Argentina, have created anti-corruption commissions or offices expressly charged with the responsibility of following up reports on corruption.[33] To be effective these offices must have independence from the political establishment, ample resources and personnel of the highest integrity. They must also have the power to enforce penalties or, at least, have others, including the judiciary, enforce the penalties. Unfortunately in some countries these offices are required to report confidentially to the president or the prime minister of the country rather than, say, to the legislative body. This goes a long way towards reducing their effectiveness and politicizing the process. In other countries these commissions do not have the power to impose penalties and their reports may not have any follow-up by other institutions.

Transparency of Rules, Laws and Processes

In many countries the lack of transparency in rules, laws and processes creates a fertile ground for corruption. Rules are often confusing, the documents specifying them are not publicly available and, at times, the rules are changed without properly publicized announcements. Laws or regulations are written in a way that only trained lawyers can understand and are often conceptually and not just linguistically opaque on important aspects, thus leaving grounds for different interpretations. Processes or procedures on policy matters and other actions, such as for competitions for public projects, are equally opaque so that, at times, it is difficult to understand the process that was followed before a decision was reached.

Some countries, for example New Zealand, have made great efforts in recent years in bringing more transparency to all the accounts and actions of the government.

Examples set by the Leadership

A final contributing factor is the example provided by the leadership. When the top political leaders do not provide the right example, either because they engage in acts of corruption or, as is more often the case, because they condone such acts on the part of relatives, friends or political associates, it cannot be expected that the employees in the public administration will behave differently. The same argument applies within particular institutions such as tax administration, customs, public enterprises and so on. These institutions cannot be expected to be corruption-free if their heads do not provide the best examples of honesty.

In some countries the leadership has been somewhat indifferent to this problem. In an African country, the president refused to fire ministers widely reputed to be corrupt. In an Asian country, a minister that was accused of corruption was simply moved to head another ministry. In a Latin American country, a president who was planning to create an anti-corruption commission proposed to appoint as head of this commission an individual widely reported to be corrupt. Examples such as these do not help create the climate that would lead to a corruption-free society.

MEASUREMENT OF CORRUPTION

If corruption could be measured, it could probably be eliminated. In fact, conceptually, it is not even clear what one would want to measure.[34] Simply measuring bribes paid would ignore a whole range of corrupt acts which are not accompanied by the payment of bribes. If one attempted to measure acts of corruption rather than the amounts of bribes paid, one would count many relatively unimportant actions, one would have to identify each act and, in any case, one would not have the information. While there are no *direct* ways of measuring corruption, there are several indirect ways of getting information about its prevalence in a country or in an institution. Some useful information can be obtained from a number of sources.

1. Reports on corruption available from published sources, including newspapers. The Internet is becoming a progressively more valuable source.[35] Newspapers such as *Le Monde*, the *Financial Times* and *The New York Times*, and magazines such as *The Economist* and *The Far Eastern Economic Review* have been producing many articles on corruption.
2. Case studies of corrupt agencies such as tax administrations, customs, police or some other institutions. Unfortunately, while there are many such studies, often the reports are internal and are kept confidential.
3. Questionnaire-based surveys. These can be related to a specific agency (in Peru or Argentina for tax administrations) or to a whole country. These surveys *measure perceptions of corruption*, rather than corruption per se. The World Bank has been making use of these surveys in its work in Tanzania, Uganda, India, Ukraine and other countries. It has used these surveys to improve the effectiveness of particular programs such as health care. Countrywide surveys are available from: Global Competitiveness Report (Geneva), Political and Economic Risk Consultancy (Hong Kong), Transparency International (Berlin), Political Risk Services (Syracuse). The Gallup poll has also conducted a major survey for 44 countries dealing with corruption in particular activities.

The results obtained from the above surveys for many countries are now widely used by researchers and by business people. The Transparency International index, for example, assesses the perception of corruption on a scale of nought to ten. Ten refers to a corruption-free country. Zero refers to a country where most transactions or relations are tainted by corruption. The variance of these indexes, which reflects how the views are spread among respondents, is also very important and has been used by some researchers in their work.[36] People may tend to confuse these indexes with actual measurements of corruption. It is important to keep in mind that the indexes reflect perceptions and not objective and quantitative measures of actual corruption. One good feature is that the various indexes available are highly correlated among themselves.

Table 7.1 shows the indexes for 1995, 1996 and 1997 provided by Transparency International. The table indicates that countries normally hold their positions over the period. The largest positive swing in the three years available is shown by Italy, the largest negative swing by Chile. How closely changes in these indexes reflect real changes within given countries is an important, open question. A single but widely reported case of corruption may easily change perceptions in a given country and lead to an index that may not correctly assess corruption in that country.

CORRUPTION AND GROWTH

The recent fairly broad consensus seems to be that corruption is unqualifiably bad but, in past years, the views on corruption have been more divergent and some economists have actually found some redeeming value in it.[37] Until the 1997 currency crisis, some countries from South-east Asia seemed to provide support for the view that corruption might promote growth. Indonesia and Thailand were often mentioned as countries growing fast in spite of, or even because of, high levels of corruption associated with a low degree of uncertainty.[38] In the case of Indonesia it was argued that institutionalized corruption made it less damaging than random corruption. One knew where to go and how much to pay. Some of the arguments in favor of the view that corruption may promote efficiency and even growth are summarized below?[39] This survey is not intended to be exhaustive, but just to provide a feel for the relevant literature.

Leff (1964) and Huntington (1968) advanced the view that corruption can be efficiency-enhancing because it removes government-imposed rigidities which impede investment and interfere with other economic decisions favorable to growth. Thus corruption 'oils the mechanism' or 'greases the process'. This reasoning has often been used to explain the high rates of growth in some countries of South-east Asia which were characterized by much corruption.

Beck and Maker (1986) and Lien (1986) have developed models that show that, in bidding competitions, those who are most efficient can afford to offer the highest bribe. Therefore bribes can promote efficiency by assigning projects to the most efficient firms.

Lui (1985) has argued that time has different values for different individuals, depending on their level of income and the opportunity cost of their time. Those for whom time is most valuable will offer bribes to public officials to be allowed to economize on time by jumping to the front of the line, that is

Table 7.1 Corruption perception index*

	1995	1996	1997
New Zealand	9.55	9.43	9.23
Denmark	9.32	9.33	9.94
Sweden	8.87	9.08	9.35
Finland	9.12	9.05	9.48
Canada	8.87	8.96	9.10
Norway	8.61	8.87	8.92
Singapore	9.26	8.80	8.66
Switzerland	8.76	8.76	8.61
Netherlands	8.69	8.71	9.03
Australia	8.80	8.60	8.86
Ireland	8.57	8.45	8.28
United Kingdom	8.57	8.45	8.28
Germany	8.14	8.27	8.23
Israel	n.a.	7.71	7.97
United States	7.79	7.66	7.61
Austria	7.13	7.59	7.61
Japan	6.72	7.09	6.57
Hong Kong	7.12	7.01	7.28
France	7.90	6.96	6.66
Belgium	6.85	6.84	5.25
Chile	7.94	6.80	6.05
Portugal	5.56	6.53	6.97
South Africa	5.62	5.68	4.95
Poland	n.a.	5.57	5.08
Czech Republic	n.a.	5.37	5.20
Malaysia	5.23	5.32	5.01
South Korea	4.29	5.02	4.29
Greece	4.04	5.01	5.35
Taiwan	5.08	4.98	5.02

by getting decisions more quickly. Thus corruption can be efficient because it saves time for those for whom time has the greatest value. In a more recent paper, Lui (1996) has argued that, while corruption may improve the allocation of resources in some circumstances, it reduces growth because it provides some individuals with the incentive to acquire the kind of human capital that can be used to improve corruption opportunities. This argument is related to those by Baumol and by Murphy and others, discussed below.

Table 7.1   Continued

	1995	1996	1997
Jordan	n.a.	4.89	4.29
Hungary	4.12	4.86	5.18
Spain	4.35	4.31	5.90
Turkey	4.10	3.54	3.21
Italy	2.99	3.42	5.03
Argentina	3.24	3.41	2.81
Bolivia	n.a.	3.40	2.05
Thailand	2.79	3.33	3.06
Mexico	3.18	3.30	2.66
Ecuador	n.a.	3.40	2.05
Brazil	2.70	2.96	3.56
Egypt	n.a.	2.84	1.94
Colombia	3.44	2.73	2.23
Uganda	n.a.	2.71	1.67
Philippines	2.77	2.69	3.05
Indonesia	1.94	2.65	2.72
India	2.78	2.63	2.75
Russia	n.a.	2.58	2.27
Venezuela	2.66	2.50	2.77
Cameroon	n.a.	2.46	2.27
China	2.16	2.43	2.88
Bangladesh	n.a.	2.29	1.80
Kenya	n.a.	2.21	2.30
Pakistan	2.25	1.00	2.53
Nigeria	n.a.	0.69	1.76

Note: * Level at which corruption is perceived by people in business, political analysts and the general public.

Source: Transparency International.

Corruption can be a useful political glue, allowing politicians to get funds that can be used to hold a country together. The latter outcome is seen as a necessary condition for growth. (See Graziano, 1979.) Bribes can supplement low wages. Thus corruption can allow the government to maintain a lower tax burden which can favor growth. (See Tullock, 1996; Becker and Stigler, 1974.) The issue here is whether a lower tax burden is more favorable to growth than a lower degree of corruption.

The above pro-corruption, theoretical arguments can be countered in a number of ways. First, rigidities and rules are not exogenous and unmovable features of a society. A society is not born with these rigidities: they are created and, in fact, they may be intentionally created by public officials, to extract bribes. When rules can be used to extract bribes, more rules will be created. Furthermore these rules are often kept opaque intentionally so that more power will remain on the side of those who enforce them. Knowledge gives power to those who have it.

Second, those who can pay the highest bribes are not necessarily the most economically efficient but the most successful at rent seeking. If bribes are seen as investments, those who pay them must figure that they are investments with a high rate of return. Baumol (1990) and Murphy *et al.* (1991) have advanced related arguments that can be used to argue that, in traditional or corrupt societies, the most able individuals will be diverted by existing incentives from pursuing socially productive activities and towards rent-seeking activities. This diversion will impose a high cost for the growth of these countries. If the potentially most socially productive individuals are in scarce supply, as they are assumed to be, the diversion of their talent toward rent-seeking activities and corruption will be particularly damaging to society.

Third, payment of 'speed money' may be an inducement for the bureaucrats to reduce the speed at which most practices are being processed. (See Myrdal, 1968.) Bribes may change the order in which public officials process the practices, say on providing permits, but they may slow down the average time for the whole process.

Finally, corruption and rent seeking as political glue or as wage supplement may be helpful in the short run, but they may lead to major problems over the longer run, as shown by Zaire under Mobutu.

Effects of Corruption on the Economy: Qualitative Effects

Corruption reduces public revenue and increases public spending. It thus contributes to larger fiscal deficits, making it more difficult for the government to run a sound fiscal policy. Corruption is likely to increase income inequality because it allows well positioned individuals to take advantage of the government activities at the expense of the rest of the population.[40] There are strong indications that the changes in income distribution that have occurred in recent years in previously centrally planned economies have been partly the result of corrupt actions such as *nomenklatura* privatization.

Corruption distorts markets and the allocation of resources because:

1. It reduces the ability of the government to impose necessary regulatory controls and inspections to correct for market failures. When the govern-

ment does not perform well its regulatory role over banks, hospitals, food distribution, transport activities, financial markets and so on, it loses part of its basic raison d'être. When, to the contrary, intervention is motivated by corruption, as for example when the government creates monopolies for private interests, it is likely to add to those shortcomings.

2. It distorts incentives. As already mentioned, able individuals allocate their energies to rent seeking and to corrupt practices and not to productive activities. In some cases the resulting activities have a negative value added.

3. It acts as an arbitrary tax (with high welfare costs). Especially when corruption is not centralized, its random nature create's high excess burdens because to the cost of negotiating and paying a bribe must be added the cost of searching for the person or persons to whom the bribe must be paid. When corruption is not centralized the contractual obligations secured by the payment of a bribe are more likely not to be complied with.[41]

4. It reduces or distorts the fundamental role of the government (on enforcement of contracts, protection of property rights and so on). When one can buy one's way out of a commitment or out of a contractual obligation, or when one is prevented from exercising one's property rights because of corruption, one of the fundamental roles of the government is distorted and growth may be negatively affected.

5. It reduces the legitimacy of the market economy and perhaps of democracy. In fact the criticisms often voiced in many countries, and especially in transition economies, against democracy and the market economy, are highly influenced by the existence of corruption. Thus corruption may slow down or even block the movement toward democracy and a market economy.

6. It is likely to increase poverty because it reduces the income earning potential of the poor.

For all the above reasons corruption is likely to reduce economic growth.

In many countries (for example, Ukraine, Russia and Indonesia) enterprises, and especially small enterprises, are forced by public officials to make payments to make things happen or to keep bad things from happening. Often these payments must be made if the enterprise is to remain in business. In Indonesia there is a term for these payments ('pungli') and, according to a recent report, these payments may raise the costs of doing business for small activities by as much as 20 per cent of total operating costs (See Sjaifudian, 1997.) This is equivalent to imposing very high sales taxes on these enterprises. Similar information has been reported for Russia (Shleifer, 1996) and for Ukraine (Kaufmann, 1997). This problem, however, may be much more general.

Corruption of a cost-increasing kind is often coercive for small enterprises and especially for new, emerging enterprises. These enterprises are often bullied by bureaucrats and by tax inspectors into making substantial payments. Pressures on them often come from local governments' officials. These officials impose high pecuniary costs, which are partly legal and partly illegitimate payments, to obtain licenses or authorizations, or simply to contribute to some alleged cause.[42] They also impose high costs in terms of the time that the managers of these enterprises must spend to comply with the many requirements imposed on them. The burden of these costs is likely to fall on these small enterprises because they operate in a far more competitive market than the large ones, so that they have greater difficulty in passing the costs on to their customers.

In most countries small enterprises are the main engine of growth. When they do not grow, economies languish and unemployment grows. This is true in most countries but especially in developing countries and, even more, in economies in transition. Obstacles to the creation of these enterprises can be particularly damaging.

Large enterprises can protect themselves more easily from these problems, because (a) they have specialized departments that can deal with aggressive bureaucrats; (b) they can use 'facilitators', that is individuals skilled at going through the jungle of opaque regulations and tax laws; (c) their size makes them more immune from the extortion of petty bureaucrats; and (d) they can use their political power to influence relevant individuals in the public administration or to pursue rent-seeking activities that give them benefits not available to others. For example, they may use bribes camouflaged as political donations or gifts to acquire market power through reduction in competition or to get tax incentives, subsidized credit or other benefits.

The reforms of recent years (such as trade liberalization) in many countries have removed obstacles to the growth of economies that had characterized earlier periods. However these were obstacles imposed mostly by the national governments. They were probably more important for large enterprises because these enterprises were more likely to trade abroad and to operate in the whole national territory. These reforms have not done much to reduce the many regulations, controls, opaque taxes and fees imposed by *local* governments, by unions, by professional groups and so on. These are probably the most important ones for the small enterprises.

Effects of Corruption on the Economy: Econometric Results

In the past couple of years several studies, using cross-section analysis and utilizing the available corruption indexes, have reported important quantitative results on the effects of corruption on economic variables. These results suggest that corruption has a negative impact on the rate of growth of countries. Some, but not all, of these studies are mentioned below. It has been found that corruption has the following negative effects.

1. It reduces investment and, as a consequence, it reduces the rate of growth. (See Mauro, 1995.) Such reduction in investment is assumed to be caused by the higher costs and by the uncertainty that corruption creates. In this analysis the reduction in the rate of growth is a direct consequence of the decline in the investment rate. In other words the analysis is based on a production function that makes growth a function of investment.

2. It reduces expenditure on education and health because public expenditure on education and health does not lend itself easily to corrupt practices on the part of those who make budgetary decisions.[43] (See Mauro, 1997.)

3. It increases public investment because public investment projects lend themselves easily to manipulations by high-level officials to get bribes. (See chapter 9.) It also distorts the effects of industrial policy on investment. (See Ades and Di Tella, 1997.)

4. It reduces expenditure on operation and maintenance of infrastructure for reasons similar to those that reduce expenditure on education and health. (See chapter 9.)

5. It reduces the productivity of public investment and of a country's infrastructure. (See ibid.)

6. It reduces tax revenue, mainly because of the impact that it has on the tax administration and on customs, thus reducing the ability of the government to carry out needed public expenditure. (See ibid.)

7. It reduces foreign direct investment because corruption has the same effect as a tax, and in fact it operates as a tax. (See Wei, 1997a.) Less predictable is the level of corruption: the higher is its variance, the greater is the impact on foreign direct investment. A higher variance makes corruption behave like an unpredictable and random tax. (See Wei, 1997b.) Thus increases in corruption and in its unpredictability are equivalent to increases in the tax rate on enterprises. Wei concludes that raising the index of corruption from the Singapore level to the Mexican level is equivalent to increasing the marginal tax rate on enterprises by 20 percentage points.

THE FIGHT AGAINST CORRUPTION AND THE ROLE OF THE STATE

In the earlier sections of this chapter many factors that contribute to corruption were discussed. These factors tend to be more common in poorer countries, and in economies in transition, than in rich countries. Thus, at some point in time, economic development reduces the level of corruption of a country. However, at similar levels of development, some countries are perceived to have more corruption than others.

Particular economies (Singapore, Hong Kong and Portugal) have managed to reduce significantly the incidence of corruption. Lindbeck (1998, p. 3) has pointed out that, even in Sweden, 'corruption flourished ... in the second half of the 18th century and in the early 19th century'. Thus governments should not be fatalistic or passive about corruption. With well focused and determined efforts, corruption can be reduced, though not to zero. Trying to bring corruption to zero would be too costly in terms of resources and in other ways. For example, it may require excessively high public sector wages; or major legal or organizational changes; or excessive limitations upon civil rights; or very harsh effective penalties. An optimal *theoretical* level would be reached where the marginal social costs of reducing it further were equal to the marginal social benefits from that reduction.[44] It is therefore realistic to think that the level will remain above zero in all countries. In fact no country is free of corruption and none scores a perfect ten in the perception index.

Corruption is a complex phenomenon that is almost never explained by a single cause. If it had a single cause, the solution would be simple. Of the many factors that influence it, some can be changed more easily than others. Because of the complexity of the phenomenon, the fight against corruption must be pursued on many fronts. It is a fight that cannot be won in months or even in a few years. The greatest mistake that can be made is to rely on a strategy that depends excessively on actions in a single area, such as increasing the salaries of the public sector employees, or increasing penalties, or creating an anti-corruption office, and so on, and expect results to come quickly.

Any realistic strategy must start with an explicit recognition that *there are those who demand acts of corruption* on the part of public sector employees and *there are public employees willing for a price to perform these acts.* There is thus a demand for acts of corruption and a supply of such acts and, as is the case with all demands and supplies, the price plays a major role. Various incentives determine the elasticities of these supply and demand functions. In the basic case the briber wants something (a reduction in a cost or an increase in a benefit) from the public official and is willing to pay a bribe for it. The official has something to sell (that is, he has some power that he can sell) and wants to be compensated for the risk and the effort involved.[45] However in the background there is the state in the totality of its actions carried out by the many agencies that constitute the public sector. To a large extent it is the state that, through its many policies and actions, creates the environment and the incentives that influence those who pay bribes and those who accept or demand them. It is the state that influences the relationship between briber and bribee. See Klitgaard (1988).

In the ideal bureaucracies described by Max Weber, the public official (as the agent of the state) is the faithful executor of the mandate and of the instructions that he receives from the state (the principal). The public official is just a conduit, or a direct and legitimate channel for the relationship between the state and the citizen. He would not distort the state–citizen relationship. In this Weberian world, no principal–agent problems would develop. Unfortunately, in the real world, Weberian bureaucracies are rare,[46] in part because the actions and the policies of the state are not always transparent and in part because of characteristics of the bureaucracies themselves. The citizens may question the legitimacy of some state actions attributing them to rent seeking by public officials and not to the pursuit of the public interest. The state may have de facto been fragmented into several power centers (ministries, public enterprises, independent institutions, subnational governments and so on) each pursuing somewhat distinct interests. Sometimes the policies of these power centers are not consistent with one another and the instructions that emanate from these public centers are conflicting.[47]

At times the instructions passed on to the agents who will carry out the execution of the policies are not clear because the top policy makers do not have clear ideas or, perhaps, may not wish to have total transparency in their actions. Total transparency in processes and in policies may imply less power for particular policy makers in the sense that their discretion in affecting the welfare of particular groups is reduced. The basic point of this discussion is that the fight against corruption is not distinct and independent from the reform of the state. The reason is that some of the measures to reduce corruption are at the same time measures that change the character of the state. Let us consider a few examples.

It is generally believed that the level of relative wages in the public sector is an important variable in the degree of corruption in a country. Singapore, a country with a good index of corruption and where corruption was much reduced over the years, has some of the highest wages for public employees. Reportedly its ministers receive the highest salaries in the world. The civil service of Singapore is small and enjoys a high status.

In countries where public sector wages are low with respect to those in the private sector, often they are low because of public policies that have inflated the number of people working for the government. In other words the governments have traded wage levels for the number of civil servants on their payrolls. The increase in the number of employees has meant lower real wages paid to them. In these situations it is not realistic or wise to suggest that these countries simply increase real wages without reducing the size of the civil service. However, for many governments, reducing the number of public employees would go counter to the objectives of their government, or at least would be difficult politically. And there are many governments that believe that unemployment can be reduced through public sector hiring.

The same argument applies to wage differentials. It has been the objective of many governments to reduce the spread in the wages they pay to their employees. In some countries the ratio between the highest and the lowest salaries has been reduced to three. This is far less than in the private sector. The effect of this wage compression is that the most qualified and the most honest employees leave the public sector to join the private sector. For many governments changing this policy would be contrary to their goals and in many cases would be opposed by the labor unions.

It is generally believed that increasing the penalties for acts of corruption would reduce a country's corruption. However the imposition of higher penalties could run into problems with employees' associations, with trade unions, with the judiciary system, and so on. Also there is the danger that an unscrupulous government would use this weapon to go after political opponents. In other words penalties could be used selectively or, worse, they could be used in connection with fabricated accusations. In democratic societies penalties are imposed after what is often a lengthy and costly process. The immediate supervisors of the corrupt officials may be reluctant to carry the brunt of some of the procedural costs (in terms of time lost, damaged friendships and so on). They may prefer to close their eyes to acts of corruption.

It is generally believed that many acts of corruption are stimulated by the existence of regulations. Some kinds of quasi-fiscal regulations at times take the place of taxing and spending actions. It is useful to point out that some of the countries perceived to be the least corrupt (Sweden, Denmark, Canada and so on) have some of the highest tax burdens. On the other hand, some of the countries with the highest indexes of corruption (Nigeria, Pakistan, Bangladesh, China, Venezuela and so on) have some of the lowest tax burdens. In the latter group of countries quasi-fiscal regulations (regulations that take the place of taxing and spending) replace taxes and public expenditures.[48] Thus, in order to reduce corruption, these countries would need to eliminate these quasi-fiscal regulations and, if necessary, replace them with taxing and spending policies. But quasi-fiscal regulations are predominant in these economies, which would have a difficult time substantially raising the level of taxation. Once again we come to the conclusion that the fight against corruption and the reform of the state are two sides of the same coin.

Tax incentives, especially when they imply discretionary decisions on the part of public officials, create conditions in which corruption develops. A simple recommendation would be to eliminate tax incentives and replace them with tax systems with broad bases and lower rates. This is a recommendation often made by tax experts. Unfortunately the roles that some governments want to play require the use of these incentives.[49] Therefore, once again, the fight against corruption requires reform in the role of the state.

Corruption often accompanies the provision by the government of goods and services at below market prices. This often occurs with credit, foreign exchange, the prices of public utility services, public housing, higher education, health services, and so on. The low or zero prices create excess demand and the need to ration the good or service. Rationing always brings corruption. Thus raising, whenever possible, these prices to equilibrium level would eliminate or reduce corruption. However it would also change the role of the state in a way that many governments are not willing to accept.

Many other examples could be provided. However the ones given above are sufficient to make the point that in many cases the fight against corruption cannot proceed independently of reform of the state. In many ways it is the same fight. Thus corruption will be reduced mainly in those countries where governments are willing to substantially reduce some of their functions.

CONCLUDING REMARKS

In this chapter we have discussed the phenomenon of corruption that affects many countries. We have shown the incidence of this phenomenon and the damage that it brings to economies and democracies. When corruption is widespread, and especially when it contaminates the actions of the policy makers in democratic, market-oriented economies, it becomes more difficult to argue in favor of such economic and political arrangements.[50] The widespread disillusion among the populations of some economies in transition and some developing countries with both market economies and democratic processes is very much prompted by the widespread corruption that prevails in these countries and that is wrongly attributed to the market economy and the democratic process.

We have also argued that corruption is closely linked with the way governments conduct their affairs in modern societies. Therefore the growth of corruption is probably closely linked with the growth of some of the activities of the government in the economy. It is unlikely that corruption can be substantially reduced without modifying the way governments operate. The fight against corruption is thus intimately linked with the reform of the state. In any case, any serious strategy to attempt to reduce corruption will need action on at least four fronts:

1. honest and visible commitment by the leadership to the fight against corruption. The leadership must show zero tolerance for it;

2. policy changes that reduce the demand for corruption by scaling down regulations and other policies such as tax incentives, and by making those that are retained as transparent and as non-discretionary as possible. Discretion must be kept to the minimum;
3. reducing the supply of corruption by increasing public sector wages, by increasing incentives toward honest behavior, and by instituting effective controls and penalties on public servants; and
4. somehow solving the problem of the financing of political parties.

In conclusion societies can do a lot to reduce the intensity of this problem, but no single action will achieve more than a limited improvement and some of the required actions may require major changes in existing policies.

NOTES

1. See Noonan (1984) for a very interesting historical overview of corruption in different societies.
2. However, much information was available on the corruption in centrally planned economies. See, for example, Simis (1982), Galasi and Gertesi (1987), Grossman (1982) and Remnick (1994).
3. An attempt by the author to create a corruption index on the basis of newspaper stories reported by the Internet indicated that for some countries these Internet entries amount to tens of thousands.
4. See, for example, the remarks by (then) Secretary of Commerce, Michael Kantor, to the Detroit Economic Club (25 July 1996) in which he stated that, since 1994, American companies had lost international contracts worth $45 billion because of bribes paid by foreign contractors to the officials of foreign countries. See also Hines (1995).
5. See, for example, Tanzi and Schuknecht (1997).
6. These norms of behavior may be different between countries and are likely to change only slowly over time.
7. This has actually happened in some countries in particular areas, such as the customs administration.
8. Reported in Galtung (1997).
9. See Nordio (1997). Carlo Nordio was one of the leading judges in the Italian fight against political corruption.
10. See Kaufmann and Siegelbaum (1996) and Goldman (1997). For a review of the Latin American experience, see Manzetti and Blake (1997).
11. A more neutral definition is that corruption is the intentional non-compliance with arm's-length relationships, aimed at deriving some advantage from this behavior for oneself or for related individuals. See Chapter 6. For other definitions, see Theobald (1990).
12. For example, when a taxi driver charges you more than the regulated price.
13. It becomes difficult to draw a distinction between some forms of rent seeking and corruption.
14. In practice those who offer gifts may expect some form of payment for them. For example, we expect love or good behavior from our children when we give them gifts, but the recipients of the gifts do not have an obligation to reciprocate.
15. For an elaboration of some of these points, see Chapter 6.
16. The state can exercise its role through various instruments. Some of these lend themselves more easily to acts of corruption. See Chapter 6. For an empirical analysis that links market structure and rents to the level of corruption, see Ades and Di Tella (1997).

17. Some economists have argued that this kind of corruption can be eliminated by setting up several offices, all authorized to provide the authorizations or permits. This would remove the monopoly power from the bureaucrats. (See Shleifer and Vishny, 1993). Unfortunately the setting up of several offices may be costly. In some cases, particular activities (say yearly inspections of cars) can be privatized.

18. In cases of political corruption, those who represent the state (president, prime minister, ministers) or their close relatives may use the tax and customs administrations to pursue rent-seeking and corrupt practices.

19. There have even been reports that in some countries these jobs can be bought.

20. See chapter 9.

21. The notorious US$600 hammers bought by the Pentagon could be explained in terms of the application of these procedures.

22. Because of the variation in the price of commodities even within a day, it may be difficult to ascertain at which price a transaction takes place. Some of the difference between the actual price and the declared price may be channeled into foreign accounts.

23. In some countries these incentives have been provided outside the normal legal process, by high-level public officials, for favored individuals.

24. One of the leading judges of *mani pulite* (clean hands), the investigation in the Italian corruption scandal, has recently described the arrangements among the parties to share the proceeds from corruption. See Nordio (1997). On the issue of political corruption, see also Cazzola (1988), Johnston (1997) and Ferrero and Brosio (1997).

25. See von Klimo (1997). Von Klimo compares the public conception of an inefficient and corrupt public administration in 19th-century Italy with the 'myth of absolute efficiency and incorruptibility' enjoyed by the administration of the Prussian state.

26. In some countries, public sector hiring has had the main objective of reducing unemployment rather than improving the quality of the public administration.

27. In Peru the wage structure in the tax administration became similar to that of the central bank and thus somewhat higher than the wage structure of the civil service. Also an incentive system was introduced which assigned to the tax administration (SUNAT) a share of the tax revenue. The average age of the employees of the tax administration was dramatically reduced.

28. A common belief is that, in situations of low wages but high possibilities of corruption, less honest individuals will be attracted to the civil service.

29. For an econometric application of Becker's theory to the Netherlands, see van Tulden and van der Torre (1997).

30. China has recently gone as far as applying the death penalty to some individuals accused of corruption. However some acts of corruption may still go unpunished, so that uncertainty prevails on the treatment of individuals accused of corruption. This may lead to the perception that penalties are applied selectively or arbitrarily.

31. Even in countries with relatively little corruption, so-called 'whistle blowers' do not seem to have an easy time.

32. Reluctance to apply harsh penalties may also be due to concerns that the penalties might be applied selectively, to political opponents.

33. For the experience of Uganda in the fight against corruption, see Ruzindana (1997) and Langseth and Stapenhurst (1997). As Table 7.1 below shows, Uganda is still perceived as a country with a high level of corruption.

34. One could measure acts of corruption or bribes paid.

35. For some countries the Internet reports tens of thousands of entries for the subject of corruption.

36. See, for example, Wei (1997a and 1997b).

37. Even today a few economists still argue that, within well confined circumstances, corruption may promote faster growth. See, for example, Braguinsky (1996).

38. Since the fall of 1997, some journalistic accounts have blamed corruption for both the enormous fires that consumed large areas of the Indonesian forests and for the currency crises caused by unproductive investments and high short-term borrowing.

39. For a review, see Bardhan (1997) and Susan Rose-Ackerman (1997).

40. For a quantitative analysis that establishes a connection between higher corruption, on the one hand, and higher income inequality and poverty, on the other, see Gupta et al. (1998).
41. Furthermore random corruption may also be accompanied by higher penalties if the act of corruption is discovered.
42. These small, economic activities may be preyed upon by the police, health inspectors, tax inspectors and by myriads of other individuals presumably representing the government.
43. Of course this does not mean that there is no corruption in the provision of these services. The provision of health is often distorted by bribes to doctors or other medical personnel to get better or faster service.
44. In practice, of course, these marginal costs and marginal benefits are impossible to measure.
45. Of course we are ignoring the cases when corruption is coercive and reflects the pressures of public officials or individuals.
46. They may be approximated only in a few countries such as Denmark, Sweden, New Zealand, Canada and perhaps one or two others.
47. This is particularly the case of tax officials in some countries with decentralized fiscal systems. In these situations the officials may be subject to conflicting pressures from the national government and the local governments.
48. For a discussion of quasi-fiscal regulations and their power to replace taxing and spending, see Chapter 3.
49. This has been a major issue in economies in transition, where governments want to continue to influence directly the activities in some sectors. Thus the policy makers have found it hard to accept the approach associated with broad-based taxes.
50. It should be remembered that many dictators or many potential dictators make the fight against corruption one of the reasons why they should be given the reins of a country. Some associate democracy with lack of discipline.

BIBLIOGRAPHY

Ades, Alberto and Rafael Di Tella (1997), 'National Champions and Corruption: Some Unpleasant Interventionist Arithmetic', *The Economic Journal*, 107 (July), 1023–42.

Bardhan, Pranad (1997), 'Corruption and Development: A Review of Issues', *Journal of Economic Literature*, XXXV (September), 1320–46.

Baumol, William. J. (1990), 'Entrepreneurship: Productive, Unproductive and Destructive', *Journal of Political Economy*, 98 (October), 893–921.

Beck, Paul. J. and Michael W. Maker (1986), 'A Comparison of Bribery and Bidding in Thin Markets', *Economic Letters*, 20, 1–5.

Becker, Gary S. (1968), 'Crime and Punishment: An Economic Approach', *Journal of Political Economy*, 76(2) (March/April), 169–217.

Becker, Gary S. and George J. Stigler (1974), 'Law Enforcement, Malfeasance and Compensation for Employees', *Journal of Legal Studies* (January), 1–18.

Braguinsky, Serguey (1996), 'Corruption and Schumpeterian Growth in Different Economic Environments', *Contemporary Economic Policy*, XIV (July), 14–25.

Cazzola, Franco (1988), *Della Corruzione: Fisiologia e Patologia di un Sistema Politico*, Bologna: Il Mulino.

Chand, Sheetal K. and Karl O. Moene (1997), 'Controlling Fiscal Corruption', IMF Working Paper, WP/97/100.

Elliot, Kimberly Ann (ed.) (1997), *Corruption and the Global Economy*, Washington: Institute for International Economics.

Ferrero, Mario and Giorgio Brosio (1997), 'Nomenklatura Rule under Democracy: Solving the Italian Political Puzzle', *Journal of Theoretical Politics*, 9 (4) (October).

Galasi, P. and G. Gertesi (1987), 'The Spread of Bribery in a Centrally Planned Economy', *Acta Aeconomica*, 34 (3–4), 371–89.

Galtung, Frederik (1997), 'Developing Agencies of Restraint in A Climate of Systemic Corruption: The National Integrity System at Work', paper presented at the Third Vienna Dialogue on Democracy, 26–27 June (Vienna).

Goldman, Marshall (1997), 'The Pitfalls of Russian Privatization', *Challenge* (May–June) 35–49.

Graziano, Luigi (1979), *Clientelismo e Sistema Politico. Il Caso dell'Italia*, Milan: F. Angeli.

Grossman, Gregory (1982), 'The Second Economy of the USSR', in Vito Tanzi (ed.), *The Underground Economy in the United States and Abroad*, Lexington, Mass.: D.C. Heath, pp. 245–70.

Gupta, Sanjeev, Hamid Davoodi and Rosa Alonso-Terme (1998), 'Does Corruption Affect Income Inequality and Poverty?', IMF Working Paper.

Hines, James R. (1995), 'Forbidden Payments: Foreign Bribery and American Business After 1977', Working Paper 5266, National Bureau of Economy Research (September).

Huntington, Samuel P. (1968), *Political Order in Changing Societies*, New Haven: Yale University Press.

Johnson, Simon, Daniel Kaufmann and Andrei Shleifer (1997), 'The Unofficial Economy in Transition', *Brookings Papers on Economic Activity*, 2, 159–239.

Johnston, Michael (1997), 'Public Officials, Private Interests and Sustainable Democracy: When Politics and Corruption Meet', in Kimberly Ann Elliot (ed.), *Corruption and the Global Economy*, Washington: Institute for International Economics, pp. 61–82.

Kaufmann, Daniel (1997), 'The Missing Pillar of a Growth Strategy for Ukraine', in P. Cornelius and P. Lemain (eds), *Ukraine: Accelerating the Transition to Market*, Washington: International Monetary Fund.

Kaufmann, Daniel and Paul Siegelbaum (1996), 'Privatization and Corruption in Transition Economies', *Journal of International Affairs*, 50(2), (Winter), 419–58.

Klimo, Arpad von (1997), 'Fra Stato Centralistico e Periferia. Alti Funzionari Statali in Italia e nella Germania Prussiana dal 1870 al 1914', in Oliver Janz and Pierangelo Schiero (eds), *Centralismo e Federalismo nel XIX e XX Secolo, Un Confronto tra la Germania e Italia* (Bologna: II Mulino).

Klitgaard, Robert E. (1988), *Controlling Corruption*, Berkeley: University of California Press.

Kopits, George and Jon Craig (1998), 'Transparency in Government Operations', IMF Occasional Paper, no. 158.

Langseth, Peter and Rick Stapenhurst (1997), 'National Integrity System: Country Studies', Economic Development Institute of the World Bank, EDI Working Papers.

Leff, Nathaniel (1964), 'Economic Development Through Bureaucratic Corruption', *American Behavioral Scientist*, 8–14.

Lien, Donald H.D. (1986), 'A Note on Competitive Bribery Games', *Economic Letters*, 22, 337–41.

Lindbeck, Assar (1998), 'Swedish Lessons for Post-Socialist Countries' (mimeo).

Lui, Francis T. (1985), 'An Equilibrium Queuing Model of Bribery', *Journal of Political Economy* (August), 760–81.

Lui, Francis T. (1996), 'Three Aspects of Competition', *Contemporary Economic Policy*, 14 (July) 26–29.

Manzetti, Luigi and Charles Blake (1997), 'Market Reforms and Corruption in Latin America: New Means for Old Ways', *Review of International Political Economy*, 662–97.

Mauro, Paolo (1995), 'Corruption and Growth', *Quarterly Journal of Economics*, 110(3) (August), 681–712.

—— (1997), 'The Effects of Corruption on Growth, Investment and Government Expenditure: A Cross-Country Analysis', in Kimberly Ann Elliott (ed.), *Corruption in the Global Economy*, Washington: Institute for International Economics, 83–107.

Murphy, Kevin M., Andrei Shleifer and Robert W. Vishny (1991), 'The Allocation of Talent: Implication for Growth', *Quarterly Journal of Economics*, 106 (May), 503–30.

Myrdal, G. (1968), *Asian Drama: An Inquiry into the Poverty of Nations*, New York: Pantheon.

Noonan, John T. Jr. (1984), *Bribes*, New York: Macmillan.

Nordio, Carlo (1997), *Giustizia*, Milan: Angelo Guerini e Associati.

Rauch, James E. and Peter B. Evans (1997), 'Bureaucratic Structure and Bureaucratic Performance in Less Developed Countries' (mimeo).

Remnick, David (1994), *Lenin's Tomb: The Last Days of the Soviet Empire*, New York: Vintage Books.

Rose-Ackerman, Susan (1997), 'Corruption and Development', paper presented at the Annual Bank Conference on Development Economies.

Ruzindana, Augustine (1997), 'The Importance of Leadership in Fighting Corruption in Uganda', in Kimberly Ann Elliott (ed.), *Corruption in the Global Economy*, Washington: Institute for International Economics, pp. 133–46.

Shleifer, Andrei (1996), 'Government in Transition', Discussion Paper No. 1783, Harvard Institute for Economic Research.

Shleifer, Andrei and Robert W. Vishny (1993), 'Corruption', *Quarterly Journal of Economics*, 108(3) (August), 599–617.

Simis, Constantine M. (1982), *USSR: The Corrupt Society. The Secret World of Soviet Communism*, New York: Simon and Schuster.

Sjaifudian, Shetifah (1997), 'Graft and the Small Business', *Far Eastern Economic Review*, 16 October, p. 32.

Tanzi, Vito (1995a), 'Corruption, Arm's-Length Relationships, and Markets', in Gianluca Fiorentini and Sam Peltzman (eds), *The Economics of Organised Crime*, Cambridge: Cambridge University Press, pp. 161–80.

—— (1995b), 'Government Role and the Efficiency of Policy Instruments', IMF Working Paper 95/100.

Tanzi, Vito and Ludger Schuknecht (1997), 'Reconsidering the Fiscal Role of Government: The International Perspective', *The American Economic Review*, 87(2) (May), 164–8.

Theobald, Robin (1990), *Corruption, Development and Underdevelopment*, Durham, North Carolina: Duke University Press.

Tullock, Gordon (1996), 'Corruption Theory and Practice', *Contemporary Economic Policy*, XIV (July), 6–13.

Ul Haque, Nadeem and Ratna Sahay (1996), 'Do Government Wages Cuts Close Budget Deficits? Costs of Corruption', *IMF Staff Papers*, 43 (December), 754–78.

van Rijckeghem, Caroline and Beatrice Weder (1997), 'Corruption and the Rate of

Temptation: Do Low Wages in the Civil Service Cause Corruption?', IMF Working Paper, WP/97/73 (June).

van Tulden, Frank and Abraham van der Torre (1997), 'Crime and the Criminal Justice System: An Economic Approach', paper presented at the 53rd Congress of the International Institute of Public Finance, August, Kyoto, Japan.

Weber, Max (1947), *The Theory of Social and Economic Organization*, London: The Free Press of Glencoe.

Wei, Shang-Jin (1997a), 'How Taxing is Corruption on International Investors', NBER Working Paper 6030, Cambridge, Massachusetts: National Bureau of Economic Research.

—— (1997b), 'Why is Corruption So Much More Taxing than Tax? Arbitrariness Kills', (Mimeo).

8. Corruption and the budget: problems and solutions

INSTRUMENTS AND EFFECTS OF CORRUPTION

Corruption affects and distorts what should be arm's-length, or objective and unbiased, relationships between government officials and private sector individuals. Through the payment of bribes, some individuals succeed in getting favorable treatment in their economic activities from public officials. Such treatment can either reduce the costs of the economic activities in which the individuals are engaged or it can create new opportunities for them that are not available to others. Acts of corruption may be initiated either by private individuals or by government officials. When it is the latter, they may offer favorable treatment in exchange for a bribe or some other favor. When this happens corruption disrupts the competitive situation that exists in the market and may give a competitive advantage to some individuals or enterprises.

Corruption in the public finances reduces the ability of the government to pursue its basic public finance functions. It distorts the allocation, distribution and stabilization roles of the government. The effect of corruption on allocation is obvious. In the public finance literature, the role of the government in the allocation of resources is justified in terms of the need for governmental action to correct for market failures. However corruption distorts markets, because of the differential treatment that individuals receive when some of them bribe public officials while others do not. In some countries corruption has led to the creation of monopolies when some individuals have been given exclusive rights to engage in particular activities. The 'crony capitalism' of the Marcos and Suharto regimes in the Philippines and Indonesia created several such monopolies, but the practice is not limited to the experience of those countries.

The distributional role is distorted because those who benefit from corruption, and especially from high-level corruption, either as corruptors or as corrupted, are often better placed and better connected than those who do not. Corruption allows them to increase their real incomes. The stabilization role is made more difficult because corruption, and especially corruption in the public finances, tends to decrease government revenue and to increase government spending, thus contributing to larger fiscal deficits. Additionally corruption obfuscates the relationship that exists between policy changes and the final results of those changes. For example, it should be possible to predict that a given change in a tax rate may result in a given change in tax revenue. When corruption is present it becomes difficult, if not impossible, to do so. And it becomes difficult to predict the impact of a change in public spending on a given social output.

CORRUPTION IN TAX AND CUSTOMS ADMINISTRATION[1]

Those who have worked on taxation in different countries have occasionally encountered cases where tax collection was much lower than estimated on the basis of available information on tax bases and tax rates. This difference reflects the known and common phenomenon of tax evasion (discussed in Chapter 10). Some, or much, tax evasion occurs when taxpayers manipulate their accounts or their declarations to reduce their tax payment. This kind of tax evasion takes place whether corruption on the part of tax officials exists or not. However some tax evasion exists *because of* corruption. This is the part that is of interest to us here.

Examples of corrupt practices undertaken by tax administration officials in return for bribes would include (a) provision of certificates of exemption from tax to persons who would not otherwise qualify; (b) deletion or removal of a taxpayer's records from the tax administration's registration, filing and accounting systems; (c) provision of confidential tax return information to a taxpayer's business competitors; (d) creation of multiple false taxpayer identifications to facilitate tax fraud; (e) write-off of a tax debt without justifications; (f) closure of a tax audit without any adjustment being made or penalties being imposed for an evaded liability; (g) manipulation of audit selection; and so on.

Examples of corrupt practices undertaken by customs administration officials include (a) facilitating the smuggling of goods across a national border to avoid tax and duty payments; (b) facilitating the avoidance or understatement of a tax or duty liability through acceptance of an undervaluation or misclassification of goods in the processing of a customs entry; (c) allowing goods that are held in a bonded warehouse to be released for consumption in the domestic market without payment of tax or duty; (d) facilitating false tax and duty refund claims through certification of the export of goods that have been consumed in the domestic market or that have not been produced at all; and so on.

These are by no means exhaustive lists of corrupt practices in which tax and customs officials may engage. Indeed, where corrupt practices are widespread in a revenue administration, its officials are likely to be continually looking for new opportunities to engage in rent seeking. In some countries the highest bribes may be paid by a businessman to a senior tax or customs official, for example, to secure a formal certificate of exemption from tax or duty. In the same countries different businessmen may rely upon their personal contacts with low-level officials to secure similar results. In some countries imports by relatives of the most senior political personalities have been given blanket exemptions, thus costing the country large amounts in forgone revenue and giving these importers an unfair competitive advantage.

Reductions in government revenue occur when corruption contaminates the tax and customs administrations, so that some of the payments made by taxpayers end up in the pockets of tax inspectors or customs officials, rather than in the government treasury. In some countries corruption in the tax and customs administrations became so pervasive that drastic measures had to be taken. In Peru and Uganda the existing tax administrations were dismantled and were replaced by new institutions with new personnel, new salary structures and new organizational arrangements. In these cases an attempt was made to provide better incentives and higher salaries for the new employees.[2] In several other countries the customs administrations were privatized by hiring the services of foreign companies which assumed control of the customs operations in exchange for a fee expressed as a share of customs revenue. Thus incentives were introduced for the foreign companies to maximize customs revenue.

When there is corruption, the tax burden *as measured from the point of view of a taxpayer* who has paid a bribe to the tax or customs inspectors is higher, and in some cases much higher, than the burden *as measured from the point of view of the government*, which excludes the bribe. The difference may lead some unwary observers to recommend increases in tax rates, or the introduction of new taxes, on the assumption that the country is highly taxed. This difference in tax burdens may explain why the taxpayers of some countries complain about the heavy taxes they pay while the revenue statistics of those countries convey a different impression.

Many aspects of the tax systems may be affected by corruption, but this phenomenon seems to be particularly significant in some areas. Prominent among these are the provision of tax incentives and the imposition of foreign trade taxes. Both of these areas have revealed major cases of corruption. In this connection it is important to emphasize that we are not dealing with the question of tax evasion in general, that may or may not require the collusion and, thus, the corruption of officials of the tax or customs administrations. Rather we are focusing especially on cases where tax revenue is lost *because of* corruption and, thus, where there is an active participation by government officials. Tax evasion that does not involve the participation of corrupt officials does not fall within our area of concern. Total tax evasion in a country is often much higher than the tax evasion caused by corruption.

In the provision of tax incentives some officials, either in the Ministry of Finance or in other ministries (such as industry or trade), have considerable discretion over the decision on whether to grant or not to grant a tax incentive to an investor. The decision often depends on subjective considerations, such as whether the investment is 'necessary', or is in the 'national interest'. Thus some official has to decide whether the investment meets these often vague criteria. Often the request for tax exemption for some economic activity is made by foreign companies and involves decisions by senior political figures.

The value of the incentive to the requesting investor can be very high because it is the present value of the taxes that would be saved over the life of the project. One can visualize the situation in which an often poorly-paid public official has to make decisions that may be worth millions of dollars to the investor.[3] Furthermore applications for tax incentives often require many contacts between the applicants and the officials so that there is ample time to develop close personal relations. In these situations the offering of a bribe, at times disguised as a gift, and the accepting of it are likely outcomes.

Political or high-level corruption has also been linked to the use of tax incentives. High level political figures, including presidents and prime ministers or their relatives or close associates, are occasionally involved in their private lives in economic activities that can benefit from tax incentives. These political figures have the power to make, or to influence, the decisions granting the incentive. These decisions can save the investors, both domestic and foreign, much money at the cost of the country's revenue. The area of tax incentives is often linked with that of foreign trade taxes because the incentives concern, not just income taxes, but foreign trade taxes and, especially, import duties. Getting an incentive that exempts an enterprise from taxes on imported inputs or imported products can save it much money.

Corruption affecting foreign trade taxes is an activity of both lower-ranking officials and high-ranking political figures. When the latter are involved, the involvement is through close relatives or associates. Serious cases of corruption in customs were reported in past years in Morocco, Argentina, Brazil and other countries. In Morocco the head of the customs administration was jailed for major cases of smuggling, and major reforms in customs administration were made. In Argentina the existence of a customs administration parallel to the official one was discovered. In Brazil smuggling by navy personnel, using military ships, was uncovered.[4] In other countries corruption has involved collusion in the faking of invoices to get rebates on non-existing exports. In some cases, as in Kenya, the magnitude of these claims became very large, thus affecting the macroeconomic situation of the country.

Many of the factors that may lead to significant corruption problems in the tax and customs administration are common to other areas of public administration. There are, however, some special factors that make the task of addressing corruption problems in tax and customs administration especially difficult. If the tax policy and legislation framework of a country is highly complex, as is normally the case with the provision of tax incentives, the taxpayers may often have to deal on a face-to-face basis with tax and customs officials to obtain explanations of the way the laws apply to their particular transactions. At the same time, officials may have wide discretionary powers to determine such things as the appropriate tax rate, timing of a liability, tariff classification or valuation to be applied to goods which are the subject of a transaction. Where such broad discretion is available to officials, opportunities for corruption are bound to arise.[5]

In poorly organized tax and customs administrations, complex, bureaucratic procedures can even make compliance with basic obligations to file returns, lodge declarations and pay taxes and duties extremely difficult. If taxpayers have to complete multiple forms and obtain multiple authorizations to complete a transaction at a tax or customs administration office, it will generally require visits to a number of offices to get appropriate official certifications, stamps and signatures. Where this occurs opportunities for rent seeking by officials will invariably arise.

Corrupt practices in tax and customs administration do great damage to the revenue collection capabilities of a country. On the one hand, there is the direct loss of revenue from each individual collusive arrangement between a taxpayer and a tax or customs official. But, more importantly, the long-term result of all these individual actions by corrupt tax and customs officials is to destroy any notion that taxpayers can be expected to comply voluntarily with their obligations under the tax laws.

When corrupt behavior is commonplace among tax and customs officials, the incidence of taxation can become completely arbitrary. When a tax or customs administration's systems and procedures are weak, there is little likelihood that a taxpayer's non-compliance will be detected and appropriate sanctions imposed. When, in addition, corrupt officials are regularly helping taxpayers to circumvent their tax and duty liabilities, voluntary compliance with the tax laws will decline and so will revenue collections. If tax rates are raised to recover revenue lost through low levels of voluntary compliance, the result may be to increase the amount of the bribe that officials will ask for to facilitate the evasion of some or all of that increased tax liability. Looked at in this way, corrupt practices in tax and customs administration might be seen as a major impediment to improving revenue performance in some countries.

If corruption problems in tax and customs administration are to be seriously addressed by a country, a commitment must be made at the highest political level to deal with these problems. If senior officials engage in corrupt behavior while embarking upon a campaign to eradicate similar behavior at lower levels in a revenue administration, it is unlikely that such a campaign will succeed. Many of the measures required to build a modern professional tax or customs administration, where opportunities to engage in corrupt practices are minimized, are of an organizational and procedural nature. However significant simplification of a tax system can lay the foundations for improvements in tax and customs administration that will reduce opportunities for corruption. A policy framework that provides for a limited number of taxes, with a limited number of rates, and minimum exemption provisions can make the tax system much easier to administer for tax and customs officials. At the same time, if the system is more transparent, its requirements will be more readily understood by taxpayers. If reform of the policy framework is accompanied by the introduction of effective penalty measures, this can provide a clear indication to taxpayers that their liabilities will be rigorously enforced in the future.

Simplification of tax declaration forms and filing and payment procedures can also reduce opportunities for day-to-day contacts between taxpayers and officials and thereby reduce opportunities for collusive behavior. Importantly the introduction of simplified procedures can also significantly reduce a taxpayer's compliance costs and increase voluntary compliance.

The most important principle that stands behind the procedures and systems of modern tax and customs administrations is that of self-assessment (or self-declaration). This means that taxpayers are entitled to present to a tax or customs administration their returns or declarations setting out their calculation of tax liabilities based upon their understanding of the law. Of course a tax and customs administration has the right to challenge and audit taxpayers' self-assessment of their liabilities on a selective basis. By reducing contacts between taxpayers and tax officials, self-assessment is likely to reduce tax evasion due to corruption of tax officials. At the same time, under some circumstances, it may increase tax evasion by the taxpayers acting on their own.

CORRUPTION IN PUBLIC SPENDING[6]

Corruption increases public spending and distorts its allocation. It increases public spending by promoting unnecessary or unproductive expenditure, by contributing to the overpayment for some services or goods that the government buys, by making payments to individuals not entitled to these payments, and in many other ways.

To address corruption in public spending properly, it is particularly useful to distinguish between political or high-level and administrative or bureau-

cratic corruption. Corrupt behavior that takes place during the budget preparation phase, a time when political decisions are made, reflects political
corruption. Corrupt behavior and/or corrupt activities that take place during
the budget execution phase reflect mostly administrative corruption. Political
corruption has particularly damaging effects on the allocation of resources
because it tends to divert resources away from the function to which they
would have been allocated in the absence of corruption.

Some of the major corruption scandals, such as those that shook Italy in
recent years, have been connected with political corruption and public investment. The intellectual bias favoring capital spending, the controls that
high-level officials have over decisions concerning public projects, and the
fact that in some way each investment project is unique and is subject to
many kinds of designs, sizes, technology and other options make public
projects an area of public spending to be watched closely.

As is true of taxes in many cases, corruption in public spending is connected with bureaucratic rather than political actions. It is thus linked to
budget *execution* rather than budget *formulation*. Budget execution involves
several phases, each providing different possibilities for corruption. During
the budget appropriation and spending authorization phase there are various
possibilities for interventions and manipulations. If the spending authorization is not granted regularly, spending units such as ministries will not be
able to make commitments and, therefore, goods and services will not be
delivered on schedule. The official in charge of issuing spending authorizations might favor a given ministry in order to allow that ministry to contract
particular suppliers which compensate the official with under-the-table re-
wards.

In spite of the often specific nature of budget laws regulating commitments, the commitment phase of the expenditure process is a fertile ground
for corrupt activities. The most frequent, and perhaps the most damaging, of
these activities is the partial or total disregard of procurement laws and
procedures. Regulations regarding prices, quality and quantity, as well as
terms of delivery, can be disregarded in favor of particular suppliers who
bribe corrupt officials. As the government is a major purchaser of goods and
services, bending the rules in favor of a few suppliers can have serious effects
on their competitors and thus favor individuals who are more efficient at
bribing than at producing. Another possible case of corruption is the ordering
of goods and services not authorized in the budget. Commitment of resources
for goods and services not authorized in the budget often pre-empt commitment for some that are authorized.

The task of officials entrusted with the receiving and verification phase is
to check whether all the regulations have been respected. The budget laws of
many countries prescribe that, if at the receiving and verification phase it is

discovered that goods and services not conforming to specifications or not authorized in the budget have been ordered, commitments must be canceled. However, because of collusion among corrupt officials, verification procedures are not carried out and the existence of illegal commitments is often not discovered.

Corrupt behavior during the preparation and issuance of payment orders phase is essentially the same as during the preceding phases. It is based on the disregard of laws, rules and regulations. If cash is not available for payment when goods and services are delivered, the government will incur arrears. Suppliers often accept arrears as a cost of doing business with the government. However some suppliers will bribe officials in charge of issuing payment orders in order to get paid before the others. When, because of bribes, some suppliers are paid first and others much later, corruption can have a detrimental effect on those enterprises not willing to pay bribes, especially in periods of inflation or when interest rates are high. Those who pay bribes may recover their 'investments in bribes' by increasing their prices or by delivering substandard goods.

In cases of severe cash shortages, when daily cash rationing must be imposed, the establishment of an order of priority among competing claims is essential. The official in charge of such a decision has enormous discretionary powers, which can be used for corrupt purposes. By manipulating the allocation of cash resources for the purpose of favoring selected spending units the official can rearrange budget priorities for the year.

Corruption has often accompanied the establishment of extrabudgetary accounts. The very purpose of establishing extrabudgetary, earmarked funds and special accounts is to exempt some transactions from standard budgetary procedures and controls. While it should not be assumed automatically that these resources will be misappropriated, a lack of appropriate control procedure can create a fertile ground for corrupt behavior.

The literature on corruption has extensively discussed the consequences of the corrupt behavior of officials and has emphasized its illegal and criminal aspects. However, while these aspects are important, other dimensions of corrupt behavior are also important. We have already mentioned the impact of corruption on the size and composition of total expenditure, but there are other costs. The total economic and social effects of corrupt actions might be very costly and out of proportion to the bribes received by corrupt officials in terms of resources wasted, the opportunity cost of resources misused and the inefficiencies introduced into the system. By diverting resources from their intended purposes, corrupt officials will change the allocation of resources as intended and approved in the budget. Thus the decisions of the legislative body will be undermined and in the end the democratic process will be altered.

The next section discusses general steps that can reduce corruption. Corruption in public spending would respond to general actions against corruption, but a few comments addressed more specifically to public spending may be appropriate at this point. Political corruption and especially that associated with budget formation rather than budget execution can only be controlled at the political level. Such control must depend on the existence of checks and balances, a powerful legislature, a vocal press and an electorate that responds to accusations of incorrect practices. When the same political parties control both the executive and legislature and when the electorate can be manipulated, this kind of corruption can go on for many years, as it did in Italy before Tangentopoli.

Bureaucratic corruption, at the budget execution stage, is much more difficult to control because there are many areas where possibilities are open for corrupt bureaucrats to take advantage of particular situations. Apart from general factors such as the level of wages and penalties, the existence of effective administrative controls is very important. These can be internal controls (that is, internal to the particular ministries) as well as effective public expenditure management systems including clear budgetary classification, well functioning treasuries and so on.

STEPS TO REDUCE CORRUPTION

Corruption has moved from being a phenomenon of little interest to being one of major concern. Many now recognize that a country with much corruption cannot have a truly efficient economy or a truly democratic state. Corruption can be a cancer for both democracy and the market economy and, if not checked, it can eventually kill both.

Corruption is tied to many activities of the government. As we have seen in our discussion of corruption in the public finances, it can be carried out at the political level, by the leaders or the most senior officials of a country, or at the administrative level, by the bureaucracy. In this chapter we have been concerned mostly with corruption as it affects government revenue and government spending. Both political and bureaucratic corruption play a role in the public finances. We have shown that it reduces government revenue while it tends to push for higher government spending, thus contributing to larger fiscal deficits. It also distorts the tax system and renders public spending less productive.

As with any other human action, corrupt behavior responds to incentives. Some incentives promote corruption, some discourage it.[7] Governments must address these issues more systematically than they have done so far. They must do so by looking at the transparency of existing laws and regulations, at the quantity of them, at the structure of government institutions, at the level of wages, at the professionalism of the civil service, at the penalty system for corrupt actions, and so on. In this process, the example provided by the leadership is very important. One should not expect to find an honest bureaucracy in an environment where political corruption is rampant.

Governments should not be fatalistic about corruption. With a well focused and determined effort, corruption can be reduced, although attempting to bring it to zero may not be an optimal policy. At some point the social benefit derived from reducing corruption further would not justify the pecuniary and social costs of doing so. For example, it may require excessively high public sector wages or major legal or organizational changes. The optimal theoretical level would be reached where the marginal social cost of reducing it further would be equal to the marginal social benefit from the reduction. This level is likely to be higher than zero. In many countries corruption is well above the 'optimal' level so that there is ample justification for trying to reduce it.

The war against corruption must be fought on at least four fronts: (1) commitment by the country leadership, (2) reduction of the demand for corruption by the private sector, (3) reduction of the supply of corruption by the public sector officials and (4) increasing controls and penalties for acts of corruption.

Commitment by the Leadership

The war against corruption must start with an explicit commitment by the leadership of the country (president, prime minister) to a clean government and the willingness to pay the price to achieve it. To be believable, this commitment must be accompanied by visible action. Leaders should not only declare that they are against corruption, but they should be seen as not tolerating any form of corruption, whether it involves family members, political associates or other members of government. They must be particularly vigilant and strict, especially vis-à-vis those closest to them who use their positions as gatekeepers to the leaders to extract rents from the private sector.

In some countries political leaders have not been considered personally corrupt or, at least, no acts of corruption have been traced back to them, but they have, at times, tolerated (or at least have closed their eyes to) questionable practices by family members, political allies and members of their government. These sins of omission are as important in creating perceptions as sins of commission. The fight against corruption requires that neither of these be committed.

Reducing the Demand for Corruption

Corruption exists mainly because government officials find themselves in positions from which, through their decisions, they can influence significantly the activities of some individuals. As a consequence particular individuals, such as investors, businessmen, importers, taxpayers or even plain citizens, can benefit from a decision that is favorable to them. In countries where governmental intervention in the economy is carried out mainly through broad, general and indirect policy tools, there is much less scope for corruption. Unfortunately, in many countries, governmental intervention in the economy transcends the use of general policy tools and is carried out through regulations, authorizations, tax incentives, special access to credit or foreign exchange, and other tools that require direct contacts between specific individuals and public officials and require decisions by public officials which are tailored for specific individuals or enterprises. Such intervention creates a strong demand for acts of corruption.

An important reason for corruption seeming to be more prevalent in developing and transition economies than in industrial countries is that in the former the role of the state is carried out substantially more through the use of rules and regulations and less through spending and taxing. As countries become richer and acquire the ability to raise the level of taxation, and as markets develop more fully, the role of the state comes to be played more through taxing and spending and less through regulations.[8] However, when in a country, individuals are required to obtain permits or authorizations (and often from several or even many different offices) to import, obtain foreign exchange, borrow, export, invest, benefit from tax incentives, open a shop, keep the shop open, start a new activity, and so on, it is inevitable that somewhere along the line bribes will be offered (or asked) to get the desired decisions. A bribe may provide a license denied to others; it may provide a license more speedily; it may reduce the cost of complying with existing regulations (for example, those related to health standards); it may provide a tax incentive or subsidized credit and foreign exchange.

Thus the fight against corruption must start with the pruning of the regulatory framework at both the national and the local level, to eliminate redundant or unnecessary regulations. This exercise may also reveal that some needed regulations are not in place. The fight must continue with an attempt to make the regulations that are retained clear and more transparent to reduce the possibility of conflicting interpretations. Also, if possible, strict time limits must be set by which a given request must be accepted or rejected in order to reduce the chance that public officials may invite bribes by simply sitting on requests. The deregulation of economic activities which is characterizing the economic policy of many countries should in time lead to a reduction in the demand for acts of corruption.

Reducing the Supply of Corruption

The widespread involvement of the government in the economy, especially when carried out with non-neutral and non-general instruments, creates conditions which lead some individuals to want to bribe public officials. In other words it increases the demand side of the corruption equation. However, as the saying goes, it takes two to tango. An act of corruption is much like tango because it usually involves two sides – one that offers a bribe and one that accepts it. It is conceivable that two countries could have the same instruments for governmental intervention, and thus the same demand for acts of corruption, but one might end up with much more corruption than the other. The reason might be that the willingness of the public officials to accept bribes could be very different. In this case one reason for the difference might be the relative level of public sector wages and the status of a civil service job.

Countries that have low corruption tend to be those where the status of a civil service job is high and these jobs are relatively well paid. In this case there is less pressure on the public employees to accept bribes (to make ends meet) and there is a higher opportunity cost to them associated with losing their government job. In some countries, however, public employees are paid so little that they are pushed, or even expected, to get additional income, either by having second jobs or by compromising their integrity. In these countries the low levels of wages are often also accompanied by little differentiation in salaries across the ranks, which creates additional pressures for some employees and especially for those with more discretion on decisions.

Although the level of wages is far from being the only factor that determines the supply of acts of corruption, it is a very important one, so that a country that sets the objective of reducing corruption must be willing to revise the salary structure for its public sector employees. Countries that over the years have made significant progress against corruption, such as Singapore and Hong Kong, compensate well their public sector employees. In Singapore, for example, ministers are among the best paid in the world. This indicates that the fight against corruption is not a costless one.

Increasing Controls and Penalties

So far we have discussed three lines of action in the war against corruption, namely the commitment by the leadership, reducing the demand for corrupt acts and reducing the incentives for public officials to accept bribes. The fourth line of action must be related to the establishment of better controls and heavier penalties. The controls would be aimed at increasing the chance that a corrupt act will be discovered. The heavier penalties would make it more costly for those who engage in corruption to continue to do so. There is now an extensive literature, that started with the work by Gary Becker, that supports this approach, with respect to crime in general.

Countries could create the equivalent of a Corruption Investigation Bureau (as in Singapore and Hong Kong) that should be a high-profile and politically independent unit staffed with well-paid and highly motivated personnel charged with investigating reports of corruption. This bureau should go after corrupt officials and also after those who attempt to bribe the officials. It should have the power to recommend adequate penalties (including dismissal) for those who are caught in acts of corruption. It is clear that the effectiveness of such a bureau will depend on its political independence, its integrity, its resources and the extent to which its investigations bring effective punishment on those who are caught either as corruptor or as corrupted. In this context the role of the judiciary is important. A criminal investigation bureau cannot be effective if its actions are not followed by the institutions which have the legal responsibility to punish those who commit crimes. Unfortunately, in many countries, the justice system has been experiencing major problems that have much reduced its effectiveness.

CONCLUDING REMARKS

In this chapter, we have discussed various issues related to the fascinating and important problem of corruption. We have discussed factors that create an environment where corruption becomes common, and we have outlined major steps to reduce corruption. It should be realized, however, that to some extent corruption is a reflection of society. Non-democratic societies, without a free press and an independent judiciary, are less likely to be relatively free of corruption. At the same time we have evidence of democratic societies where corruption has been and is still a major problem. But all societies can do a lot to scale down the problem. The costs of *not* doing so are becoming progressively higher in a globalizing context. But the fight against corruption must be carried out on many fronts. There are no magic solutions to this problem.

NOTES

1. Some of the issues discussed in this section are drawn from Crotty (1997).
2. For example, in Peru the salary structure of the new tax administration (SUNAT) became

the same as that prevailing in the central bank. SUNAT also has discretion over a share of the revenue increase.

3. There is now some empirical evidence that supports the intuition that low public sector wages encourage acts of corruption. See Van Rijckeghem and Weder (1997).

4. Smuggling protected by corrupt officials is at times tied to the import of narcotics or even weapons. Customs officials on the border between Mexico and the United States have often been suspected of contributing to the smuggling of illicit drugs into the United States.

5. In these situations interpersonal relationships come to acquire a particularly important note. In Morocco, for example, before the reforms the average waiting period for clearing goods at customs was 16 days and required 17 documents. In some other countries the situation is even worse. By contrast, in Singapore the clearing of goods takes 2–3 hours and is mostly done by computers.

6. Some of the issues dealt with in this section are discussed in greater depth in Garamfalvi (1997) and in Chapter 9.

7. For an attempt to link incentives to corruption, see Chand and Moene (1997).

8. It should be recalled that some of the countries with the best indexes of corruption, that is those that are perceived to be least corrupt (Denmark, Sweden, Canada, Norway and so on) have some of the highest levels of taxes and public spending.

BIBLIOGRAPHY

Chand, Sheetal K. and Karl O. Moene (1999), 'Controlling Fiscal Corruption', *World Development*, 27(7), 1129–40.

Crotty, John (1997), 'Measures to Address Corruption Problems in Tax and Customs Administrations', paper presented at The Eighth International Anti-Corruption Conference in Lima, Peru, 7–11 September.

Garamfalvi, Laszlo (1997), 'Corruption in the Public Expenditure Management Process', paper presented at The Eighth International Anti-Corruption Conference in Lima, Peru, 7–11 September.

Mauro, Paolo (1995), 'Corruption and Growth', *Quarterly Journal of Economics*, 110(3) (August), 681–712.

—— (1997), 'The Effects of Corruption on Growth, Investment and Government Expenditure: A Cross-Country Analysis', in Kimberly Ann Elliot (ed.), *Corruption and the Global Economy*, Washington: Institute for International Economics.

Tanzi, Vito (1995), 'Corruption, Arm's-Length Relationships and Markets', in Gianluca Fiorentini and Sam Petzman (eds), *The Economics of Organized Crime*, Cambridge: Cambridge University Press, pp. 161–80 (Chapter 6 in this volume).

Tanzi, Vito and Partho Shome (1993), 'A Primer on Tax Evasion', *IMF Staff Papers*, 40(4).

Ul Haque, Nadeem and Ratna Sahay (1996), 'Do Government Wage Cuts Close Budget Deficits? Costs of Corruption', *IMF Staff Papers*, 43(4) (December), 754–78.

van Rijckeghem, Caroline and Beatrice Weder (1997), 'Corruption and the Rate of Temptation: Do Low Wages in Civil Service Cause Corruption?', IMF Working Paper, WP/97/73 (June).

9. Corruption, public investment and growth

INTRODUCTION

Up to the time when a huge corruption scandal, popularly labeled 'Tangentopoli' (bribe city), brought down the political establishment that had ruled Italy for several decades, that country had reported one of the largest shares of capital spending in GDP among the OECD countries. After the scandal broke and several prominent individuals were sent to jail, or even committed suicide, capital spending fell sharply. The fall seems to have been caused by a reduction in the number of capital projects being undertaken and, perhaps more importantly, by a sharp fall in the costs of the projects still undertaken. Information released by Transparency International (TI)[1] reports that, within the space of two or three years, in the city of Milan, the city where the scandal broke in the first place, the cost of city rail links fell by 52 per cent, the cost of one kilometer of subway fell by 57 per cent and the budget for the new airport terminal was reduced by 59 per cent to reflect the lower construction costs. Although one must be aware of the logical fallacy of *post hoc, ergo propter hoc*, the connection between the two events is too strong to be attributed to a coincidence. In fact this chapter takes the view that it could not have been a coincidence.

The basic hypothesis of this chapter is that corruption, and especially political or 'grand' corruption,[2] is often tied to capital projects. Corruption is likely to increase the number of projects undertaken in a country, and to change the design of these projects by enlarging their size and their complexity. The net result is (a) an increase in the share of public investment in GDP (b) a fall in the average productivity of that investment, and (c) because of budgetary constraints and other considerations, a possible reduction in some other categories of public spending, such as 'operation and maintenance', education and health. As a consequence of these and other effects of corruption on the economy, the rate of growth of a country where corruption is significant is negatively affected.

In the second section we discuss reasons why we assume that public investment is particularly sensitive to the existence of (political) corruption. The third section presents empirical evidence on the basic hypotheses. In the final section we draw conclusions.

CORRUPTION AND GOVERNMENT SPENDING

At least from the time, after World War II, when influential economists such as Harrod, Domar, Rostow and others argued that countries need capital to grow and, more importantly, that there is an almost mechanical relation (the capital–output ratio) between increased capital spending and increased growth, there has been a strong intellectual bias in the economic profession in favor of capital spending. For example, when economists evaluate the allocation of public money between current and capital spending in government budgets, they tend to be critical of countries that allow the share of current spending to grow. On the other hand, they generally praise countries where the share of capital spending in total government expenditure goes up.

The above bias is enshrined in the 'golden rule' that many economists advocate for countries. That rule essentially states that it is all right to borrow as long as the borrowing is for investment projects.[3] Thus it is all right to borrow to finance the building of new roads, but not to finance the repairs of existing roads; or to borrow for the building of a new hospital, but not for the hiring of doctors or nurses or for buying medicines. This rule continues to be invoked as a good guide to policy even in the face of much evidence that some current spending – such as 'operation and maintenance' that keeps the existing infrastructure in good condition or spending that contributes to the accumulation of human capital – can promote growth more than capital spending.

Politicians have internalized this bias and to some extent have exploited it. For example, ribbon-cutting ceremonies, when new investment projects related to roads, dams, irrigation canals, power plants, ports, airports, schools and hospitals are completed and inaugurated, are very popular with politicians. They like to be pictured in newspaper articles in the act of cutting the ribbons and, thus, presumably, contributing to the future growth of the country. In a particular Latin American country, capital projects completed under the current administration have been painted orange to send a clear signal to the population that the present government is promoting growth. This pro-investment bias increases the investment budget. We will argue that another factor that also increases the size of the investment budget is corruption.

There is nothing routine about the investment budget and its composition. While much current government spending reflects, to a large extent, explicit or implicit entitlements or previous commitments,[4] thus allowing limited discretion, in the short run, to politicians and, especially, to specific politicians, capital spending is highly discretionary.[5] For the latter, high political figures – members of parliament, general secretaries, ministers or even heads of state – must make some of the basic decisions. These decisions relate to (a) the size of the total public investment budget, (b) the general composition of that budget, that is, the broad allocation among different categories of capital spending, (c) the choice of the specific projects and their locations, and (d) even the size and the design of each project. In these decisions, and especially those in (c) and (d), some high-level individuals will have considerable control or influence. This will happen especially when some of the essential controlling or auditing institutions are not well developed and, therefore, institutional controls are weak.

Public investment projects tend to be large and in some cases they are very large. Their execution is often contracted out to domestic or foreign private enterprises. There is thus a need to choose the enterprise that will be responsible for undertaking the project. For a private enterprise, getting a contract to execute a project, and especially a large one, can be very profitable. Therefore the managers of these enterprises may be willing to pay a 'commission' to the government officials that help them win the contract.[6] In some countries commissions paid by their enterprises to foreign politicians are both legal and tax-deductible. Such 'commissions' are often calculated as percentages of the total cost of the projects.

A commission of even a few percentage points on a project that costs millions or even hundreds of millions of dollars can be a large sum, one large enough to exceed the temptation price of many individuals.[7] When commissions are calculated as a percentage of projects' costs, the public officials who receive the payments for helping the enterprises win the bid will have a vested interest in increasing the scope or the size of the projects so that they can get larger commissions.[8]

The process of approval of an investment project involves several phases. For example, a civil construction project (roads, buildings, ports) requires decisions related to (a) specification and design issues, (b) issue of tender (limited or open?), (c) tender scrutiny, (d) tender negotiations, and (e) tender approval and contracting process. The completion of the project will require verification that the work has been done according to the stipulated contract. It will also require some arbitration about points of disagreement. The writing of contracts for complex projects is very difficult and inevitably there will be many areas of uncertainty and eventual disagreement.

In some of these phases it will be possible for a strategically placed high-level official to influence the process in ways that lead to the selection of a particular enterprise. For example, the specifications of the design can be tailor-made for a given enterprise. The issuance of tenders can be accompanied by the provision of insider information to favored enterprises, and so on.

The enterprise that pays the commission will not suffer from the payment of the bribe if it is able to recover that cost in a number of ways: (a) it can achieve 'up-front' cost recovery if it can win the bidding competition with an offer that includes the cost of the commission; (b) it can have an understanding with the influential official that the initial low bid can be adjusted upward along the way, supposedly to reflect modifications to the basic design;[9] or (c) it can reduce its project costs be skimping on the quality of the work done and on the materials used, thus delivering, at completion, an inferior product.[10] In cases where the contract is stipulated in a cost-plus fashion, the enterprise can recover the cost of the commission by overpricing.

In all these alternatives which require the collaboration of the corrupt official the country will end up either with a higher cost for the specified project than would have been the case in the absence of corruption; with a bigger or more complex project than would have been necessary; or with a project of inferior quality that will not perform up to the anticipated standards and will require costly upkeeping and repairs. The experience with public sector projects, especially in developing countries, is full of stories about roads that needed to be repaired a short time after completion, power plants that worked at much lower capacity than anticipated, and so on.

The above discussion has highlighted cases where corrupt high-level officials or political personalities steer the approval of investment projects toward particular domestic or foreign enterprises in exchange for bribes. This is an important part of the way in which corruption, defined in the broader sense of rent seeking, affects public investment. However it is not the full story. Important cases of corruption exist also when political personalities steer public investments toward their home districts or their own land. In a case reported in the *Financial Times* of 29 July 1997, the president of a country was accused of having built an airport with public funds in his small home town even though there seemed to be little economic justification for it. This is far from being an isolated case. At other times projects are steered toward particular areas in order to increase the value of assets (such as lands owned by political personalities) in those areas.

In all of these cases the productivity of the capital spending is reduced, thus reducing the growth rate of the country. Therefore corruption can significantly distort the relationship between the capital input and the output generated by that capital, thus increasing the capital–output ratio.

When the approval of investment projects comes to be much influenced by corrupt, high-level officials, the rate of return of projects as calculated by cost–benefit analysis ceases to be the criterion for project selection.[11] Capital spending becomes much less productive and much less of a contributor to growth than generally believed. Unfortunately situations of this type are far from rare. In these situations those who carry out the projects (the executing enterprises) come to care mostly about the profits that they make. And the political figures that authorize the projects and choose the enterprises care mostly about the bribes, or the other advantages that they get. Thus corruption distorts the whole decision-making process connected with the investment budget. In the extreme case of a totally corrupt country, projects are chosen exclusively for their bribe-generating capacity and not for their productivity. The productivity of the projects becomes almost irrelevant.[12]

When corruption plays a large part in the selection of projects and contractors, the result of this process is a capital budget that is highly distorted. 'White elephants' and 'cathedrals in the desert' are produced. Some projects are completed but never used. Some are much larger and complex than necessary. Some are of such low quality that they will need continuous repairs and their output capacity will be much below initial expectations. In these circumstances it is not surprising that capital spending does not generate the results in terms of growth that economists expect.

Widespread corruption in the investment budget will not only reduce the rate of return to *new* public investment, but will also affect the rate of return that a country gets from its existing infrastructure. The reasons are several. First, to the extent that corruption is not a new phenomenon but one that has been around for some time, the existing infrastructure has also been contaminated because *past* investments were also misdirected or distorted by corruption.

Second, higher spending on capital projects will reduce the resources available for other spending. Of the other spending one that is not protected by the existence of entitlements or implicit commitments is 'operation and maintenance', that is the kind of current public spending that is required to keep the existing physical infrastructure of a country in good working condition. Therefore a frequently observed phenomenon is the poor condition of the existing infrastructure (roads with potholes, buildings badly in need of repairs, and so on). One often observes situations where new projects are undertaken while the existing structure is left to deteriorate.

Third, and more speculatively, in cases of extreme corruption, operation and maintenance on the physical infrastructure of a country may be intentionally reduced so that some infrastructure, such as roads, will deteriorate quickly to the point where they will need to be rebuilt, thus allowing some high-level officials the opportunity to extract another commission from the enterprise that will undertake the project. Some World Bank reports have hinted that this may have happened in some countries.

A country can squeeze more output out of the existing infrastructure by keeping it in good working condition so that it can be used at close to 100 percent capacity.[13] It is easy to think of situations where the deterioration of this infrastructure retards growth more than the new capital projects add to growth. Additionally, when generalized corruption in a country reduces resources because of the negative impact on tax revenue that is caused by corrupt tax administrators, operation and maintenance will be reduced far more than public investment because of the intellectual bias listed above that supports borrowing for capital projects but not for current expenditure.

EMPIRICAL ANALYSIS

Data Description

In our empirical analysis we use indices of corruption data from two sources: Business International (BI) and Political Risk Services, Inc. The BI index has been used by Mauro (1995), among others, and is available for 68 countries over the 1980–83 period (one observation per country). The second source publishes a closely related index in the *International Country Risk Guide* (ICRG). Unlike the BI index, the ICRG index is annual; it covers the 1982–95 period and, depending on the year, is available for 42 to 95 countries. This index has been used by Knack and Keefer (1995) and many others.

Both indices are assessments of the degree of corruption in a country by informed observers, the BI's network of correspondents, in the case of the BI index, and foreign investors, in the case of the ICRG index. The BI index has been discontinued, while the ICRG index is updated annually and is sold as part of a package to potential investors worldwide. Corruption in the BI indicates 'the degree to which business transactions involve corruption or questionable payments'. The index ranges from 0 (most corrupt) to 10 (least corrupt). In the ICRG index higher corruption indicates that 'high government officials are likely to demand special payments' and 'legal payments are generally expected throughout lower levels of government' in the forms of 'bribes connected with import and export licenses, exchange controls, tax assessment, police protection or loans'. The ICRG index ranges from 0 (most corrupt) to 6 (least corrupt).

We have rescaled the ICRG index by multiplying it by 10/6 so that both indexes range from 0 to 10, and have spliced them to form a single corruption index from 1980 to 1995.[14] For ease of interpretation of the regression results we have multiplied the resulting index by minus one so that higher values of the index imply higher corruption.

The discussion in the previous section underscored the interaction between corruption, public investment, operations and maintenance (O&M) expenditures and other aspects of the government's budgetary position. For public investment, capital expenditure data from the International Monetary Fund's *Government Finance Statistics* (GFS) are used. Unfortunately cross-country data on O&M expenditures are not available. We have therefore chosen two proxies called 'expenditure on other goods and services' which includes O&M expenditures, and 'wages and salaries as a fraction of current expenditures'. The rationale behind these proxies will be explained below.

To investigate the impact of corruption on the *quality* of public investment, we use the following indicators of quality of infrastructure:

- paved roads in good condition as a percentage of total paved roads,
- electric power system losses as a percentage of total power output,
- telecommunication faults per 100 mainlines per year,
- water losses as a percentage of total water provision,
- railway diesels in use as a percentage of total diesel inventory.

The above data are often referred to as performance indicators of infrastructure and seem adequate for our purpose; they are measured from the perspective of both infrastructure providers and the users; they cover a large number of countries and, most importantly, they have many characteristics that make them the responsibility of governments. These data are taken from International Telecommunications Union and the World Bank's World Development Indicators data base. Paved roads in good condition are roads substantially free of major problems and requiring only routine maintenance. Electric power system losses consist of technical losses such as resistance losses in transmission and distribution and non-technical losses such as illegal connection to the electricity and other sources of theft. System losses are then expressed as a fraction of total output. Water losses include physical losses (pipe breaks and overflows) and commercial losses (meter under-registration, illegal use including fraudulent or unregistered connections, and legal, but not usually metered, uses such as firefighting). Railway diesels in use as a percentage of total diesel inventory measures technical and managerial performance.

Finally government revenue data, taken from the GFS, are expressed as fractions of GDP. Data on GDP and real per capita GDP (the latter is a control variable in regression) come from the World Bank's World Development Indicators data base.

Regression Results

The discussion in the previous section suggests testable hypotheses about the relationship between corruption, on the one hand, and public investment, government revenue, O&M expenditures and quality of infrastructure on the other. We use regression analysis to test these hypotheses using cross-country data. It is of course difficult to draw causality statements from regression equations, and one must guard against spurious regression results. We do so by controlling for other variables, such as real per capita GM government revenue–GDP ratio and public investment–GDP ratio.

Corruption and public investment
Hypothesis 1: other things being equal, high corruption is associated with high public investment To test this hypothesis we regress the public invest-

ment–GDP ratio on a constant and the corruption index. We subsequently add real per capita GDP and the government revenue–GDP ratio to see if the corruption–investment relationship is robust to the inclusion of these two variables. We add real per capita GDP since it is typically a proxy for the stage of economic development and different levels of development may require different needs for public investment. The government revenue–GDP ratio is added because the higher are these revenues the easier it is to finance public investment. The results are three regressions, shown in Table 9.1. In all the regressions, we cannot reject hypothesis 1 at the 1 per cent significance level.[15] The government revenue–GDP variable has a statistically significant positive coefficient indicating that such revenues are important sources for financing public investment. The results shown in Table 9.1 are for the world sample, but they also hold up for the subsamples of developing countries and members of the Organization for Economic Cooperation and Development (OECD).

Table 9.1   *The effects of corruption on public investment, 1980–95 (as a ratio of GDP, annual data)*

Independent variables	(1)	(2)	(3)
Constant	6.75	6.47	4.71
	(23.4)	(19.5)	(13.9)
Corruption index	0.38	0.27	0.48
	(8.97)	(4.15)	(7.48)
Real per capita GDP*		−0.71	−1.21
		(−2.94)	(−5.18)
Government revenue–GDP ratio			0.13
			(12.6)
Adjusted R^2	0.069	0.082	0.207
Number of observations	1 081	1 011	1 000

Note: * Indicates that the coefficient is multiplied by 10 000.

Sources: IMF, *Government Finance Statistics, World Tables*; *Business International*; *Political Risk Services*. The corruption index is taken from Mauro (1995) and *International Country Risk Guide* compiled by Political Risk Services. A high value of the index means a country has high corruption; *t*-statistics are in parentheses. Estimation technique is OLS.

Corruption and government revenues

Regressions in Table 9.1 show the direct impact of corruption on public investment and do not rule out the possibility of an indirect impact, say, through government revenues. Corruption can reduce government revenues if it contributes to tax evasion, improper tax exemptions or weak tax administration. This leads to the second hypothesis.

Hypothesis 2: other things being equal, high corruption is associated with low government revenue   To test this assertion we regress the government revenue–GDP ratio on a constant and corruption. We then add real per capita GDP to control for stage-of-economic development effects. The results given in Table 9.2 for the world sample show that we cannot reject hypothesis 2 at the 1 per cent significance level. Similar results also hold up for subsamples of developing and OECD countries.

Table 9.2   The effects of corruption on government revenues, 1980–95 (as a ratio of GDP, annual data)

Independent variables	(1)	(2)
Constant	9.99	12.9
	(12.1)	(13.7)
Corruption index	–2.51	–1.71
	(–20.4)	(–9.28)
Real per capita GDP*		3.73
		(5.34)
Adjusted R^2	0.272	0.28
Number of observations	1 114	1 042

Notes: * indicates that the coefficient is multiplied by 10 000.

Sources: IMF, *Government Finance Statistics*; *World Tables*; *Business International*; *Political Risk Services*. The corruption index is taken from Mauro (1995) and *International Country Risk Guide* compiled by Political Risk Services. A high value of the index means a country has high corruption; *t*-statistics are in parentheses. Estimation technique is OLS.

Corruption and O&M expenditures

An observation made in the previous section, and one closely related to hypotheses 1 and 2, is the underfunding of O&M expenditure. Since corruption and bribery are more effectively related to new investments, corruption may result in lower O&M expenditure. These observations lead to the third hypothesis.

Hypothesis 3: other things being equal, high corruption is associated with low O&M expenditures   As stated earlier, direct cross-country data on O&M expenditures are not available.[16] We therefore use two proxies: (1) 'expenditures on other goods and services', a component of current expenditure, expressed as a fraction of wages and salaries; and (2) 'wages and salaries expressed as a fraction of current expenditure'. These data are taken from the IMF's GFS data base. The rationale behind the first proxy is obvious since, according to the GFS manual on government finance statistics, expenditures on other goods and services include O&M expenditures. We have expressed this expenditure relative to wages and salaries in order to highlight potential trade-offs between O&M expenditure and expenditure on wages and salaries. The ratio of wages and salaries to current expenditure is a reasonable proxy for O&M expenditures because governments often tend to award wage increases but cut O&M expenditures. Hence increases in wages and salaries can be interpreted as cuts in O&M expenditures.

To test hypothesis 3 we regress each of the above proxies on a constant and a corruption index and, as usual for sensitivity analysis, we add real per capita GDP to each regression. The results are shown in Table 9.3. Unlike the previous regressions, we present the results for three samples (world, OECD and developing) as there are differences across these samples. With respect to the first proxy, results in Table 9.3 indicate that high corruption is indeed associated with low O&M expenditures. However one can reject hypothesis 3 at the 1 per cent significance level only for the developing country sample. Once we control for real per capita GDP, hypothesis 3 is rejected at the 1 per cent significance level for all three samples. One interpretation of this finding is that the first proxy is a noisy indicator of O&M expenditure.

As regards the second proxy for O&M expenditures, we cannot reject hypothesis 3 for all three samples at the 1 per cent significance level whether or not we control for real per capita GDP (Table 9.3, panel (b)). Countries with high corruption do tend to have a high ratio of wages and salaries to current expenditure.[17] The evidence is much stronger statistically and economically for the developing country sample than for the OECD sample.

Corruption and quality of public investment

Infrastructure investments are often lumpy and require substantial 'up-front' financial capital. It has been known for some time that corruption is most prevalent in the infrastructure sector (Wade, 1982; Rose-Ackerman, 1996). Regressions in Table 9.1 have provided evidence that high corruption is indeed associated with high public investment. (See also Mauro, 1997.) However this evidence links corruption to *quantity* of investment, and not the *quality*. In the previous section we argued that countries take on new infrastructure investment without maintaining the existing infrastructure capital stock. Therefore we expect the quality of the infrastructure to deteriorate, and more so if corruption leads to O&M expenditure cutbacks. These observations lead to the fourth hypothesis.

Table 9.3   The effects of corruption on O&M expenditure

(a) Expenditures on other goods and services, 1980–95 (as a ratio of wages and salaries, 1980–95)						
	World		OECD		Developing	
Independent variable	(1)	(2)	(1)	(2)	(1)	(2)
Constant	72.9	97.2	–20.2	43.4	84.2	82.3
	(8.15)	(9.29)	(–0.558)	(1.19)	(7.08)	(6.65)
Corruption index	–3.54	4.44	–14	5.96	–1.24	1.43
	(–2.69)	(2.20)	(–3.53)	(1.23)	(–0.57)	(0.60)
Real per capita GDP*		0.42		0.81		0.63
		(5.55)		(6.99)		(3.93)
Adjusted R^2	0.006	0.038	0.037	0.182	–0.01	0.021
Number of observations	999	927	300	273	699	654

(b) Wages and salaries, 1980–95 (as a ratio of current expenditure, annual data)						
	World		OECD		Developing	
Independent variable	(1)	(2)	(1)	(2)	(1)	(2)
Constant	47.3	42.2	34.2	30.8	39.7	39.7
	(41.7)	(33.2)	(12.2)	(11.3)	(26.1)	(25.2)
Corruption	3.1	1.48	2.17	0.75	1.22	1.16
	(18.5)	(6.03)	(7.02)	(2.07)	(4.43)	(3.83)
Real per capita GDP**		–0.84		–0.65		–0.067
		(–9.13)		(–7.54)		(–0.327)
Adjusted R^2	0.255	0.319	0.139	0.31	0.026	0.023
Number of observations	1 000	925	300	273	700	652

Note: * and ** indicate that the coefficients are multiplied by 100 and 1000, respectively.

Sources: IMF, *Government Finance Statistics*; *World Tables*; *Business International*; *Political Risk Services*. The corruption index is taken from Mauro (1995) and *International Country Risk Guide* compiled by Political Risk Services. A high value of the index means a country has high corruption; *t*-statistics are in parentheses. Estimation technique is OLS.

Hypothesis 4: other things being equal, high corruption is associated with poor quality of infrastructure   To test this hypothesis we regress indicators of quality of infrastructure on a constant, the corruption index and real per capita GDP. The results are given in Table 9.4 for five indicators of quality of infrastructure. Hypothesis 4 cannot be rejected at the usual significance levels:

Table 9.4   Corruption and quality of infrastructure, 1980–95 (annual data)

Dependent variable	Constant	Corruption Index	Real per capita GDP*	Adjusted R²	N
Paved roads in good condition	19.2	–3.84		0.052	513
	(4.97)	(–5.40)			
Paved roads in good condition	15.5	–2.22	5.4	0.268	373
	(3.87)	(–2.89)	(9.85)		
Power outages	18.7	1.1		0.07	997
	(27.7)	(8.69)			
Power outages	18.8	0.95	–0.56	0.162	922
	(32.5)	(8.17)	(–7.07)		
Telecommunication faults	97.6	4.17		0.007	241
	(6.93)	(1.63)			
Telecommunication faults	94.5	–0.54	–9.33	0.127	201
	(6.31)	(–0.18)	(–5.01)		
Water losses**	43.8	2.25		0.089	26
	(6.89)	(1.86)			
Water losses**	43.6	1.52	–2.92	0.186	25
	(7.19)	(1.14)	(–1.63)		
Railway diesels in use***	47.1	–3.66		0.17	67
	(7.45)	(–3.80)			
Railway diesels in use***	59.4	–0.58	1.37	0.285	67
	(8.62)	(–0.46)	(3.39)		

Note: * indicates that the coefficient is multiplied by 10 000; ** and *** denote averages of data over 1980–89 and 1990–95 periods, respectively.

Sources: IMF, *Government Finance Statistics*; *World Tables*; *Business International*; *Political Risk Services*. The corruption index is taken from Mauro (1995) and *International Country Risk Guide* compiled by Political Risk Services. A high value of the index means a country has high corruption; *t*-statistics are in parentheses. Estimation technique is OLS.

countries with high corruption do tend to have poor quality of infrastructure. In terms of statistical significance, the impact of corruption is strongest on the quality of roads (paved roads in good condition), power outages and railway diesels in use. When we control for real per capita GDP, corruption changes its sign in only one regression (telecommunication faults) and loses its statistical significance at the usual levels in three regressions (telecommunication faults, water losses and railway diesels in use). The fit of every regression improves, as judged by the adjusted R-squared, when we add real per capita GDP. Moreover real per capita GDP in every regression has the right sign: countries with higher real per capita GDP tend to have better quality of infrastructure. An important implication of the results in Table 9.4 is that the costs of corruption should also be measured in terms of the deterioration in the quality of the existing infrastructure. These costs can be very high in terms of their impact on growth.

Does corruption reduce the quality of infrastructure through public investment? To answer the above question, we conduct a more rigorous test of hypothesis 4 for the quality of roads.[18] We regress paved roads in good condition on a constant, real per capita GDP, the corruption index (that is, the same regression as in Table 9.4) and two additional variables: the public investment–GDP ratio and its interaction with the corruption index. Results are shown in Table 9.5. Columns (1) and (2) show that, even when we control for public investment, we still cannot reject hypothesis 4 at the 1 per cent significance level. The regression in column (3) shows that corruption is still significant in the presence of the interaction variable. If corruption reduces the quality of roads through public investment, we should find that corruption loses its significance when the interaction variable is added to the regression, given the presence of the public investment–GDP ratio and real capita GDP.

Table 9.5   The effects of corruption on quality of roads, 1980–95 (dependent variable: paved roads in good condition as a percentage of total paved roads, annual data)

Independent variable	(1)	(2)	(3)	(4)
Constant	−1.03	7.55	1.83	19.6
	(−0.150)	(1.01)	(0.193)	(1.82)
Corruption index	−7	−2.56	−6.51	−0.32
	(−8.68)	(−2.20)	(−4.74)	(−0.17)
Public investment–GDP ratio	2.03	3.09	1.15	−0.2
	(2.65)	(4.00)	(0.53)	(0.10)
Public investment–GDP ratio × corruption index			−0.16	−0.58
			(−0.44)	(−1.56)
Real per capita GDP*		0.24		0.25
		(6.38)		(6.57)
Adjusted R^2	0.186	0.326	0.184	0.329
Number of observations	322	269	322	269

Note: * indicates that the coefficient is multiplied by 100.

Sources: IMF, *Government Finance Statistics*; *World Tables*; *Business International*; *Political Risk Services*. The corruption index is taken from Mauro (1995) and *International Country Risk Guide* compiled by Political Risk Services. A high value of the index means a country has high corruption; *t*-statistics are in parentheses. Estimation technique is OLS.

Comparison of columns (4) and (2) – with and without the interaction term respectively – shows this to be the case. In addition the statistically significant interaction term in column (4) shows that the impact of corruption on the quality of roads depends on public investment. The negative sign on the interaction term suggests that the higher the public investment, the higher the negative impact of corruption on the quality of roads. This additional evidence is consistent with the finding in Table 9.1 that higher corruption is indeed associated with higher public investment.

Does higher corruption reduce the productivity of public investment? Suppose that we measure productivity of public investment by improvements, in the quality of roads per dollar of public investment. The regression in column (4) of Table 9.5 shows that the impact of investment on the quality of roads depends on the existence of corruption. Specifically the negative sign on the interaction term shows that higher corruption can reduce the productivity of public investment.

CONCLUDING REMARKS

There are many channels through which higher corruption reduces economic growth. Mauro (1995, 1997) provides evidence and summarizes some of these arguments. The new evidence presented in this chapter supports four additional arguments. First, corruption can reduce growth by increasing public investment *while reducing its productivity.*[19] This finding is consistent with typical reduced-form cross-country growth regressions. For example, Devarajan *et al.* (1996) have found that higher public investment is associated with lower growth, given other determinants of growth, and Tanzi (1994) found that the relation between growth and investment is highly sensitive to the inclusion of a couple of countries.

Second, corruption can reduce growth by increasing public investment that is not accompanied by its recurrent current expenditure: adequate non-wage O&M expenditures. Our evidence shows that higher corruption is associated with higher total expenditure on wages and salaries. Wages and salaries are a large component of government consumption and higher government consumption has been shown to be unambiguously associated with lower growth (Commander *et al.*, 1997; Barro, 1996; Barro and Sala-i-Martin, 1995).

Third, corruption can reduce growth by reducing the quality of the existing infrastructure. A deteriorating infrastructure increases the cost of doing business for both government and private sector (congestion, delays, break-downs of machinery and so on) and thus leads to lower output and growth. The importance of infrastructure in growth has been shown in many cross-country growth regressions (Canning and Fay, 1993; Easterly and Levine, 1996; Hulten, 1996).

Finally, corruption can reduce growth by lowering government revenue needed to finance productive spending.

The implication of this chapter is that economists should be more restrained in their praise of high public sector investment spending and of rules such as the golden rule, especially in countries where corruption, and especially high level corruption, is a problem. The chapter has focused on the problem of corruption and not on solutions. As far as corruption relates to the activities of foreign enterprises, the OECD is currently attempting to induce industrial countries (a) to make the payment of bribes to foreign officials not tax-deductible and (b) to criminalize the payment of bribes. So far the ministers representing the OECD countries have accepted these recommendations, but the legislative bodies of some of those countries must still act. The OECD proposal, however, would not affect public investment projects in non-OECD countries carried out by domestic contractors or by other contractors from non-OECD countries.[20]

NOTES

1. TI is a non-governmental organization with headquarters in Berlin which traces corruption trends around the world and which has as its goal the elimination of corruption.
2. The literature distinguishes between petty or bureaucratic corruption and 'grand' or political corruption.
3. The rule simply states that only current expenditure needs to be balanced by ordinary revenue: a country can have a fiscal deficit equal to the net capital spending of the government.
4. Pensions, interest payments on the debt, salaries, subsidies and so on.
5. Specific politicians generally do not have the power to change the pensions, salaries or subsidies of specific individuals.
6. 'Commission' is often a euphemism for what is essentially a bribe.
7. Actually, in many cases the act of bribery may start, not with the enterprises, but with the officials who control the decisions. Foreign enterprises report that in some countries it is impossible to get a government contract without paying a bribe.
8. For a useful discussion of corruption in public investment, see Patrick Meagher (1997).
9. This second option may be less attractive to the enterprise if it fears that the official may require additional payments when the cost-increasing modifications are made or if it fears that the official may no longer have the power to influence the process. In countries where the same individuals remain in power for a long time, the strategy of the low initial bid followed by adjustments over the period when the project is executed is a common one.
10. This has been a frequent occurrence in road building, where the thickness of the base of the road may be much reduced. It has also been an occurrence in the building of bridges and buildings which, at times, have collapsed, causing loss of lives and economic costs.
11. In Italy, before Tangentopoli, those hired to evaluate projects often found that they were totally ignored.
12. This may be part of the reason why we observe extremely high capital–output ratios in some countries.

13. World Bank studies indicate that in many countries public infrastructure including roads, power plants and irrigation canals often can be used only at a fraction of their full capacity.
14. The two indices are highly correlated with a correlation coefficient of 0.81. Other indices are also available, including one issued by Transparency International. These indices are also highly correlated.
15. Note that corruption reduces aggregate investment (Mauro, 1995) which is the sum of public and private capital investment. Thus corruption must reduce private capital investment by more than it increases public capital investment.
16. Ideally we want shortfalls in O&M expenditures. This requires knowledge of the so-called 'r' coefficients and actual O&M expenditures. The 'r' coefficient is the ratio of net recurrent expenditure requirements to the total investment cost of a project (see Heller, 1991).
17. This does not mean that the level of salaries in corrupt countries is higher. In fact a recent study has found a negative relationship between salary levels in the public sector and corruption. See Van Rijckeghem and Weder (1997).
18. Results with other measures of quality of infrastructure are similar.
19. Please note that, because corruption reduces tax revenue, the relative increase in public investment (that is, its share of the total government budget) is likely to be higher than the absolute increase in public investment.
20. For a discussion of steps to reduce corruption, see previous chapters.

BIBLIOGRAPHY

Barro, Robert J. (1996), 'Determinants of Economic Growth: A Cross-Country Empirical Study', NBER Working Paper, no. 5698.
Barro, Robert J. and Xavier Sala-I-Martin (1995), *Economic Growth*, New York: McGraw-Hill.
Canning, David and Marianne Fay (1993), 'The Effect of Transportation Networks on Economic Growth', Columbia University (mimeo).
Commander, Simon, Hamid R. Davoodi and Une J. Lee (1997), 'The Causes of Government and the Consequences for Growth and Well-Being', World Bank Policy Research Working Paper no. 1785.
Devarajan, Shantayanan, Vinaya Swaroop and Heng-fu Zou (1996), 'The Composition of Public Expenditure and Economic Growth,' *Journal of Monetary Economics*, 37, 313–44.
Easterly, William and R. Levine (1996), 'Africa's Growth Tragedy', The World Bank (mimeo).
Heller, Peter S. (1991), 'Operations and Maintenance', in Ke-Young Chu and Richard Hemming (eds), *Public Expenditure Handbook*, Washington, DC: IMF.
Hulten, Charles R. (1996), 'Infrastructure and Economic Development: Once More Unto the Beach', World Bank and University of Maryland, College Park (mimeo).
Klitgaard, Robert E. (1988), *Controlling Corruption*, Berkeley: University of California Press.
Knack, Stephen and Philip Keefer (1995), 'Institutions and Economic Performance: Cross-Country Tests Using Alternative Institutional Measures', *Economics and Politics*, 7(3), 207–27.
Mauro, Paolo (1995), 'Corruption and Growth', *Quarterly Journal of Economics*, 110(3) (August), 681–712
——(1997), 'The Effects of Corruption on Growth, Investment and Government

Expenditure: A Cross Country Analysis', in Kimberly Ann Elliott (ed.), *Corruption and the Global Economy*, Washington: Institute for International Economics.

Meagher, Patrick (1997), 'Combating Corruption in Africa; Institutional Challenges and Response', paper presented at the IMF Seminar on Combating Corruption in Economic and Financial Management. Lisbon, 19–21 May.

Olson, Mancur (1996), 'Big Bills Left on the Sidewalk: Why Some Nations are Rich and Others Poor', *Journal of Economic Perspectives*, 10(2), 3–24.

Pritchett, Lant (1996), 'Mind Your P's and Q's: The Cost of Public Investment is not the Value of Public Capital Stock', World Bank Policy Research Working Paper, no 1660.

Rose-Ackerman, Susan (1997), 'Corruption and Development', paper presented at the Annual Bank conference on Development Economies, Washington D.C., World Bank, April 30 and May 1.

Svensson, Jacob (1996), 'Foreign Aid and Rent-Seeking', World Bank, Macroeconomics and Growth Division (mimeo).

Tanzi, Vito (1991), *Public Finance in Developing Countries*, Aldershot: Edward Elgar.

—— (1994), 'The IMF and Tax Reform', in Amaresh Bagchi and Nicholas Stern (eds), *Tax Policy and Planning in Developing Countries*, Delhi: Oxford University Press.

—— (1995), 'Corruption, Arm's Length Relationships and Markets', in Gianluca Fiorentini and Sam Peltzman (eds), *The Economics of Organised Crime*, Cambridge Cambridge University Press, pp. 161–80.

—— (1997), 'Corruption, Governmental Activities and Policy Instruments: A Brief Review of the Main Issues' (mimeo).

Van Rijckeghem, Caroline and Beatrice Weder (1997), 'Corruption and the Rate of Temptation: Do Low Wages in the Civil Service Cause Corruption?', IMF Working Paper, WP/97/73 (June).

Wade, Robert (1982), 'The System of Administrative and Political Corruption: Canal Irrigation in South India', *Journal of Development Studies*, 18, 287–328.

Wei, Shang-Jin (1997), 'How Taxing is Corruption on International Investors?', NBER Working Paper 6030, Cambridge, Massachusetts: National Bureau of Economic Research.

10. A primer on tax evasion

INTRODUCTION

Tax evasion is a universal phenomenon. It takes place in all societies, in all social classes, in all professions, in all industries, in all religions and in virtually all economic systems. Two thousand five hundred years ago, Plato was already writing about this phenomenon and on the Ducal Palace of Venice built many centuries ago there is a stone with a hole in it, through which people who knew about tax evaders could inform the Republic about the culprits. The only surprise is how little attention this phenomenon had received in some places and especially in the United States until recent years. For example, there is no reference to it in the index to Richard Goode's (1964) classic *The Individual Income Tax*, none in Richard Musgrave's (1959) *The Theory of Public Finance* and none in Joseph Pechman's (1966) *Federal Tax Policy*. These authors either did not think that tax evasion was important or opted to ignore it.

In recent years, however, there has been growing attention paid to this phenomenon. In the United States the attention to it may have started with a somewhat political view that the problem of the rising fiscal deficit could be solved by reducing the so-called 'tax gap' rather than by raising tax rates or cutting public spending.[1] Because of its policy of reducing tax rates and its inability to reduce public spending, the Reagan administration promoted the idea that the fiscal deficit could be reduced by reducing or eliminating the tax gap. In other countries the concern for tax evasion was in part prompted by a growing preoccupation with horizontal equity. The realization that people with similar incomes often ended up paying very different taxes because of different possibilities of tax evasion led many governments to worry about the implications of tax evasion. Also a growing concern about underground economic activities and how these affected economic policies, and the realization that the underground economy was often the other face of tax evasion, led in the 1980s to increasing attention being paid to tax evasion.[2] This is certainly true of Latin America, where the authorities, after introducing major tax policy reforms, have demonstrated increasing interest in the measurement and diminution of evasion of both income taxes and consumption taxes.[3]

The next section surveys some of the sources of tax evasion and recounts how economists have attempted to provide a theoretical underpinning for them. It also discusses some of the limitations of this theoretical literature. The third section reviews the role of tax administration and sanctions in limiting tax evasion and mentions, briefly, the relation between society at large and tax evasion. The fourth section provides some concluding remarks.

THEORETICAL UNDERPINNINGS FOR CAUSES AND EFFECTS

Sources and Implications of Tax Evasion

Tax evasion comes in different forms. It comes, for example, through the non-declaration of income, through the underreporting of income, sales or wealth, through the overreporting of deductible expenses, through smuggling activities, and through many other forms. In fact the variety of tax evasion is truly remarkable, and one is always finding new ways by which taxpayers attempt to reduce their tax burden.[4] The many authors who have reviewed these matters include Sisson (1981) and Richupan (1987), among IMF studies and, more recently, Cowell (1990) and Webley *et al.* (1991). Such findings are reported in technical assistance works which are often confidential.

The opportunity for tax evasion varies between sectors, and this may lead to social turmoil. In Italy, for example, salaried workers have demonstrated in large numbers in the streets to call for reduction in tax evasion by independent professionals and other groups. Activities in which tax evasion is easier are those of independent contractors, of professionals such as doctors, lawyers and architects, and those of people who engage in agricultural activities. There is increasing evidence that enterprises that operate in different countries can also reduce their tax burden through the judicious use of transfer pricing.[5]

Tax evasion has much to do with the structure of the economy. The more atomized is production, the more likely it is that tax evasion will flourish. A country where much production takes place in large enterprises or establishments is unlikely to have a lot of tax evasion. However a country where much economic activity takes place in small shops, in small farms and on the part of single individuals is likely to experience a lot of evasion.

Tax evasion is also strictly connected with the structure of the tax system. It is likely to vary according to the use of different tax bases. For example, in the case of income taxes it is likely to vary between dependent and non-dependent income sources, as well as between large, small and multinational enterprises. In the case of sales taxes it is likely to be connected with the underreporting of sales or the overreporting of purchases. In theory, at least, tax evasion is connected with the accounting concepts of tax liabilities. When a country relies on presumptive concepts of taxation, tax evasion is likely to be more limited unless there is hiding of the assets on which the presumptive estimate of the tax payment is based. The tax structure will also influence tax evasion by its number of taxes. At times governments introduce additional taxes in order to neutralize the losses connected with tax evasion associated with existing taxes. However an increase in the number of taxes will produce inefficiencies in the tax system and will facilitate for taxpayers the search for new ways of avoiding paying taxes.

The policy implications of tax evasion would be quite different according to whether evasion is an individual or a social phenomenon. A single tax evader in a country of honest taxpayers typifies the behavior of just that individual. However a tax evader in a country where tax evasion is a national sport is a somewhat different phenomenon. Tax evasion has implications for the equity of the tax system, for both its horizontal and its vertical equity. It has implications for the efficiency of the tax system and even for the competitive market framework. For example, it is impossible to have pure competition when some of the sellers can evade taxes while others cannot. In this case the former will be able to undersell the latter. Tax evasion affects the productivity of the tax system, reducing the amount of revenue that could be raised given the statutory system. It affects the general attitude of citizens vis-à-vis the government, often building cynicism about the role of the public sector. Often it affects even the statutory system in the sense that the tax laws begin to anticipate the tax evasion by particular groups and try to penalize tax evasion by increasing the tax rates for those particular groups. This often results in increased horizontal inequity since not all the taxpayers in those groups behave like the average.

The Theory of Tax Evasion and its Limitations

Since Allingham and Sandmo (1972) wrote a classic theoretical paper on tax evasion, the problem of tax evasion, seen from the point of view of the taxpayer, has been discussed as a kind of game theory.[6] The taxpayer is faced with the decision whether to evade or not to evade. In other words the decision on whether to pay the tax becomes similar to playing a lottery where one is free to buy or not to buy a lottery ticket. For a rational individual the choice will be made on the basis of the expectations of gains or losses associated with the decision made. The objective is to maximize the utility of the taxpayer.[7]

The benefit derived from tax evasion is related to the expected value of the money (and thus to the utility of the money) that the individual does not pay. The cost of tax evasion is connected to the probability of being caught and the consequences of this outcome. These consequences, in the Allingham and

Sandmo model, are associated with fines which can considerably exceed the original tax due. But, of course, the probability that the individual will pay these fines depends on the probability of being caught and that probability can be very low.

The Allingham and Sandmo theory has some important implications for tax administration. In fact the theory implies that tax evasion can be reduced by either increasing the penalties associated with it or by increasing administrative expenses, assuming that this increase raises the probability that the tax evader will get caught.[8] In an extreme interpretation of the Allingham and Sandmo theory it has been argued that the penalties should become so high and the cost of administration so low that at the limit the tax evader who gets caught should be hanged, but that the probability of being caught would approach zero.

The theoretical and, especially, the practical limitations of the theoretical literature have not received the attention they deserve, but some of these have been discussed by various writers. A first limitation has to do with risk aversion, which may vary among individuals and may depend on the level of the taxpayer's income or wealth. In the more recent theoretical advances, the taxpayer's behavior toward tax compliance turns entirely on his attitude toward risk. For example, treating tax evasion in the context of intertemporal choice models, Banerji (1991) concludes:

> Is there a more subtle way of enforcing compliance without such elaborate calibration – by simply increasing the risk of detection for the evader, and thereby making him or her switch from the riskier asset to the safer one of declared income? Unfortunately, this plan would work with certainty only if we were willing to assume that all possible evaders in the economy had constant absolute risk aversion, i.e., that their willingness to take risks did not depend upon their level of income or consumption. (p. 98)

A second limitation has to do with the use of penalties which are applied to only those unfortunate fellows who get caught. In other words there are many tax evaders who should be penalized but who do not get caught and who are, thus, not affected by those penalties. This raises the question of whether the judiciary system and the community at large will be willing to penalize fully the unlucky few individuals who get caught when many more individuals are committing the same offenses but are not being punished. Anecdotal evidence from many countries indicates that the judiciary system is unwilling to fully apply the penalties under these conditions. This means that one of the basic conclusions of the theoretical literature is unlikely to hold fully if the penalties actually implemented differ from those which are in the books.

Third, the theory assumes that the taxpayers know precisely the probability of being caught and the penalties that they will receive so that they can make the cost–benefit calculations. However tax administrations often keep this information highly confidential, so that for most, if not all, taxpayers the probability of being caught is an unknown. And the penalties may be highly uncertain.[9]

Fourth, the theory ignores costs in terms of embarrassment, loss of self-esteem and social status, and so on experienced by those who get caught. These costs vary from society to society and from individual to individual. In a society where tax evasion is condoned because of the unpopularity of the government, tax evaders may be admired and the social costs associated with tax evasion, consequently, may be low or even negative. In a society where tax evasion is taboo, these costs can be very high.

Finally, many countries rely on means-testing based on declared income for determining access to many government-provided benefits such as food stamps, free health care, free education or scholarships, and so forth. Therefore the advantages from tax evasion may far exceed those measured by the non-payment of the tax.

The Role of Penalties and Amnesties

Perhaps a few comments on the penalties themselves would be appropriate. Some of these comments have relevance for the theoretical literature on tax evasion. The higher the penalties, the more probable it is that they will not be applied to those who get caught. If the high penalties had led to a reduction in the cost of administration, this would have reduced the probability of detection and thus the number of cases requiring the imposition of penalties. Many societies would feel uncomfortable about singling out and punishing particular individuals, almost by a lottery process, when many other individuals may have committed the same offenses. Second, for the penalties to be effective, they must be applied quickly. A penalty that is delayed for years, because of appeals on the part of the taxpayer, is unlikely to have the same effect, as a deterrent to evasion, as one that is expected to be applied immediately. In some legal systems, such as the Italian and Tunisian ones, it has at times been possible to postpone for many years, through appeals, the application of the penalties.[10] The impact of penalties on tax compliance may not always be great under the circumstances described above. For example, using a model of varying attitudes toward risk and applying econometric estimation techniques to Mexican data for 1982–9, Dunn (1992) concludes:

> large changes in the odds of being detected and the penalty for illegal evasion are required to even modestly alter compliance ... a doubling of the fines for tax evasion would increase declared taxable income by about 10 percent. Similarly, a large increase in the number of audits would achieve only a modest rise in compliance. (p. 14)

Of course, in the pre-penalty period, the appeal may be successful or a tax amnesty may come along.[11] Appeals mechanisms and tax amnesties bring a lot of confusion to the theory which assumes that the probability of application of the penalty and the penalty itself are known and are precisely defined. The theory is also affected by the existence of administrative corruption. If the individual who gets caught can bribe some tax officials, and if the bribe is less than the penalty, then the theory becomes ambiguous. Tax amnesties which continue to be used in some countries also have important implications for tax evasion because in many ways they encourage tax evasion at least over the longer run and, by so doing, they have an impact on the equity of the tax system, on tax revenue, on the future of the tax system and on the tax administration. For example, using a game-theoretic approach to an economic analysis of tax amnesties, Stella (1989) concludes:

> while in general it may be correct to impose a reduced penalty on individuals who voluntarily disclose tax evasion, short-lived amnesties of the type most frequently observed in practice are unlikely to generate significant revenue when judged against the potential danger of reducing future tax compliance. (p. i)

Also, analyzing the sustainability of revenue intake from tax amnesty experiences in different countries, including Argentina, Colombia and India, during the 1980s, Uchitelle (1989) concludes: 'most of the programs have not led to a widening of the overall tax base, and many have failed to produce even very large one-time revenue gains' (p. 53).

TAX ADMINISTRATION AND TAX EVASION

The tax administration of a country plays an important role in the extent to which tax evasion prevails in that country. To the best of our knowledge the theory of the firm has not yet been applied to the activities of a tax administration,[12] but a tax administration is not very different from a firm, even though it should be compared to a monopolistic firm. The tax administration has a given budget assigned to it by the state and with this budget it has the task to maximize an output, that is, tax revenue, taking into account certain important constraints. The allocation of resources within the tax administration is obviously very important for determining the output. Under optimal conditions the tax administration would not be able to increase its output by shifting resources within its various activities such as assessment, collection, auditing and so on.[13]

Size and Allocation of Administrative Resources

Some of the constraints on the tax administration are imposed by tax policy, others are objectives that the tax administration needs to take into account (equitable treatment of taxpayers). How much revenue a country should allocate to the administration of taxes remains a subject that has received little attention. There is a remarkable variance among countries in both the share of resources allocated to tax administration in the national income of the country and the share of these resources in the total tax collection by the tax administration.[14] It should not be concluded that a low share of resources going to either of those two denominators is necessarily good. In fact a country that wanted to minimize collection costs would simply collect the taxes which are easiest to collect and collect them from the largest taxpayers. This behavior would condone a lot of tax evasion and would generate tax revenue in a way that would be far from optimal. It would also conflict with other objectives of taxation, such as neutrality and equity.

A tax administration should be careful to minimize not only the explicit costs borne by itself (its collection costs) but also the costs borne by the taxpayers and by the economy. These latter costs do not show up in the balance sheet of the administration and, thus, often tend to be ignored. These are essentially welfare costs, compliance costs and perhaps those that could be called 'good relations' costs.

Welfare and Compliance Costs

The welfare cost per dollar collected can be defined as the excess cost to society of collecting $1 of tax revenue. These are the costs that have attracted the attention of economists. They have been estimated for the United States by various authors, such as Ballard *et al.* (1985a, 1985b) and Hansson (1987). They have shown that the marginal dollar raised by the US tax administration may have cost the country more than $1.50. Usher has discussed the marginal cost of taxation in the presence of tax evasion (see Usher, 1986). Clearly the above estimates indicate that the tax system is far from optimal. These welfare costs are often imposed by the particular tax policy followed by the country. However attempting to make the system optimal may raise other costs, such as administrative and compliance costs, which have not received much attention from economists. There is still no literature that has attempted to deal with the administrative and compliance costs of trying to pursue 'optimal' tax policies (but see Slemrod, 1990). However some recent literature has been trying to assess the implications of tax evasion for optimal taxation (see Cremer and Gahvari, 1993).[15]

The compliance costs are more closely associated with the behavior of the tax administration, and are more likely to be connected with tax evasion. These compliance costs refer to the cost to the taxpayers in terms of lost time, payments to tax accountants and lawyers, trips to the tax office, and so forth, associated with a given tax payment.[16] In some countries, and for some taxes, these compliance costs can be enormous, especially if the taxpayers have to stand in line for hours and sometimes for days, and perhaps several times a year, in order to meet their tax obligations. They are also likely to be extremely high when the tax laws are so complicated that the taxpayer has to rely on experts' advice or, in the case of enterprises, has to hire experts whose only function is to comply with the tax obligations. There have been reports from Latin American countries that even relatively small enterprises sometimes have had to establish sizable tax departments simply to find their way through the jungle of fiscal laws and regulations. When this situation prevails, the tendency to begin to evade taxes is likely to rise. There must be a direct and positive relationship between the size of tax evasion and the cost of compliance. When firms create tax departments to comply with existing tax obligations, those same departments will be used to scrutinize the laws for any possible loopholes or for any ambiguity that might justify tax avoidance.

Public Relations

Let us now turn briefly to what could be called 'good relations' costs. This is essentially the public relations activity of a tax administration. This public relations activity is connected with the way in which tax administrations are organized, with the number of employees and with the use of these employees, with the level of their salaries, the quality of their working conditions and the controls that the tax administration is able to extend over the behavior of the tax inspectors. These controls are necessary to minimize or eliminate the possibility that these inspectors, or other tax administrators, will take advantage of their positions for their own benefit.[17]

A tax administration that wants to improve taxpayer compliance and minimize tax evasion must be available to the taxpayer who needs information, forms, specific instructions and so forth. It must show courtesy toward the taxpayers, since resentment on their part is likely to lead to a lower propensity to pay taxes. It must also show punctuality in sending refunds to those who have overpaid, since a taxpayer who expects to wait for years to get a refund is likely to begin to underpay.

Use of Withholding, Presumptive and Minimum Taxes, and Cross-controls

Collection systems are also important for minimizing tax evasion. There is now overwhelming evidence that evasion is minimized whenever there is withholding at source. In the United States, for example, the difference in tax evasion between independent contractors, for whom there is no withholding at the source, and dependent workers, whose taxes are withheld by enterprises, is enormous. The same evidence is available on taxes on interest incomes and dividends.

Various countries have tried to minimize evasion by resorting to minimum taxes or to presumptive methods of taxation. In these presumptive methods, now in use in a large number of countries, the government tries to assign a particular income to taxpayers on the basis of their standard of living, the value of the houses in which they live, the value of the cars they drive, and so forth.[18] It also tries to estimate, for example, the value added of a company on the basis of sales statistics or other criteria (employees, floor space and so on). The minimum income tax of a company or individual can also be based on their gross assets, a system that has been introduced in Argentina and Mexico, for example.

Tax administrations utilize various instruments of control to limit tax evasion. For example, cross-controls between the information available to the tax administration, to the social security institution and to the customs administration can play a very important role. The assignment of a taxpayer identification number which can be used in this cross-control is extremely important, since it facilitates the use of computers. Instruments of control which also play a role are (a) the government's ability to gain access to the accounts of individuals or companies in the banks, (b) detailed audits of taxpayers, and (c) reporting requirements by employers or by those who make payments.

Social Ethics

Before leaving the section dealing with the role of the tax administration vis-à-vis tax evasion, it may be worthwhile to refer to another relationship, that between society at large and tax evasion. Tax evasion prospers when society condones it. In a society that does not condone tax evasion, this phenomenon will remain isolated and will concern relatively few individuals. When, however, society condones it, the phenomenon becomes much more widespread. Citizens at large should have a responsibility in preventing tax evasion. Since tax evasion is often facilitated by the acquiescence, on the part of some citizens vis-à-vis the tax-evading behavior of other citizens, laws should be passed that penalize not just the tax evaders but also those who collaborate either passively or actively in the tax-evading activities of other individuals. For example, in many countries the tax evasion of professionals, such as doctors or independent contractors, is facilitated by requests to their customers on the part of these individuals that payments should be made in cash or by the acceptance, on the part of those who buy the services, of invoices given by these professionals which underestimate the payment. Also the examples provided by those who govern are very important. When those who govern themselves engage in tax evasion or similar activities, they send an unmistakable signal that non-compliance with the law is acceptable.

Penalties

As can be anticipated from the preceding discussions, the severity of the penalties would have some impact on the extent and spread of tax evasion. Taxes may be paid in arrears without the intention to evade them, especially if the interest charges are low. Usually interest charges and pecuniary penalties are applied to any tax in arrears which do not reflect tax-evading motivation. Tax evasion or fraud, however, are a more serious matter and, at least in the tax laws, carry much heavier sanctions against them.

Interest on and penalties for tax arrears

Usually the amount of interest charged on taxes paid in arrears is calculated in one of two ways: either fixed percentage points above some key central bank rate or above the average of bank rates; or a specified percentage per month of amount due in taxes up to a maximum amount. In some countries additional surcharges are also applied.

Penalties on taxes paid in arrears vary according to whether the cause is late filing of returns, failure to file returns at all or filing incorrect returns. In the case of taxes withheld at source, penalties depend on the type of infraction. For example, penalties differ according to whether the correct amount has been withheld or whether the amount withheld has been surrendered to the tax authorities. In all cases repeated offenses or offenses not corrected or admitted within a specified time period are subject to higher penalties. Sanctions are often in the form of a percentage of the tax due and range between 25 per cent and 100 per cent; several countries also charge penalties fixed in nominal terms.

Sanctions for evasion or fraud

Sanctions for tax evasion and tax fraud are much more severe, with higher penalties (up to 15 times the amount of the defrauded amount), possible closure of establishments for a specified time period, and/or jail sentences ranging from a few months to several years. Giving the tax administration the power to close establishments for a few days without the possibility of appeal has been an effective deterrent to tax evasion in Argentina and in other Latin American countries.

CONCLUDING REMARKS

This chapter has surveyed the factors that give rise to tax evasion as well as its ramifications. Tax evasion varies by sector (agriculture, industry, commerce), organization of production (small trader or business, companies) or type of economic agent (salaried, self-employed, capital owner). It is also affected by social ethics and the standards set by those that govern. Given those standards, it is further affected by the attitude toward risk of a potential taxpayer.

Tax evasion affects the horizontal and vertical equity of a tax system, as well as the efficiency of the free market in general and of its tax system in particular. It certainly affects the revenue productivity of the tax system. Unchecked or deficiently controlled tax evasion builds cynicism about the role of the public sector. It tends to complicate the tax structure as legislators begin to anticipate tax evasion through the tax legislation. The use of effective and quickly applied penalties to counter tax evasion has an impact on its extent and spread. However their application does not necessarily imply even a second-best solution for the correction of inequities or for the efficiency of the competitive mechanism if many tax evaders are not caught and remain unaffected by penalties.[19]

The theoretical foundation for modeling tax evasion remains somewhat wanting. It is really too simple to be of much practical use. The theory relates the taxpayers behavior toward tax compliance to his attitude toward risk, while ignoring other factors that influence tax evasion. The theory assumes that taxpayers know precisely the probability of being caught and the consequences of such an event; however tax administrators often keep this information confidential and the consequences of being caught may not be fully predictable.

Estimates of tax evasion of income and consumption taxes have been selectively reported in the published literature for many countries. More information of a confidential nature exists as a result of exercises carried out by tax authorities or in the context of technical assistance by international organizations. The methodologies utilized leave much to be desired because of lack of data but also, more importantly, because of what the data are able to capture. The data may only partially capture the effects of tax evasion while including the effects of other leakages (for example, legitimately used tax incentives or deductions whose total effect may be difficult to remove). Thus it would not be prudent to base economic policy solely on the results that emerge from these estimations.

Given their limitations, methods of estimation include the matching of information from tax declarations with either national accounts data or survey (or sample) data blown up to population levels. Because of the lack of reliability of surveys (for example, respondents may not reveal the truth regarding tax evasion, even in surveys) and because of their cost, the national accounts approach is more commonly used. If the objective is to estimate evasion of the VAT, however, a national input–output framework has to be utilized because of the VAT's method of collection at different stages of production, some of which may be exempted from the VAT base. An indirect way of estimating tax evasion has been to estimate the extent of the underground economy and, once that has been done, to estimate the taxes that should have been paid. It appears from the published literature that perhaps a third of potential tax revenue may be evaded in selected Latin American and in some Mediterranean countries. Some estimates would indicate even higher percentages. These estimates, however, must be taken with a grain of salt since they would at times imply very high tax burdens in the absence of tax evasion.

If tax evasion is so high, the role of the tax administration becomes doubly important. The size of tax administration resources, the main target groups (large enterprises or all taxpayers), the efficiency with which the resources are utilized (collection costs), the ease with which taxpayers can pay taxes (compliance costs), the relation between the tax administration and the taxpayer (good public relations rather than the spreading of fear) and the methods of tax collection (withholding, presumptive taxes, minimum taxes and cross-controls) all play a role in determining the level and lowering of tax evasion.

Finally one interesting aspect of the evasion phenomenon is that it has a counterpart on the expenditure side of the budget but the counterpart has not as yet received the attention that tax evasion is receiving today.[20] While tax evasion is the non-payment of taxes duly owed to the government, the equivalent phenomenon on the expenditure side is the abusive receipt of government payments. In a way one finds a parallel in a comparison between indirect taxes and consumer subsidies, one being the negative of the other. Activities connected with the illegal receipt of government expenditures may be those associated with corruption: for example, the receipt of a percentage of government contracts; the receipt of pensions not deserved, for example by claiming disability when one is not disabled; the payment of wages to so-called 'ghost workers', a phenomenon common in several developing countries; the taking of leave on the basis of fictitious illnesses; and so forth. This is the other side of the coin of tax evasion: the government loses when taxes are not paid, but it also loses when payments that should not have been made are made. Economic theory and the law should treat the two phenomena in the same way and economists should pay the same attention to both.

NOTES

1. The tax gap is the measure of tax evasion that emerges from comparing taxable income declared to tax authorities with taxable income calculated from other and presumably more accurate sources.
2. Scholars have often made a distinction between tax evasion and tax avoidance. In theory tax evasion implies violation of the law, whereas tax avoidance implies the taking advantage of ambiguities in the law to reduce the tax burden. This distinction, however, is not always easy and in fact in some countries, such as India, the courts have considered tax avoidance with the intention of evading taxation as tax evasion.
3. Several requests by Latin American countries for IMF technical assistance have had the objective of measuring tax evasion.
4. In recent years new developments in industrial organization and in technology have introduced totally new ways of evading taxes, for example through transfer pricing and thin capitalization.
5. During the electoral campaign, President Clinton argued that the reduction of tax evasion by multinationals could generate a lot of revenue. Recent work by the US Internal Revenue Service has given some support to this view (see US Treasury, 1992).
6. There is actually a close relationship between Allingham and Sandmo's theory of tax evasion and Becker's theory of crime (1968).
7. Becker's theory assumes that individuals evaluate the expected benefits and costs of various activities including criminal activities and choose those that provide the highest income.
8. The theory assumes a close relationship between increasing the costs of administration and increasing the probability of catching tax evaders. The importance of this assumption has to be kept in mind.
9. In some cases they may be so delayed in time that they lose their deterrence effect.
10. Sometimes the taxpayers benefit from the delay as a consequence of the low interest rates charged on the taxes that were due. Some countries require an advance payment of the tax assessed after the tax evasion is discovered, even when the taxpayer contests the assessment.
11. However appeals are not costless in terms of time, worries and lawyers' and other fees.
12. But see Goode (1981).
13. For a recent important contribution to the literature on tax administration, see Bird and Casanegra (1992).
14. See Sandford *et al.* (1989).
15. This literature concludes that, in the presence of tax evasion, some of the standard conclusions of optimal taxation do not hold.
16. Thus the compliance cost per dollar paid can be defined as the excess cost to the taxpayer in terms of lost time, payments to lawyers and accountants, and so on of $1 of tax payment.
17. Anecdotal reports have referred to countries where some key posts in the tax administration have been in high demand by those who took civil service exams, or have even been 'sold' to the highest bidders. Obviously these posts provided possibilities of high 'incomes'.
18. Italy has perhaps been the most imaginative in the use of presumptive taxes in recent years.
19. In fact the theoretically advocated and practically followed procedure of selecting

taxpayers through audits to detect tax evaders raises serious questions of equity when many other tax evaders remain undetected and unpunished.
20. For some discussion of this issue, see Smith (1986, ch. 8).

BIBLIOGRAPHY

Allingham, M.G. and A. Sandmo (1972), 'Income Tax Evasion: A Theoretical Analysis', *Journal of Public Economics*, 1(3/4) (November), 323–38.

Ballard, Charles L., John B. Shoven and John Whalley (1985a), 'General Equilibrium Computations of the Marginal Welfare Costs of Taxes in the United States', *American Economic Review*, 75, 128–38.

—— (1985b), 'The Total Welfare Cost of the United States Tax System: A General Equilibrium Approach', *National Tax Journal*, 38, 125–40.

Banerji, Arup (1991), 'Tax Evasion, Enforcement, and Intertemporal Choice', *Proceedings of 1991 National Tax Association Conference*, Williamsburg, Virginia: National Tax Association, 90–100.

Becker, Gary (1968), 'Crime and Punishment: An Economic Approach', *Journal of Political Economy*, 76, 169–217.

Bird, Richard and Milka Casanegra de Jantscher (eds) (1992), *Improving Tax Administration in Developing Countries*, Washington: International Monetary Fund.

Cowell, Frank A. (1990), *Cheating the Government: The Economics of Evasion*, Cambridge: MIT Press.

Cremer, Helmuth and Firouz Gahvari (1993), 'Tax Evasion and Optimal Commodity Taxation', *Journal of Public Economics*, 50, 261–75.

Dunn, D. (1992), 'Tax Compliance with Untaxed Fringe Benefits: Evidence from Mexico', unpublished; Washington: International Monetary Fund.

Goode, Richard (1964), *The Individual Income Tax*, Washington: The Brookings Institution.

—— (1981), 'Some Economic Aspects of Tax Administration', *Staff Papers*, International Monetary Fund, 28, 249–74.

Hansson, Ingemar and Charles Stuart (1987), 'The Welfare Costs of Deficit Finance', *Economic Inquiry*, 25, 479–96.

Musgrave, Richard (1959), *The Theory of Public Finance: A Study in Public Economy*, New York: McGraw-Hill.

Pechman, Joseph A. (1966), *Federal Tax Policy*, Washington: The Brookings Institution.

Richupan, S. (1987), 'Determinants of Income Tax Evasion: Role of Tax Rates, Shape of Tax Schedule, and Other Factors', in Ved P. Gandhi (ed.), *Supply-Side Tax Policy: Its Relevance to Developing Countries*, Washington: International Monetary Fund.

Sandford, Cedric T., M. Godwin and P. Hardwick (1989), *Administrative and Compliance Costs of Taxation*, Bath, England: Fiscal Publishers.

Sisson, C.A. (1981), 'Tax Evasion: A Survey of Major Determinants and Policy Instruments of Control', IMF Departmental Memorandum DM/81/95, Washington: International Monetary Fund.

Slemrod, Joel (1990), 'Optimal Taxation and Optimal Tax Systems', *Journal of Economic Perspectives*, 80, 157–78.

Smith, Stephen (1986), *Britain's Shadow Economy*, Oxford: Clarendon Press.

Stella, Peter (1989), 'An Economic Analysis of Tax Amnesties', IMF Working Paper 89/42, Washington: International Monetary Fund.

Tanzi, Vito (1983), 'The Underground Economy in the United States: Annual Estimates, 1930–80', *Staff Papers*, International Monetary Fund, 30(2) (June), 283–305.

Uchitelle, Elliott (1989), 'The Effectiveness of Tax Amnesty Programs in Selected Countries', *Quarterly Review*, Federal Reserve Bank of New York, 14, 48–53.

Usher, Dan (1986), 'Tax Evasion and the Marginal Cost of Public Funds', *Economic Inquiry*, 24, 563–86.

U.S. Department of the Treasury (1992), Internal Revenue Service, *Report on the Application and Administration of Section 482*, Washington: Internal Revenue Service.

Webley, P. and others (1991), *Tax Evasion: An Experimental Approach*, Cambridge: Cambridge University Press.

11. Money laundering and the international financial system

GLOBALIZATION AND MONEY LAUNDERING

One of the most important economic developments of recent years has been the growing globalization of the world economy and, especially, of the world capital market. The globalization of the economy has led to an expansion of the world trade twice as fast as that of the world economy. Most economies have become much more open that they were in the past. The globalization of the world capital market, which allows individuals and firms to shift money from one country to another with few or no impediments, has made it possible for huge amounts of money to move freely and rapidly across frontiers in search of the most desirable economic habitat and the highest rate of return.

While the potential benefits of greater economic integration and of freedom of capital movements are obvious and significant, there are inevitably some costs. For example, with the freer and larger movement of goods and the increased volume of trade, it has become easier for drug dealers and weapon smugglers to move their wares across countries.[1] As far as the globalization of the capital market is concerned, one such cost is the occasionally large, sudden, capital movements promoted by speculators in search of quick gains, or by legitimate investors who may be influenced by herd instincts to take their money out of the country where they had invested it. The growth of hedge funds and the increasing importance of derivatives may have contributed to these sudden capital movements that may create difficulties for the countries involved.

Another potential cost of globalization is that it allows countries with structural fiscal deficits, that is with deficits not caused by the economic cycle, to postpone making the necessary corrections to their fiscal accounts because of their easier access to foreign borrowing. These countries may thus tend to accumulate more debt than may be wise. Still another cost, and one of particular relevance for this chapter, is the greater facility with which the integration of capital markets has provided criminal elements to launder internationally the money that they acquire from their illegal or criminal activities in particular countries.

The international laundering of money has the potential to impose significant costs on the world economy by (a) harming the effective operation promoting poorer economic policies, especially in some countries; (b) slowly corrupting the financial market and reducing the public's confidence in the international financial system, thus increasing risks and the instability of that system; and (c) as a consequence of (a) and (b), reducing the rate of growth of the world economy.

QUANTITATIVE ASPECTS OF MONEY LAUNDERING

Several studies, including the annual reports of the Financial Action Task Force (FATF), have documented the growing importance of the criminal activities that generate large monetary gains for those who engage in them.[2] These are not the activities of the petty criminals who engage in minor or random crimes. Rather they are the activities of well-organized groups. They include, first of all, the production and distribution of illegal drugs. Over the years this activity has acquired immense international dimensions. It concerns most countries as consumers and few countries as producers and major distributors. The criminal activities extend to the smuggling and the illegal sale of weapons and, in worrisome recent developments, to the smuggling and sale of nuclear material. They also cover usury, fraud, embezzlement, high level corruption,[3] kidnaping, extortion, prostitution, theft of artworks and other valuable assets, and large-scale tax evasion.

Some of these illegal activities attract significant economic resources, such as those that go into the production and the distribution of illicit drugs and, perhaps, weapons. These resources are subtracted from the regular economy, thus reducing its output and its rate of growth. This reduction is an important economic aspect of these criminal activities but it is related more to the criminal activities per se than to the laundering of the proceeds from those activities. These activities at times generate far more 'income' for those who engage in them than these individuals can reasonably or prudently spend in the short run. In order to be enjoyed over a longer time horizon these 'incomes' need to be stored (or invested) in ways that will, to the extent possible, preserve their value and possibly convert them into assets that can later be claimed legitimately or without attracting the attention of the authorities.[4] This, then, is what money laundering attempts to do: to maintain, to the extent possible, the value of the acquired assets and to transform them (that is, to launder them) into more legitimate or more usable assets.[5] This process of storage of value and conversion into more accessible and usable forms may have macroeconomic consequences when it involves, as it often does, large sums.

Because the activities that generate the money to be laundered are illegal activities that, by necessity, must take place far from the eyes of the authorities, it is impossible to measure directly or precisely the size of the net financial gains that they bring to those who engage in them. In some cases, as with narcotics, major costs may have to be met at the stage of production of the raw material (say, coca leaves) and its transformation into a usable product (such as cocaine) or at the stage of distribution of the finished product. These costs sustain the standard of living of the producers or the distributors; thus they do not enter the circuit of money laundering and especially of international money laundering.[6] Those who manage and control the whole process, the 'drug lords', are the ones who end up with the large profits. Anecdotal reports, as well as the guesses or the estimates of well-informed observers, including some of the official agencies with jurisdiction in these areas, such as the US Customs Office, suggest that the total earnings from these activities are likely to be very large.[7]

Some 'guesstimates', and they cannot be more than that, have pointed to total annual gains from these criminal activities that, for the whole world, may reach US\$500 billion.[8] How much of these gains need to be laundered is difficult to say. It is even more difficult to assess the value of the stock of all assets, including cash, acquired with laundered money. This stock would, of course, include this year's as well as past years' laundered money (at its present value) less the money that has been spent. Changes in exchange rates and in the rates of return to the previously 'invested' profits would influence the total present value. The laundering of money is reported to be very expensive. According to some reports, sometimes fees of 30 per cent or even higher of the amount to be laundered have to be paid or loss-making activities have to be bought. With all these qualifications, a reasonable conclusion must still be that the value of the total stock of laundered money must be larger, and perhaps much larger, than the yearly figure.[9] The value of this stock is likely to exceed the gross domestic product of many countries.

The proceeds from criminal and illegal activities to be laundered are not evenly distributed among countries. In some countries the proceeds from crime tend to be small and atomized among many petty criminals who spend them as soon as they receive them. In others, and especially in those engaged in the management of the drug trade, or where crime is organized or corruption is on a large scale, the proceeds from illegal activities tend to be large and to be concentrated into a relatively few hands. In the latter case the money needs to be laundered, especially when it is received in countries other than the ones where the managers of these activities reside. This is the case, for example, when cocaine produced in Colombia is sold in the United States.

Because of the volume of money to be laundered, because of the concentration of this money in a few countries and in relatively few hands, and because the countries' authorities are more likely to uncover or to be interested in the domestic laundering of illegally obtained money, there have been progressively more sophisticated attempts to launder these assets internationally. Recent developments, such as (a) the large-scale privatization of public enterprises in many countries, (b) the growth of stock markets in developing countries, (c) the growing diversification of financial instruments in the international financial market, (d) the growing share of international capital controlled through entities which report tax haven countries as their legal place of residence, (e) the as yet non-stringent regulatory controls in many countries and especially in economies in transition and in several developing countries, and (f) the great need for foreign capital on the part of economies in transition and many developing countries, have created both a strong demand for foreign financial capital and the conditions that facilitate the anonymous investment of this capital.

The globalization of the capital market and its increasing technical sophistication have oiled the process. The much larger volume of legitimate capital moving at any one time in the world and the relatively limited official controls over that movement have made it possible for money of questionable origin to enter this huge money stream without attracting much attention. It is often impossible to distinguish between capital movements encouraged or induced by differences in economic policies and capital movements that reflect attempts at laundering money. Currently available statistics and controls do not allow this distinction to be made.[10] Furthermore the fact that many countries welcome the inflow of foreign capital implies that the authorities of the capital-importing countries are not likely to look too closely at the origin of the incoming capital.[11] Some corruption of the private institutions that manage capital flows (such as the banks and the exchange houses) or of some of the officials who are charged with regulating these flows has also contributed. When the money involved is so large, the power to corrupt is also great.

THE ALLOCATION OF LAUNDERED MONEY

Available information suggests that, while the activities that generate the money to be laundered tend to be country-specific and somewhat fragmented, the laundering of the money tends to be more international. There is thus increasing distance between the places where the criminal activities that have generated the money have taken place and the places where that money is laundered.

The international laundering of money is often not done by the same individuals who engage in the criminal and illegal activities, but by experts who are familiar with the workings of the international capital market and who are thus able to determine risks of detection and to exploit differences in controls and regulations among countries.[12] They can thus channel the funds toward financial instruments and other assets such as real estate and small enterprises and toward countries in which the money can more easily be invested without too many questions asked about its origin. Often the money is first channeled, perhaps in cash, toward offshore countries or centers from which it is subsequently invested in other countries.[13] The economies of the offshore countries are not large enough to be able to absorb domestically the volume of money that searches for places where it can be invested. Therefore these countries are used mainly as conduits for financial or real investments made elsewhere.

There have been reports that some of these highly trained and skilled professionals have carried out, or have commissioned others to carry out, sensitivity analyses on behalf of those who wished to launder money. These analyses attempt to assess the probability that the origin of the laundered money will be uncovered, or they aim at spreading the risk among many investments and/or countries. As long as major differences exist in controls and in regulations among countries, there will be scope for well-informed professional money launderers to exploit them.

There are still enormous differences in controls and regulations among countries with respect to the activities that lend themselves to money laundering. In this area the international playing field remains highly uneven.[14] Some of the tax haven countries and many other capital-starved countries, as well as some economies in transition, have almost no controls. They may welcome any capital inflow, regardless of its origin.[15] Therefore money can be exported to these countries and, if necessary, it can be reinvested in third countries. By the time it is re-exported, the original provenience of the capital invested is no longer an issue.

EFFECTS ON ECONOMIC POLICY

The globalization of the capital market has allowed professional money launderers to exploit differences in controls and regulations far more efficiently and easily than was possible when capital movements were controlled and restricted. In a way the freedom of movement of capital without the necessary steps of leveling controls and regulation, has increased the importance of the differences in controls. Capital movements induced by attempts at laundering money are not promoted by differences in economic fundamentals, such as differences in after-tax rates of return to real investment, or in real interest rates. Rather they are largely induced by differences in controls and regulations which make money laundering a safer activity in some countries than in others.[16]

Those who wish to launder money are generally not looking for the highest rate of return on the money they launder but for the place or the investment that most easily allows the recycling of the criminally or illegally obtained money, even when this requires accepting a lower rate of return. Therefore these movements may well be in directions opposite to those that would be expected on the basis of economic fundamentals. Money may move from countries with good economic policies and higher rates of return to countries with poorer economic policies and lower rates of return, thus seeming to defy the laws of economics. This implies that, because of money laundering, the world capital tends to be invested less optimally than would be the case in the absence of money laundering activities. The world rate of growth is thus reduced not only because of the effects of the criminal activities on the allocation of resources but also because of the allocation of the proceeds from those activities. As a consequence of these counterintuitive capital movements, the policy makers may get confused as to the policies to be pursued. For example, the policy makers of a country that, in the face of high inflation, an overvalued exchange rate and a large fiscal deficit, experienced capital inflow might be less inclined to change their current policies.

If the reported estimates of the proceeds of crime are broadly of the right order of magnitude, the value of all the assets controlled by criminal organizations must be very large. A sizable share of this value may be invested in countries other than the ones in which reside those who own and control these organizations.[17] Some of these assets may be held in the form of deposits in foreign banks and especially in those that respect bank secrecy; some in shares in foreign enterprises;[18] some in real estate; others in public bonds; others still may be held in cash, either domestic or foreign. On the basis of the advice they receive from their financial advisers, those who own and control these assets make the decisions on whether to leave them where they are or to move them to other habitats. These decisions may be influenced more by the attempt to escape controls and to avoid detection than by the search for the highest rate of return. In a way they are still maximizing rates of return adjusted for risk of detection. However this private maximization is not consistent with an optimal allocation of resources. Therefore, as already mentioned, there may be a large misallocation of world resources associated with the allocation of laundered money in different countries.

Apart from the issue of the optimal or at least the efficient allocation of resources, a large stock of laundered capital may bring some inherent instability to the world economy. The total assets controlled by criminal organizations or criminal elements or by their agents may be so large that the transfer of even a small fraction of them from one country to another could have important economic consequences. If the annual total flow of laundered money is in the hundreds of billions of dollars, and if the stock of all laundered money is even larger, it is not too farfetched to imagine that billions of these dollars could be moved around at particular times. These movements could create macroeconomic difficulties for the countries that receive or lose this money and, at least in theory, could have a potentially significant impact on the world economy.

At the national level, large inflows or outflows of capital could significantly influence variables, such as the exchange rates and the interest rates, or even the prices of particular assets toward which the money is invested, such as land and houses. In some countries identified with money laundering activities there have been increases in asset prices (land and houses) that often could not be explained by the changes in the countries' policies.[19] When the exchange rate is free to fluctuate, the inflow of large amounts of laundered money into a country would lead to its appreciation and/or to an expansion of the country's monetary base. The appreciation of the exchange rate would reduce the competitiveness of traditional exports and would encourage more imports. The expansion of the monetary base, in the absence of sterilization, would also put some upward pressure on domestic prices. Faced with this version of the 'Dutch disease', the policy makers of the country would be forced to tighten its fiscal policy in order to try to create a budgetary surplus to use to sterilize the monetary effects of the capital inflows. A country experiencing a capital outflow would have opposite effects.

These capital movements originating from money laundering activities, especially when they are considered to be of a temporary nature, could have internationally destabilizing effects because of the integrated nature of global financial markets. This integration implies that financial difficulties originating in one center can easily spread to other financial centers, thus transforming a national problem into a systemic one. The destabilizing effects could arise because these capital movements would not be seen to reflect differences in economic fundamentals across countries. Thus they send confusing signals to the world economic community. International coordination of economic policy cannot be completely successful without addressing the causes of these perverse capital flows. These causes are, of course, the criminal or illegal activities and, perhaps as importantly for the international policy coordination, the differences in controls and regulations among countries.

An interesting aspect of international money laundering worth mentioning is the role that American dollar bills play in it. Being by far the largest market for narcotics, the United States generates a large share of the 'income' produced by this activity. The sale of illegal drugs alone has been estimated to generate as much as US$100 billion a year in the United States. These drugs are imported from Colombia and some other places. When drugs are sold in the streets of the American cities, they are bought with American currency, that is, with actual dollar bills.[20] These dollars, normally collected in small amounts reflecting the purchases by individual drug users, are used by the local distributors to buy their merchandize from the wholesalers. These in turn use them to pay the distributors who represent the drug lords. These dollar bills are generally smuggled out of the country.[21] As far back as 1984, the US President's Commission on Organized Crime had estimated that US$5 billion a year in the form of currency was being taken out of the United States through the illegal drug trade. Recent estimates indicate much larger amounts.

Other indirect evidence points to a large stock of US dollars held abroad. For example, there is a great disparity between the total amount of dollar bills known to have been issued by the American authorities, and thus known to be in circulation (about US$350 billion), and the amounts reported to be in the hands of Americans by periodic surveys made by the Federal Reserve System. On the basis of the known quantity of dollar bills issued by the American authorities, each American should be carrying about $1500 in cash in his or her pocket. Obviously this is not the case. Richard Porter of the US Federal Reserve System has estimated that the amount held abroad is at least US$200 billion out of a total of about US$350 billion.[22] How much of this has left the United States because of money laundering activities is unknown.

Important macroeconomic implications follow from this. First, the holding of these dollars by foreigners implies that an interest-free loan is given to the US government because no interest is paid by it to those who hold them. Second, by reducing the demand for *domestic* money in the countries where the US dollars are held (that is, through the phenomenon of currency substitution), the holding of dollars abroad raises the rate of inflation in those countries, or at least it reduces the seigniorage that the governments of those countries receive from issuing their own money. Finally, it creates some potential instability for the world financial system because of the possibility that at some point (if, say, the value of the dollar were predicted to fall significantly) these dollars could suddenly be unloaded in exchange for other foreign currencies.

The development of an efficient world capital market requires that those who participate in this market have full confidence in it. If this market came to be significantly contaminated by money controlled by criminal elements, this confidence would inevitably be affected. The trust that normal individuals have in the capital market would be reduced. The market would then react more dramatically to rumors and to false statistics, thus generating more instability.

The transparency and the soundness of financial markets are key elements in the effective functioning of economies, and both may be threatened by money laundering. Criminally obtained money can corrupt some of the officials who make decisions concerning the financial market of countries. If some damage should occur to the financial markets, it could be long lasting because the credibility of markets can be reduced instantaneously but it takes a long time to rebuild.[23] Thus countries that do not make a substantive effort to control money laundering are de facto imposing negative externalities on other countries.

It is not farfetched to imagine that, through the use of proxies, criminal elements could intentionally seek to subvert financial markets by corrupting some of the designers and administrators of the laws governing banking, currency and financial markets in particular countries and the administrators of the financial market. In a worst-case (and admittedly unlikely, but not impossible) scenario, a cartel of criminal organizations, with control over large financial resources, could attempt to destabilize a national economy by intentionally coordinating a transfer of funds (controlled through proxies) out of that economy. They might do this, say, to punish the authorities of that country for becoming extra vigilant or for introducing stricter controls. These shifts could create difficulties for some of the countries involved. Of course these criminal elements may also corrupt the political process of particular countries by financing candidates who may be more likely to let these elements have their way.[24] When the money involved is so large and the pay-off to the criminal elements is so significant, it seems realistic to expect that attempts will be made by criminal elements to install more friendly administrations in some countries.

ON POLICY COORDINATION AND MONEY LAUNDERING[25]

While domestic money laundering can often be fought at the national level, by each country acting with determination and good policies, an effective solution to the *international* money laundering problem can be found only at the international level. The reason is that the scope for international money laundering activity is provided by differences in controls and regulations across countries and jurisdictions. Thus the more effective the controls introduced in some countries, the more attempts will be made to exploit the less stringent environment of other countries. The international coordination of economic policy cannot be fully effective as long as the controls and the regulations imposed by individual countries differ and as long as there is a large pool of unstable money in search of the habitat that is most attractive from a regulatory point of view.

The solution to the international money laundering problem must be sought via international mechanisms: it is an international problem which requires an international solution. International money laundering is based on the exploitation, by sophisticated financial operators, of differences in financial and banking regulations of countries across the globe. Therefore the solution to the problem of eliminating the scope for this form of money laundering must be found in a mechanism that reduces, if not eliminates, these differences among countries.

When they met in Paris in 1989, the representatives of the G-7 established the Financial Action Task Force (FATF), which was mandated to examine measures that could be adopted *by each country* to combat money laundering. In April 1990, FATF issued a well-balanced set of 40 recommendations which it urged its members to implement in order to control money laundering. The FATF comprises 28 jurisdictions and regional organizations: 24 members of the OECD, Hong Kong, Singapore and representatives of the European Commission and the Gulf Cooperation Council.

Many members of the FATF have made significant progress in recent years in implementing the 40 FATF recommendations. The FATF has also monitored developments in money laundering methods and examined refinements to the countermeasures that it suggested in its recommendations. In addition it has pursued external relations activities to promote widespread international action against money laundering. The main focus of the FATF had initially been to counter the laundering of money related to illegal drug activities. More recently it has paid more attention to the laundering of the proceeds of other serious criminal activities or other offenses which also generate large funds. Proceeds from non-drug-related illegal activities are now estimated to be a significant proportion of the total money laundered.

Initiatives have also been undertaken in the United Nations system, particularly in the area of illegal drug trafficking. Most notable is the UN Convention on this matter agreed on in Vienna in 1988. The Council of Europe and the European Communities have issued a number of statements on this question, including recommendations on banking practices. The Basle Statement of Principles in 1988 also recognized that public confidence in the banking system could be undermined through association with criminals and made recommendations intended to reduce this possibility. The Commonwealth has pursued the matter by seeking to facilitate programs of mutual assistance.[26]

Despite the substantial progress achieved by the FATF, and in other international fora, there remain significant drawbacks to the current arrangements. In particular, as long as the membership of the organization is not comprehensive, there will be free-riders who will seek to benefit from the fact that other countries have adopted rules that discourage the inflow of illegal capital. The development of the various offshore tax havens and, more recently, the growth of illegal activities and organized crime in the previously centrally planned economies, together with weak controls on their banking system, suggest that the present measures to counter money laundering need to be strengthened. Moreover the guidelines of the FATF and other groups are in any case only recommendations. The question is whether the framework established by the FATF can be applied internationally. The time may have come to take the next step: to build on the experience of the FATF and on the work already done.

The international financial system is an international public good which can provide its full benefits to the world community *only if all its participants ensure that it remains transparent and credible*: activities by any one participant that seek short-term gains can impose high costs on all.[27] Unfortunately, as recent experiences show, the incentives for some countries or territories to gain economic advantages by attracting, through lax controls and regulations, criminal money are very high. So far there are no mechanisms to penalize them for the costs they impose on others. As long as these possibilities continue to exist, international laundering will remain a problem. It is now easy for criminals to invest their money through convenient conduits provided by offshore countries or by countries with inadequate controls.

The G-7, or possibly a group representing more countries, could, for example, take the initiative by issuing a strong statement that financial practices, by any country, that facilitate international money laundering will no longer be tolerated. This group could announce the intention that it would reflect this view in its countries' dealings with the countries that follow practices that facilitate money laundering. The objective would be to raise the cost to these countries of continuing to follow these practices.

However the international community may need to go beyond that. It could consider the establishment of a set of rules which will form the basis for full participation by any country in the international financial market. This market should become an exclusive club with benefits and obligations for those who wish to belong to it. An international meeting, which *all* countries or economic entities would be invited to attend, should (building on the work of the FATF) establish *minimum* worldwide standards of statistical, banking, prudential and financial rules that would be binding *on all countries*. These rules would eliminate, or at least drastically reduce, the differences in domestic regulations that encourage and to some extent make possible international money laundering. The support of the international organizations should be enlisted to effectively establish these minimum standards and, subsequently, to monitor and enforce these rules.

This leaves unanswered a fundamental question: how can countries be encouraged to participate in the meeting and to enforce the agreed set of minimum standards of financial behavior which would limit the scope of money laundering? All countries can share in the economic gains that flow from the free movement of capital. These gains, however, are not enough if some countries feel that they can gain even more by attracting to them capital of doubtful origin. Therefore some punitive measures must be introduced to induce all countries to play by the same rules.

Consideration could be given to denying international legal recognition for any financial operations transacted and rights acquired within countries that did not agree or did not adhere to the terms of the international agreement. Moreover part of the agreement could involve the imposition of substantial or punitive withholding taxes on capital flows to or from countries not participating in, or not adhering to, the rules of the international agreement. For example, an offshore country that attracted criminal money and served as a conduit to channel it to the main international financial centers would have its capital flows, in and out of the financial centers, taxed at significant punitive rates.[28] This kind of quarantine for those not willing to play by the internationally agreed rules of the game could come into effect after a given period during which the countries would make the required changes. This code of conduct for participation in the international financial system would have the objective of moving the world's allocation of resources closer to an optimum.

The International Monetary Fund (IMF) views international money laundering as an obstacle to its task of maintaining an effectively operating international monetary system. There is some, though small, risk either that international money laundering operations may destabilize the international financial system or that countries, frustrated by the behavior of those countries offering shelter to the proceeds of criminal behavior, may eventually introduce controls on the free flow of capital. Both of these outcomes would impose serious costs on the global economy that should and could be avoided by international agreement. In Article VIII of its Articles of Agreement, the IMF requires that its members furnish information necessary for the discharge of its mandate. If its members requested it, the IMF could, in its surveillance activities, monitor in more detail the rules governing capital flows and the capital operations in the balance of payments to facilitate the monitoring of an internationally agreed upon set of rules for capital transactions. However many offshore centers are not Fund members, so that other channels must be used to control them.

CONCLUDING REMARKS

This chapter has discussed briefly some of the macroeconomic implications of international money laundering activities. It has pointed out that the allocation of world resources is distorted not only when labor and capital are used in criminal activities and in the production of illicit products and services but also when the proceeds of these crimes are invested in ways that are not consistent with economic fundamentals. The chapter has also speculated on other macroeconomic consequences of these activities, showing the potential dangers to individual economies and to the international financial system.

We have suggested a way to reduce international money laundering by imposing a common code of conduct on all countries that are part of the international financial system. However we have not discussed the political, legal, administrative and financial implications of that proposal. It is clear, however, that detailed analyses, reflecting different angles – legal, political, and so on – would need to be made before that proposal was seriously considered. It would be easy to anticipate many objections to it. However we live in a world of second best, so that it would be impossible to find a solution that met all the objections. The alternative of ignoring the problem may become progressively more costly to the international community.

The chapter has relied on published estimates or, better, 'guesstimates' of the size of the money laundering phenomenon. The issues discussed above become more important the larger is the volume of money being laundered internationally each year. It is therefore essential to generate firmer estimates than we have so far. There is no question that the size of this phenomenon is very large but there are still major questions about just how large it is.

It may be worthwhile to add that, if international money laundering became much more difficult because of better controls on it, the incentive to engage in some criminal activities might be reduced because those who engage in them would have to spend (or to launder) their illicit earnings domestically. Thus the benefits to those who engage in these activities would fall while the probability of getting caught would increase. Both changes would tend to make them less attractive to those who engage in them, as the analysis of criminal activity by Gary Becker predicts.[20]

NOTES

1. During the deliberations leading to the North American Free Trade Association (NAFTA) of Canada, Mexico and the United States, some opponents to the agreement called attention to this factor, especially in relation to the drugs trade. Some newspaper articles have attributed to NAFTA the growing importance of Mexico in the drugs trade.
2. The FATF was set up following the 1989 Paris meeting of the G-7. The FATF has developed recommendations related to financial transactions (deposit in cash, banking secrecy, and so on) that member countries are advised to follow.
3. Especially bribes related to large government projects.
4. There is thus a kind of life-cycle character to these 'incomes'. Their earning is more concentrated in time than the consumption based on them.
5. The golden rule of investing, that it is better not to put all of ones eggs into one basket, applies also to money laundering.
6. The peasants who produce the coca leaves used to produce cocaine generally spend the

money they receive. They have no need to launder their earnings. This may apply also to the 'foot soldiers' who distribute the drugs in the streets.

7. As a supporting bit of evidence, on 9 May 1996, an article by Robert Graham in the *Financial Times* (page 3) reported that 'anti-mafia investigators in Sicily ... froze U.S. $640 million of assets in a crackdown on suspected laundered drug money'. Some of the captured shipments to the United States have had street values of hundreds of millions of US dollars.

8. See, for example, William C. Gilmore, *Dirty Money, The Evolution of Money Laundering Counter-Measures* (Strasbourg Council of Europe Press, 1994).

9. The measurement problems extend beyond the lack of statistics. They cover also conceptual questions such as when money that has been laundered in the past stops being considered 'laundered'.

10. See the *Report on the Measurement of International Capital* Flows (Washington, D.C.: IMF, September 1992), pp. 89–95.

11. Recently some small countries have almost advertized their willingness to accept laundered money.

12. International money laundering on a large scale requires a technical preparation and a sophistication that relatively few individuals have.

13. With increasing frequency, cases have been discovered in which employees of legitimate institutions such as banks, foreign exchange offices, investment houses and real estate agents have lent their services to money launderers in exchange for large payments.

14. Most countries are still not members of the Financial Action Task Force. Furthermore not all the countries that are members have equally effective controls. For example, many countries still do not require the reporting of large cash transactions.

15. It has been reported that some banks in these countries are in the hands of criminal groups; thus they facilitate the process of money laundering.

16. The professionals, when engaged in money laundering activities, are likely to be well informed about these controls.

17. For example, a large proportion of the assets controlled by the Colombian drug lords is likely to be invested outside Colombia and a large proportion of the assets controlled by Russian criminal elements is invested outside Russia.

18. Some reports have indicated that the privatization of public enterprises has attracted some of the money to be laundered.

19. The same conclusion has often been reached for some regions, such as Sicily.

20. These transactions are normally conducted with the use of cash. Thus they lead to an increase in the demand for dollar bills.

21. As a report by the United States General Accounting Office has put it: 'Smuggling currency out of the country is relatively easy'. See *Money Laundering, U.S. Efforts to Fight It Are Threatened by Currency Smuggling* (March 1994), p. 3. This report outlines the efforts by the US government to control currency smuggling. However these efforts are unlikely to be very successful. The use of dollar bills in these transactions has led to greater demand for large denomination bills because they are easier to carry.

22. See Richard Porter, 'Foreign Holdings of U.S. Currency', in *International Economic Insights* (November/December 1993). See also Vito Tanzi, 'A Second (and More Skeptical) Look at the Underground Economy in the United States', in Vito Tanzi (ed.), *The Underground Economy in the United States and Abroad* (Lexington, Massachusetts: Lexington Books, 1982), pp. 103–18.

23. The experience with the Bank of Credit and Commerce International (BCCI) raised some questions about the effectiveness of the supervisory role of central banks.

24. This may have already happened in some countries.

25. I owe to Michael Camdessus the basic idea outlined in this section. However some details have been added with which he may not necessarily be in agreement.

26. For details on money laundering countermeasures, see William Gilmore, *Dirty Money.*

27. In a Pigouvian world, this negative externality would justify a punitive tax on the country that generates it.

28.   For similar ideas related to the tax area, see Vito Tanzi, *Taxation in an Integrating World* (Washington, DC: The Brookings Institution, 1995).
29.   See Gary Becker, 'Crime and Punishment: An Economic Approach', *Journal of Political Economy*, 1968, 76(2), 169–217.

12. The underground economy and the unemployment rate

INTRODUCTION

Two decades ago some economic observers realized that not all relevant economic activities are reported to the countries' fiscal or statistical authorities and not all activities are recorded and measured by them. Some activities are intentionally hidden from the official eye. Others are just not reported and may thus be simply missed by the authorities. These activities form part of a phenomenon that has gone under many names, including unobserved, black, hidden, parallel or, more commonly, underground economy.

When discussing the unobserved economy one can focus on the output side of economic activity or on the input side. In other words, one can focus on the value of the output or on the income that unobserved economic activities generate; alternatively one can focus on the resources, such as capital and, especially, labor, that these activities use. Much of the attention over the years, especially in connection with the underground economy, has been directed at the output side and various authors have tried to estimate how many of these unobserved activities are not included in the national accounts statistics. But, obviously, if something is produced and if incomes are generated, regardless of whether the output or income is reported to the authorities, it must have required the work and the effort of some people. Thus a different strand of the literature has focused on unobserved labor.

In this chapter we focus on non-observed labor. In particular we shall discuss the relationship between the underground economy *properly defined* and the official unemployment rate. This is an important relationship because, if the individuals who are reported as unemployed by the official statistics can be assumed to be busy producing a large underground output, the unemployment problem, so common now in many countries and especially in many European countries, and so worrisome to the governments of those countries, would be less of a social problem than it is generally believed.

NON-OBSERVED LABOR: SOME DEFINITIONAL AND INCENTIVE ISSUES

Definitions

The new system of National Accounts (SNA 93) recognizes the existence of *non-observed* or *undeclared work*. This is work that may escape official measurement either because of deliberate actions on the part of the individuals or because of shortcomings on the part of the statistical officers. Individuals may hide their activities because the latter are illegal, because they are not complying with particular regulations, or because they want to avoid paying taxes on the incomes, the sales or the labor input associated with these activities. Alternatively the statistical offices may fail to include in their employment statistics some economically active individuals because their employment surveys or other procedures miss individuals who are economically active but are not working in well established and easily controlled institutions. Furthermore the information obtained from reporting may not have been processed and used. Lack of financial and manpower resources, or low efficiency in the use of those resources by the statistical offices, may contribute to these results.

The new system of National Accounts distinguishes three categories of non-observed labor. The first is *illegal labor*. This is labor employed in activities that are inherently illegal or criminal. Criminal or illegal activities produce an output that, by definition, does not contribute to social welfare and that should therefore not be included in the national accounts. Employment statistics should, consequently, not include the individuals engaged in these activities. Problems may arise when certain activities, for example prostitution, gambling or the production and distribution of certain drugs, are illegal in some countries but legal in others. In this case the comparability of national accounts and of labor statistics across countries can be affected. However in most cases the number of people making a living out of these illegal activities is not likely to be large.

The second category is *informal labor*. The Bureau of Statistics of the International Labor Organization (ILO) has given a precise definition of this informal labor:

> The informal labor may be broadly characterized as consisting of units engaged in the production of goods and services with the primary objective of generating employment and incomes to the persons concerned. These units typically operate at a low level or organization, with little or no division between labor and capital as factors of production and on a small scale. Labor relations – where they exist – are based mostly on casual employment, kinship or personal and social relations rather than contractual arrangements with formal guarantees. (ILO, 1993, pp. 3–4)

The ILO adds:

> Activities performed by production units of the informal sector are not necessarily performed with the deliberate intention of evading the payment of taxes or social security contributions, or infringing labor or other legislations or administrative provisions. *Accordingly, the concept of informal sector activities should be distinguished from the concepts of the hidden or underground economy.* (Ibid., p. 4, emphasis added)

It should be recalled that in many countries incomes below certain levels are exempt from income taxes, sales below a certain threshold are exempt from value added taxes, and casual employment is exempt from social security taxes. Thus much informal labor is likely not to be part of the underground economy as the latter is defined in relation to tax evasion. Informal activities also generally do not have reporting requirements until they achieve certain dimensions. To the extent that the national accounts authorities estimate the output of these informal activities through various indirect means, the output of the informal economy should also not be part of the underground economy as the latter is defined in relation to the measurement of national income. Thus the basic question is how accurately the statistical offices estimate the size of these informal activities.

The informal sector is very important in developing countries. See, inter alia, ILO (1999), Thomas (1992) and Rokotomanana and Rouband (1998). As the latter authors state, 'it is impossible to know whether [the] informal sector is, totally or partially, included in official statistics'. It depends largely on the ability and the resources of the statistical offices. It is easy to guess that often the national accounts suffer from lack of accuracy, but it is less easy to determine the direction of the errors. In some countries the size of the informal sector may well be overestimated, so that the gross national product officially calculated is larger than in reality.

Some activities may start as genuine informal activities but may progressively become underground activities when they acquire a size at which their incomes and sales should be taxable, their use of labor should be subject to social security taxes and reporting requirements should become operational. Thus, to some extent, the informal economy (and informal labor) and the underground economy (and underground labor) become overlapping sets. However statistically it is difficult or impossible to determine how much activity belongs to the truly informal sector and how much to the truly underground economy. The literature on, and the estimations of, the underground economy often mix the two and count within the underground economy activities that more properly belong to the informal economy. This tends to inflate the estimates of the underground economy.

The third category is *underground labor*. This category should include individuals who enter certain activities with the explicit intention of avoiding taxes or some regulations. It also includes activities that may have started as informal but that have achieved a size or a level at which taxes should be paid and regulations should be observed. Those who have operated in a tax-free environment (as informal activities) may not show much enthusiasm toward entering the world of taxation.

Incentives

It is generally assumed that, the higher the tax rates, the greater the use of dependent labor, and the higher the value of the output, the greater will be the incentives for both individuals and enterprise to operate underground. Equally the more restrictive the regulations, especially those related to labor contracts and to freedom of entry to some occupations or activities, the greater will be the incentive to operate underground.

These incentives are sometimes more important for the workers and at other times more important for the employers. High income tax rates on labor income clearly provide a strong incentive for individuals to moonlight or perform services off the books. Those who buy services from the underground economy may also benefit if the saving in taxes on the part of the provider is partly shared with those who use these services through a lower price for the services. In this case the net loser will be the government, which will receive less tax revenue. Statistics from various countries indicate that tax evasion by independent contractors tends to be particularly high (see Mirus and Smith, 1997).

When value added taxes have high rates, a strong incentive is created for employers to hire underground labor and to sell 'in the black'. These enterprises will have two sets of books: one which reflects the reality and one kept for a possible audit by the tax authorities which excludes both the underground output and the underground labor used. If high value added taxes are accompanied by high personal income taxes, the incentives for the employer and for the employee will go in the same direction and both will have an interest in staying underground. The decentralized nature of some productive activities, where part of the production can be done within households, facilitates this process.

For social security taxes the story is a little more complicated, first, because these taxes may be levied either on the employer or on the employee and, second, because the payment of these taxes may be linked to benefits that the worker receives from the government in the form of pensions, health services, and others. To the extent that the social security taxes are mostly levied on the employers and that the benefits from welfare programs that individuals receive are tied to their social security contributions, the incentives for the employees to work underground are much reduced. However, if a large part of the social security taxes are on the employees, if the benefits from welfare programs are general rather than person-specific, if the employees can get access to these benefits through the participation of family members (fathers, husbands and so on) and if jobs in the official economy are scarce, then the pull by the underground economy will be strong. All these conditions seem to have existed in European countries.

All the above considerations affect the two basic decisions that a potential worker must make (see Garonna, 1998).[1] The first is whether to work in the official economy or not. Such a decision is not an academic one for an American worker, because of the availability of jobs in the United States. However it may appear so for workers who live in countries with high unemployment rates and rigid labor markets. These workers, especially if they are looking for jobs with well-defined characteristics, may not have the choice of working in the official economy. Also many potential workers who might like to work in the official economy may find the road to jobs blocked by various personal characteristics such as age, nationality, lack of particular skills or education, and so on. This means that only some workers (those belonging to the official workforce) will have the choice of being *officially* unemployed or of benefiting from unemployment compensation.

The second decision is whether to stay inactive or to become part of the non-observed labor force. Those who are part of the official workforce, often meaning that they have held a job in the official economy in the recent past or that they have been actively looking for a job and reporting regularly to an employment office, may find it worthwhile to draw unemployment compensation, although some of them may become officially unemployed but busy in underground occupations. Those who are not part of the official labor force will have the alternative of remaining unemployed, and without the benefit of unemployment compensation, or of entering the world of the non-observed labor market.

Figure 12.1 provides a schematic view of the three categories of non-observed economy and non-observed labor distinguished by the new system of National Accounts. The illegal economy, or illegal labor, is by definition outside the law and obviously not registered. The informal economy is partly not registered because it is not required to do so, but it may also intentionally underreport parts of its (larger) activities. The underground economy is not registered and/or underreports by intention.

Because individuals and enterprises that operate in the underground economy intentionally underreport or hide their activities, it is obviously much more difficult for the statistical officers to get information on these activities through surveys and other means. It is thus more difficult to estimate the size of the

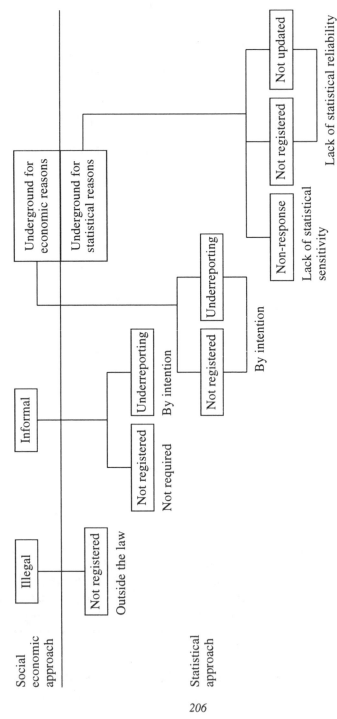

Source: Italian Statistical Office (ISTAT).

Figure 12.1 Non-observed economy

Table 12.1 *Matrix of potential workers and activities*

	Potential Activities				
Potential workers	Official employment	Official unemployment	Illegal economy	Informal economy	Underground economy
1. Officially employed	✓✓				✓✓
2. Officially unemployed		✓✓			✓✓
3. Recent graduates		✓			?
4. Students				✓	
5. Institutional population*					
6. Housewives				✓✓	✓
7. Minors				✓✓	?
8. Pensioners				✓✓	✓✓
9. Non-resident				✓✓	✓

Note: ✓ indicates some relations; ✓✓ indicates a strong relation; ? indicates the possibility of some (but not strong) relation; * indicates individuals in jails, in the military service, in hospitals, in monasteries, etc.

207

underground economy and to make adjustments to the national accounts and the labor statistics. In this case the direction of the error is more predictable.[2] But once again it must not be assumed that the informal economy and the underground economy are the same thing and that they have the same impact on the official statistics.

Table 12.1 attempts a classification of potential workers and potential activities. The potential activities for individuals are those in the official economy (official employment and official unemployment) and those in the non-observed economy (illegal, informal and underground activities). The table shows nine categories of potential workers, including those in the official labor force (both employed and unemployed) and many others who may be mostly outside the official labor force. It would be nice if the proportional participation of potential workers in each of the five potential activities could be determined, but this is not possible because of lack of information. The table marks the most likely activities in which the potential workers are to be found. For example, both the officially employed and the officially unemployed are likely to have some participation in the underground economy, but probably much less or not at all in the informal economy.[3] Housewives, pensioners and non-resident foreigners are likely to be active mostly in the informal economy but also, to a lesser extent, and especially in industrial countries, in the underground economy. Others may be found predominantly in the informal economy. In the table we have ignored participation in the illegal economy.

Table 12.1 points to the difficulty in connecting the unemployment rate with the underground economy. The officially employed – through second jobs and evening and weekend work – and the officially unemployed are often considered to be the major contributors to the underground economy. However housewives, pensioners and non-residents without work permits may also play some role in that economy. The proportions are likely to vary among countries.

SOME STATISTICAL INFORMATION

As already mentioned, it would be useful if one could allocate the activities of each one of the nine categories of potential workers in Table 12.1 to the five potential activities. Unfortunately this is not possible.

There is very little statistical information on the number of people who make a living out of illegal or criminal activities. For most countries the number is probably, and it is hoped, not large unless one considers those engaged in the production of the raw material that goes into the production of narcotics or, for some countries, those who engage in prostitution.[4] In some countries, such as Bolivia, Peru, Jamaica and some countries of South-east Asia, these numbers can be significant because of the large number of peasants engaged in the production of marijuana, coca leaves and poppies, that go into the production of narcotics, and because of significant prostitution.

The informal sector is especially important in developing countries where, according to the 1998–9 *World Employment Report* of the ILO, it accounts for over 60 per cent of total urban employment in Africa and very high proportions in Latin American and Asian countries. (See ILO, 1999, p. 167.) Studies for individual countries confirm these figures. The report attributes these high proportions to the increasingly capital- and skill-intensive character of jobs in the formal sector which excludes large portions of the population. Table 12.2 provides data on the informal labor force for selected developing countries.[5] In these countries employment in the informal sector is likely to be much more important than employment in the underground economy. However informal activities are likely to play a much less important role in industrial countries.

When we come to underground activities and underground employment, it would seem realistic to assume that in relative terms these activities are much more important in developed than in developing countries. One basic reason is that it is easier to be underground in developed than in developing countries. For example, the exemption levels for income taxes and value added taxes, expressed as shares of per capita national income, are much lower in developed countries. The social security taxes are much higher and the restrictions to enter some activities, as well as the reporting requirements, are much more stringent especially in an effective sense.

Table 12.2   Informal labor force in selected developing countries

Country	Year	Percentage of urban employment
Bolivia	1996	57
Colombia	1996	53
Ecuador	1997	40
Indonesia	1995	34
Madagascar	1995	57.5
Peru (Lima)	1996	51
Tanzania	1991	56.1
Thailand	1994	48
Venezuela	1997	46

Source: B. Du Jeu, 'Contribution of Informal Sector to Employment and Value Added in Selected Countries', paper presented to the second meeting of the Expert Group on Informal Sector Statistics, Ankara, 28–30 April 1998 (Geneva: ILO, 1998).

Several studies have provided statistical information for particular countries both on the sectors of the economy that lend themselves to the use of non-observed labor and on the characteristics of the individuals that go into these sectors. We will refer to some of these studies, starting with a few general observations.

The very high unemployment rates that now exist in many European countries do not seem to generate the kind of social tension that one would have expected from these rates. There are at least two possible explanations for this lack of tension. First, as indicated by the prevalent skepticism in some quarters about the official unemployment rates, there is a widespread belief that, at least in some countries, a large proportion of those officially classified as unemployed in fact have some form of employment in the underground economy. Two decades ago De Grazia had already reported: 'With regard to the unemployed, a Spanish government investigation showed that half of those receiving unemployment benefit in the Seville region had jobs.[6] In France the employers' organization in the Bouches-du-Rhône department estimated in 1976 that 80 percent of the unemployed were working clandestinely' (De Grazia, 1982, p. 37).

Faini *et al.* have cited Sylos-Labini, a prominent Italian economist, to the effect that, in general, 'the unemployed is not a person that does not work but, as a rule, one who works in an irregular or occasional way or, even systematically in the so-called underground economy' (Sylos-Labini, 1989, p. viii; my own translation). In Italy there have been frequent newspaper reports that enterprises that had wanted to hire workers in areas with high official unemployment had received remarkably few applications. Obviously the unemployed had other, and perhaps more attractive, alternatives.

Second, at least in some countries, such as Italy, the unemployment rate among heads of households is generally very low while it is very high for other, and especially younger, members of the family. According to Faini *et al.*, only 20 per cent of the unemployed are heads of families, while 63 per cent are either dependent children or other dependants and 17 per cent are spouses. Thus the combination of the possibility of obtaining at least some income from non-observed activities and of benefiting from income transfers within the families reduces the economic burden of being unemployed.

The differences in the ratios of officially employed population and population of working age may also be taken as an indication of non-official employment. The ratios are 51.2 per cent for Italy, 59.0 per cent for France, 62.6 per cent for Germany, 66.5 per cent for the United Kingdom and 73.2 per cent for the United States (see Faini *et al.*, p. 283). However different cultural habits must also play a role.

Which are the sectors that lend themselves to the use of irregular labor? Several studies have attempted to answer this question. The Commission of the

European Community (1998, p. 8) has identified three groups of sectors: (a) 'the traditional sectors such as agriculture, construction, retail trade, catering or domestic services', (b) 'manufacturing and business services where costs are the major factor of competition', and (c) 'modern innovative services (primarily self employed)'. The Italian statistical office has estimated that a large proportion of all the irregular labor in Italy is accounted for by agriculture and by services, although activities in construction also have a large share of irregular labor. In agriculture the share of irregular labor in total is as high as 72.3 per cent. It is 38.5 per cent in construction. In the south of Italy the rate of irregularity in agriculture is 82.1 per cent, in construction it is 63.0 per cent. Meldolesi (1998) has estimated even higher rates for the Mezzogiorno. These irregular activities are probably equally important in other countries.

Who are the participants in the irregular economy? According to the Commission of the European Communities, the main participants are 'second and multiple job holders; the "economically inactive" population; the unemployed; and third country nationals resident in the EU' (Commission, 1998, p. 2). Detailed data on participants are provided, for Spain, by Ahn and De la Rica (1997) and for the South of Italy by Mendolesi (1998). Given the mixture of participants it is difficult to tie the unemployment rate to the estimates of the underground economy.

To translate irregular jobs into national output requires several steps and several assumptions. First, the irregular occasional or part-time occupations must be translated into full-time jobs. Second, the productivity level of the irregular jobs must be estimated or assumed. Third, the total full-time jobs must be multiplied by some average productivity level to determine the presumed output produced by these irregular occupations. Finally, this total must be compared with whatever estimate for the output of the irregular labor is already included in the official national accounts. The difficulties of these steps are obvious.

Let us take the Italian case as an example. For 1995, ISTAT estimated four types of non-regular workers:

Irregular workers	2 473 000
Non-declared workers	442 000
Non-resident	684 000
Workers with a second employment	7 151 000
Total	10 749 000

It estimated that this 10 749 000 corresponded to about five million full-time jobs or about 22.5 per cent of total full-time occupation.

ISTAT estimated the contribution of this five million to total output at about 8 per cent of GDP. There is no question that the average productivity of irregular workers is lower than that of official workers. Many of them work in low-productivity jobs (agriculture, services), many work in lower-productivity areas (Mezzogiorno) and many have lower skills and fewer modern tools.

These estimates have been challenged by economists that have generated estimates of the underground economy that are much higher. However these alternative estimates are often based on rather questionable methods or assumptions; furthermore, often, the range of estimates available for the same country and for the same year is so large as to leave one perplexed about what to conclude (see Tanzi, 1999, for an elaboration of this point).[7]

CONCLUDING REMARKS

The underground economy and the high rates of unemployment are two phenomena that have attracted considerable attention over the past two decades. In the view of several observers the two phenomena are linked, in the sense that a high unemployment rate implies a large underground economy, which in turn may cast doubts on the accuracy of the national accounts data. For example, Schneider and Enste have written that the 'shadow' economy explains the high unemployment rate in Germany. The evidence available does indicate that countries with high unemployment rates also have reportedly high underground economies. However the direction of the causation is not obvious. Is a high unemployment rate a cause of a large underground economy or is it the other way around?

This chapter has not addressed the issue of causation and has not challenged the basic contention that the unemployment rate and the underground economy are somehow linked. However it has tried to show that the concept of the underground economy often used by researchers is somewhat vague. When one uses the more precise concept adopted by the ILO one finds that, depending on the countries, in some the informal economy may be more important than the underground economy. Those who are active in the informal economy often are not part of the official labor force, and statistical offices often attempt to include an estimate of their output in the national incomes. Thus a distinction must be made between the informal economy and the underground economy. Also the productivity of the workers who are active in the underground economy is important in determining the link between the underground economy and the unemployment rate.

In conclusion, it is difficult to translate a measure of the underground economy into full-time occupations. And it is difficult to translate irregular or unreported labor into a measure of the underground economy. Much more work remains to be done out to allow these conversions.

NOTES

1. Garonna's paper was particularly useful in the preparation of this chapter.
2. Statistical offices may attempt to compensate for the error. For example, the Italian Statistical Office adds 8 per cent to the GDP to account for the underground economy.
3. Work in the underground economy may require skills or tools more easily available to those who are part of the official workforce.
4. However a study by Enzo Mingione, in Commission of the European Communities (1990), reports estimates for workers in illegal activities in Italy that amount to almost a million. This seems much too large. (See Enzo Mingione, p. 355.)
5. For additional data see Thomas (1992) Tables 4.1 p. 67, and Table 4.2, p. 68.
6. A major survey in the mid-1980s for the whole country confirmed this conclusion.
7. For an estimation of such a range, see Schneider and Enste. For five industrial countries they show that the mean value of the shadow economy using different methods ranged from 3.1 per cent to 24.4 per cent. See Table 11.

BIBLIOGRAPHY

Ahn, Namkee and Sara De la Rica (1997), 'The Underground Economy in Spain: An Alternative to Unemployment', *Applied Economics*, 29,733–43.

Commission of the European Communities (1990), *Underground Economy and Irregular Forms of Employment*, Brussels and Luxembourg: ECSC–EEC–EAEC.

—— 'On Undeclared Work', Communication from the Commission, Brussels, July 4.

De Grazia, Raffaele (1982), 'Clandestine Employment: A Problem of Our Time', in Vito Tanzi (ed.), *The Underground Economy in the United States and Abroad*, Lexington, Mass.: D.C. Heath.

Faini, Riccardo, Gianpaolo Galli and Fulvio Rossi (1996), 'Mobilitá e Disoccupazione in Italia: Un Analisi dell'offerta di Lavoro' in G. Galli (ed.) *La Mobilita delle Societé Italiana*, Roma: Sipi, 253–296.

Galli, Giampaolo (ed.) (1996), *La Mobilita della Societa Italiana*. Rome: Editore SIPI.

Garonna, Paolo (1998), 'Misure e Teorie del Mercato del Lavoro: il Ruolo della Statistica Ufficiale', *Rivista di Politica Economica*, LXXXVIII (June), 3–46.

Hayes, Keith and Enrique Lozano (1998), 'Validating the Exhaustiveness of the GNP Estimates of the European Union Member States', Proceedings of the Joint IASS/IAOSS Conference, Statistics for Economic and Social Development, Aguas Caliente, Mexico, September.

Hirata, Helena and John Humphrey (1991), 'Workers' Response to Job Loss: Female and Male Industrial Workers in Brazil', *World Development*, 19(6), 671–82.

ILO (1999), *World Employment Report,* 1998–99, Geneva: ILO.

ILO, Bureau of Statistics (1993), 'Fifteenth International Conference of Labor Statistics', Resolution II Concerning Statistics of Employment in the Informal Sector, Geneva, 19–28 January.

Meldolesi L. (1998), 'Rapport Intérimaire: Sintesi delle Conoscenze Sull' Economia Sommersa Nell 'Italia Meridionale', 2 February (mimeo).

Mirus, Rolf and Roger S. Smith (1997), 'Self Employment, Tax Evasion and the Underground Economy: Micro-Based Estimates for Canada', International Tax Program, Harvard Law School, Working Paper 1002, October.

Pozo, Susan (ed.) (1996), *Exploring the Underground Economy*, Michigan: W.E. Upjohn Institute for Employment Research.

Rokotomanana, Faly and François Rouband (1998), 'Statistical Measurement of the Informal Sector in Madagascar: Experience from the 1-2-3 Surveys', Proceedings of the Joint IASS/IAOSS Conference, Statistics for Economic and Social Development, Aguascaliente, Mexico, September.

Schneider, Friedrich and Dominik Enste (1999), 'Increasing Shadow Economies All Over the World – Fiction or Reality? A Survey of the Global Evidence of Their Size and of Their Impact from 1970 to 1995' (mimeo).

Sylos-Labini Paolo (1989), *Nuove Tecnologie e Disoccupazione*, Bari: Laterza.

Tanzi, Vito (1999), 'Uses and Abuses of Estimates of the Underground Economy', in the *Economic Journal*, June.

Thomas, J.J. (1992), *Informal Economic Activity*, Ann Arbor: University of Michigan Press.

Vale Souza, Aldemindo, Leonardo Guimaraes Neto and Tarcisio Patricio de Araujo (1988), 'Employment Implications of Informal Sector Policies, A Case Study of Greater Recife', *International Labor Review*, 127(2).

13. International dimensions of national tax policy

INTRODUCTION

It was not too long ago that tax policy had predominantly a national dimension. Policy makers who considered reforming their tax systems worried about their political ability to do so; about the ability of the tax administration to cope with the changes; about the revenue impact of the changes; about the efficiency aspects; and about the effect on the prices of consumer goods and, perhaps, of assets. They may even have worried about the relationship between the tax system and the growth of the economy. However policy makers did not give much thought to the international dimensions of tax policy, and they did not consider using the tax system to gain competitive advantages vis-à-vis other countries or to influence international capital movements. There were, nonetheless, two aspects of national tax policy that did have international implications, namely foreign trade taxes and tax incentives for foreign direct investment.

Import duties were used, not only to generate revenue, but also to influence the level and the composition of imports (and the domestic allocation of resources) by providing protection for some domestic activities and encouragement for 'infant industries'. Tariffs were also used to discourage 'unnecessary' or 'luxury' imports. When a country was large enough to dominate the production of an internationally traded commodity, so that it could have an impact on world prices, export taxes were occasionally used to influence the world price of the exported commodity.

After World War II, tax incentives became a popular instrument for encouraging foreign direct investment. Especially in the 1950s and 1960s, tax incentives in the form of tax holidays, accelerated depreciations or in some other form, were offered to foreign investors to induce them to invest in the particular country rather than elsewhere. 'Incentive shopping' on the part of foreign investors became common and representatives of foreign companies often visited several countries to negotiate with one of them the most attractive tax incentive package. Under these circumstances, reluctant countries were at times forced to provide generous tax incentives because, without them, they would have no chance of attracting foreign investors. Outside of these two aspects, national tax policies did not have a truly international dimension.

This chapter will describe how the situation has changed in recent decades and how, under current circumstances, the international dimension of tax policy has become important and will continue to become even more important. As a consequence, national policy makers may have experienced a reduction or, in some cases, an increase, in their degrees of freedom in tax policy. The paper will be structured as follows. The next section will describe the relevant economic characteristics of the past period when major elements of modern tax systems were developed, or even came into existence. Those characteristics influenced the tax systems that came into existence. The third section will describe the current situation and elaborate on why the international dimension of tax policy has become important. The fourth section will outline, briefly, some potential tax reforms made necessary by the changed situation. The fifth will discuss the potential use of taxes to deal with the financing of international public goods, while a final section will draw some general conclusions.

THE PAST

Major features of current tax systems, such as personal income taxes, value-added taxes and social security taxes, largely developed, or became important, in the period around World War II or shortly after. In that period, international economic relations were guided or influenced by economic characteristics very different from today's. Let us consider some of these.

Trade Restrictions

The economies of many countries were relatively closed because of high import tariffs or quotas and other quantitative restrictions. Consumer goods especially were subjected to high import duties or were even prohibited, while raw materials and, to a lesser extent, intermediate and capital goods were subject to much lower import duties. Thus a change in the tax rates of other countries did not have much of an impact on the consumption pattern of a given country.

Limited Capital Movements

In many countries domestic currency could not be converted freely into foreign currencies and, in many countries, exporters had an obligation to sell their foreign currency to the central bank, often at rates that contained high implicit taxes. The official capital movements that did take place were largely connected with foreign direct investment, while the capital flight that occurred took place through the manipulation of import–export accounts. Capital flight happened on a large scale in Latin America in the 1980s when tens of billions of dollars left the region to be invested in the United States and in other industrial countries. However the capital flight did not take place because of actions by other countries, but because of what was happening within the Latin American countries.

The role of multinational enterprises was mostly limited to the exploitation of natural resources. Thus questions related to transfer pricing, thin capitalization, valuation of trademarks and so on did not arise or were not important.

Mobility of Individuals

There was little mobility of labor except for the mobility associated with migration which involved a permanent change of residence on the part of those who left their country of birth and moved to their adopted country. Few individuals operated internationally or earned income in more than one country, and the overwhelming majority of individuals received income from one country and often from one income source. Individuals spent most of their income in the country in which they resided even though, of course, their consumption basket might include some imported goods. Cross-country shopping on the part of individuals was very limited, for the simple reason that relatively few individuals could travel for this purpose or could obtain the required foreign exchange. Furthermore the cost of travel (in money and time) was very high. The limitation on the mobility of individuals implied that countries were free to set income tax and sales tax rates. It also made the task of collecting taxes easier.

Portfolio Investment

Short-term capital movements were limited. In the 1970s, because of the great supply of petrodollars associated with large balance of payments surpluses on the part of oil-exporting countries, which resulted in a great deal of liquidity for banks in major financial centers, lending by banks to public sector institutions in foreign countries became common. The large fiscal deficits experienced by many developing countries created a ready demand for these funds. This lending led to an accumulation of foreign debt and, eventually, to the debt crisis of the 1980s. It was for the most part fixed-term lending for specific periods of time. At that time, institutions such as *hedge funds*, capable of shifting large amounts of money across frontiers, within short periods of time, were still non-existent. Neither the existing countries' policies nor the existing technology would have allowed these activities, at least not on a large scale. *Tax havens*, though already in existence, were not playing a significant role for most taxpayers. They mainly assisted individuals in evading taxes and in laundering money obtained from illegal activities.

The modern tax systems came into existence in this environment. It should be recalled that the value-added tax, which is now a major source of revenue for many countries, was not introduced, in France, until the late 1950s, and it did not cross the French border until the 1960s. Its popularity came even later. At that time the countries that introduced it were relatively free to set any rate that they wished. The modern version of the personal income tax, that is the progressive, global income tax, did not become a major source of revenue in many countries until well after World War II and did not achieve its popularity until the 1950s and 1960s, when it became the major generator of tax revenue in most industrial countries and came to be seen as the fairest of all taxes. At that time it was applied with marginal tax rates that for high incomes (normally incomes from capital sources) could reach 90 per cent. In developing countries this tax never contributed much to total tax revenue. Because of the embryonic state of pension systems, and because of fiscally friendly demographic developments, social security taxes did not become important until recent decades. In earlier years they were applied with low rates to limited groups of workers. In industrial countries the growth of revenue associated with these three taxes made possible the achievement of high tax burdens and the development of the modern welfare state.

In the environment described above, tax competition between countries was almost non-existent, except for the two areas mentioned above, namely the provision of tax incentives for foreign direct investment and foreign trade taxes. Tax policies did not have an international dimension and, as already stated, policy makers were free to choose their tax systems and the rates at which they levied their taxes without fear of repercussions. As we shall see in the next section, the changes that started taking place in that period, and that accelerated in the 1980s and the 1990s, would force countries to begin to worry systematically about the international implications of their tax policies.

THE PRESENT

Especially since the mid 1980s, economies have become much more open. Nominal tariffs that had often reached three-digit levels in earlier years have fallen sharply and, in several countries, have practically disappeared. At the same time quotas and other quantitative restrictions on trade have become much less common and are now confined to particular sectors.[1] The result of trade liberalization has been a large expansion in world trade, an expansion that for many years proceeded at a rate twice as fast as the rate of growth of the world economy. This year (1998) and perhaps next year, may see a change in this trend because world trade is growing at a much slower pace owing to the financial difficulties faced by several countries. It is hoped that this will be a transitory development and the previous trend will reassert itself. The liberalization of trade which has led to a significant integration of the world's economies has generated large efficiency gains for many countries, because of the reduction of major distortions that had been associated with high tariffs and other constraints on trade, and a better allocation of world resources. The reduction or the elimination of import duties may have reduced tax revenue from this source, thus requiring countries to make up from other sources the lost revenue.

A second trend has been the growing importance and role of multinational corporations, a role extensively analyzed by the United Nations over the years, which has become overwhelming in world trade. A large proportion of total trade among countries is now trade among different parts (branches or subsidiaries) of the same multinational companies. This aspect has major implications for the taxation of the profits of multinationals.

Until the early 1980s a lot of criticism was directed at the multinationals; they were accused of exploiting the countries in which they operated and of making the modernization and the growth of these countries more difficult. In more recent years the criticism has been much muted and many countries have come to welcome the impact that multinational corporations have on employment, exports and productivity in the countries in which they operate. The growing awareness that these corporations often bring new technology and new management skills with positive spillovers onto domestic enterprises has made these multinationals more welcome. The new theories of growth have emphasized these effects.

The multinationals have also expanded their activities into manufacturing and, thus, away from the traditional exploitation of natural resources which in the past tended to make them enclaves without major links to the domestic economies in which they operated. Countries have continued to provide tax incentives for foreign direct investment, although the competition that existed in the 1960s in providing these incentives may have been reduced, in part because of the worldwide fall in the rates of the corporate income taxes. Some of these companies have become so international in their activities that their links to the countries in which they originated have become much attenuated. In many cases the domestic content of products produced in a country by 'foreign' multinational corporations has become higher than the domestic value added of similar products produced by 'national' companies.

A third major development has been the growth of short-term capital movements. In the 1970s most of the capital movement not associated with foreign direct investments was in the form of fixed-term loans by major foreign banks to the public institutions of debtor countries. The 1982 Latin American debt crisis was the direct result of the large loans made to public sector institutions during the late 1970s and early 1980s and the subsequent inability of the governments to meet their obligations vis-à-vis foreign banks. Many of these loans had financed largely unproductive public spending and had made it possible for countries to have large and growing fiscal deficits.

In the 1980s, and especially in the 1990s, this picture started changing fast and dramatically. Capital movements were no longer limited to the two categories mentioned above – direct investment and bank loans to governments – but, to an increasing degree, reflected short-term loans to the private sector, including domestic private banks. This type of capital movement reflected changes in national policies, which were allowing capital movements that had previously been prohibited, and changes in technology, which made possible the transfer of information and of large sums of money across countries within very short periods of time. Electronic money came to play an increasingly important role and made it possible to transfer huge sums of money across countries in seconds. See Group of Ten (1997). This kind of capital movement was not monopolized by large banks and the money was not going to government borrowers or to activities associated with foreign direct investment as it had been in earlier years. Rather the new money was going directly into stock markets, domestic securities and domestic banks; indirectly, it was going into real assets, including real estate and other investments. In South-east Asia many luxury buildings, shopping centers and other domestic investments were directly or indirectly financed by these short-term capital movements.

In this connection the role of investment funds and hedge funds deserves special mention. The growing role of these institutions is a relatively recent development with implications which are still difficult to grasp. They have acquired enormous importance in recent years. Their activities, strategies and investments are kept secret, even when the capital that they control or influence through their actions can be incredibly large. The recent difficulties of the Long-Term Capital Management hedge fund has been a spectacular illustration of the huge amount of resources that some of these institutions come to control or manipulate.[2] With these lenders it is difficult to determine when income occurs, where it occurs and who benefits from it. Often these hedge funds are able to convert incomes into capital gains. Thus it is very difficult for *national* authorities to tax the earnings of these funds. This is especially the case when these institutions operate, as they often do, from offshore and from tax havens.

The combination of the large amounts of money invested (or, at times, even laundered) and the existence of many tax havens happy to provide shelters for these activities has created situations very different from those which existed in the past. The complexity of the international financial market in which 'rocket scientists' have been developing progressively harder-to-understand market and investment strategies, and the lack of a clear national identity for the money invested or even for the institutions that make the investment, render the regulation of these activities very difficult, or impossible. In fact there is practically no regulation for hedge funds operating from tax havens and little for those registered in countries which are not tax havens. According to a reliable but non-official estimate, offshore deposit holdings now total somewhere around $7–8 trillion, or close to the GDP of the United States.

A fourth major development, closely linked to the three previously mentioned, is the growing ability of individuals to travel abroad and to work, spend and invest in more than one country. When 60 million tourists visit France in one year, about 10 per cent of the population of Japan goes abroad and a large number of individuals work abroad without permanently changing residence, it is clear that, economically speaking, national borders have become much less constraining than they used to be. This has made the task of tax administrators much more difficult as it is far harder to tax activities that take place abroad than to tax those that take place domestically. With the use of the Internet and a credit card one can now shop in many countries without even leaving one's house. A recent television program reported that even prescription drugs can now be obtained abroad in this way.

The trends described above could not fail to have major consequences for the national tax systems. First, inevitably, cross-border tax spillovers have become common. A spillover occurs when the tax policy of one country has a significant impact on other countries. Second, international tax competition is also growing in the sense that countries are becoming increasingly aware of the possibility that through well-aimed changes in their tax system, they may acquire a competitive advantage vis-à-vis other countries. For example, they may be able to export part of their tax burden by inducing foreign shoppers to shop in their countries (see OECD, 1998a). Closely associated with tax competition is what in Europe is often referred to as 'tax degradation'. The meaning of this term is a bit vague, but it broadly refers to the fact that globalization and tax competition may bring about changes in the tax system that make it less desirable either technically or politically. Countries are forced to make unwanted changes in their tax systems because of the action of other countries. For example, many Latin American countries feel that they cannot tax interest income because individuals have the option of investing their capital in countries that allow the tax-free investment of these funds for foreigners. Likewise some countries have been forced to lower their taxes on cigarettes because their neighbors did not raise them, thus providing the citizens of the former country with the opportunity to avoid the higher taxes.

Globalization, in all its aspects, and tax competition are likely to affect tax revenue by forcing many countries to cut marginal tax rates. A continuation of current developments is likely to lower the politically or technically sustainable tax burden for many countries, thus reducing the governments' ability to maintain their level of spending without widening fiscal deficits. This potential problem may be especially serious for the welfare states which have the highest tax levels. Economists who believe that governments tend to spend too much and spend inefficiently welcome this trend because it will force governments to cut spending and to reduce tax rates. Some tax theorists may also welcome tax competition because it forces a lowering of taxes on capital, thus reducing welfare costs. However policy makers who are faced with what they consider inflexible spending obligations are concerned about the likely reduction in the level of taxation.

The developments described above are also likely to increase tax evasion or tax avoidance and, because of this, to reduce even more the level of taxation. Tax evasion and tax avoidance may be associated with many actions on the part of the taxpayers. For example, multinational corporations may use transfer prices, thin capitalization, strategic allocation of fixed costs among the parts of the whole enterprise or the arbitrary valuation of trademarks or other inputs for shifting profits from parts of the corporation operating in countries where tax rates are high to parts operating in countries where tax rates are low. This strategic use of transfer prices and other maneuvers is giving lots of headaches to tax administrations and is generating very high incomes for tax experts assisting the corporations.

Tax evasion may be associated with the activities of individuals who earn their income in different countries and who do not report the income earned abroad in the tax declaration they present to their national authorities. Foreign earned income often becomes unreported income because many taxpayers are not likely to report them and because of the difficulty that national tax administrations have in ascertaining these incomes. These foreign incomes are growing at a much faster pace than the domestic incomes. Tax evasion or avoidance also results from activities operating from tax havens. It is unlikely that much of the income earned by the $7–8 trillion estimated to be held in accounts in tax haven countries is reported to the national authorities by the owners of these accounts. Also banking secrecy in several countries facilitates the non-reporting of income.

There is now a growing literature that argues that exchange of information among the tax administrations would eliminate or sharply reduce tax evasion originating from foreign incomes. However, under present circumstances, the scope and usefulness of exchanges of information are limited by political, legal, technical or administrative obstacles. (See Tanzi, 1995.) It is unlikely that, under current arrangements, the exchange of information will improve enough over the foreseeable future to make a big difference.

In conclusion, we see a growing gap between the tax systems that were largely created at a time when economies were closed, capital did not move and individuals did not travel much, and the tax systems that would fare well in the current environment. It seems likely that changes will need to be made in the international architecture that characterizes the existing systems.

POSSIBLE SOLUTIONS

In the previous pages we have tried to convey, in a concise manner, reasons why, in recent years, national tax policy has acquired an international dimension. We have also referred to some of the possible implications of this development and to the potential fragility of existing tax systems. This section will sketch some of the steps that might be taken to prevent current developments from seriously damaging the tax systems and from reducing excessively the policy makers' discretion about the tax systems that they can have in their countries. We shall start from major steps and move to actions specifically aimed at particular taxes. In most cases, we will only mention the options without subjecting them to any rigorous analysis. We take for granted that letting the market forces, through tax competition, determine the final shape of the tax systems and the level of tax revenue may not be a desirable alternative. Some may strongly disagree with this position, but systems that ignore the market forces might face a very stormy future.

In different writings since 1988 I have argued that the time may have come when some sort of world organization responsible for dealing with tax issues will become necessary. One could think of a world organization with the power to impose and collect taxes. Although only time will tell whether such an organization will ever see the light of day, at this time, this does not appear to be a realistic idea. The obstacles are great and are as much political as technical. Many powerful governments would simply not allow this development to take place, because such an organization would sharply reduce the role of nation states and of national policy makers in a highly sensitive area.

Ten years ago, before these issues became popular, I wrote:

The 'information-revolution', now well under way, and the large amounts of information on individuals that it has caused to be stored away in computers, may give governments tax handles, if they succeed in getting access to it. The governments of various countries will increasingly need to share some of this information. *It is conceivable that the day may come when the countries create an 'International Revenue Service' to collect taxes that could not be collected by separate*

> *governments and to allocate them either to the provision for international public goods or back to the countries.* Such an international institution might also collect information on taxpayers for the benefit of the member tax administrations. (Tanzi, 1988, p. 277; emphasis added).

A less ambitious proposal is the one made in *Taxation in an Integrating World* (1995) and developed more fully in a later paper (Tanzi, 1996). In this less ambitious and more realistic proposal, it was suggested that the time may have come to create a World Tax Organization that would (a) exercise a kind of surveillance function over tax developments in the whole world; (b) provide a world forum for discussing international dimensions of tax policy; (c) suggest solutions to arguments about tax competition; (d) subject countries that try to earn free rides at others' expenses – by introducing tax changes that are damaging to other countries – to some sort of moral pressure from other countries; (e) gather tax statistics; (f) inform countries about best practices; (g) develop a code of conduct for good behavior in tax legislation and in tax administration; and so on.

Such an institution would *not* collect taxes and would *not* have the power to legislate tax changes. Its role would be that of monitoring developments and advising countries, perhaps with some power of moral suasion. Its main objective would be that of trying *to make tax systems consistent with the public interest of the whole world rather than with the public interest of specific countries.* Because of the limited role of such an organization, the countries' opposition to its creation might be less strong than it would be to an International Revenue Service. However, depending on the allocation of power in the decision-making activities of such an organization, strong objections on the part of powerful countries might still be anticipated.[3]

If such an organization came into existence, it could promote a policy of tax coordination among the countries of the world. By tax coordination, it is not meant that all countries of the world would have the same tax system or the same tax rates, but simply that particular elements of tax systems that lend themselves to tax competition could be discussed among countries. It should be clear that many elements of tax systems do not require such coordination. Without a tax organization on a worldwide scale, international agreements aimed at reducing potential tax competition would be more difficult to achieve.

Let us discuss briefly taxes on consumption, on the income of enterprises and on the income of individuals. These are the areas where tax competition or tax avoidance which takes advantage of the international dimension of taxation are most likely to be found. Possible solutions will only be mentioned without any detailed discussion.

For taxes on consumption, the general sales taxes and the excise taxes should be considered separately. The general sales taxes (normally value-added taxes) do not need to be applied with identical or even similar rates because they are for the most part levied on products that are bulky, perishable or of low value. It is unlikely that, in shopping for their daily needs, individuals would go abroad to make their purchases, because of lower tax rates in other countries. The international evidence, and the evidence from the United States where different states have different sales tax rates and from the countries of the European Union where differences of ten percentage points prevail, indicate that significant rate differences may continue to prevail without major impact on the pattern of spending. See Tanzi and Zee (1998a). But, of course, the higher the difference in the rates and the closer the available alternatives, the greater the distortions that may arise.

Excise taxes imposed with high rates on products that are not perishable, are not bulky and are valuable (such as cameras and other electronic gadgets, jewelry, and so on) can generate changes in the location where individuals do their shopping because individuals will shop around during their foreign travels or by mail, using information that is becoming more and more available on the Internet. For these taxes international competition may force a progressive leveling off of the tax rates, thus reducing the rate differences among countries as well as the average rate. In some ways this has already happened. It is unlikely that international agreements would be able to determine a tax rate acceptable to all countries. Different cultural backgrounds would make some countries consider some products more necessary than would other countries. Thus tax competition will eventually determine the rates at which excise taxes on highly valuable and easily transportable products are imposed. These rates are likely to be lower than the ones that have prevailed in past years.

Consider the taxes on corporations. The nominal rates applied to corporate incomes by different countries have fallen significantly during the 1980s and 1990s, and they are now much closer to one another than they used to be. Tax competition as well as efficiency considerations have generated major changes in these taxes. However there are still substantial differences in the tax rates and, especially, in the rules applied to the determination of taxable income. In the current environment in which multinationals operate in several countries, these differences allow these corporations to exploit them to their advantage. This is an area in which reforms will be essential and these reforms must involve the international community rather than being left to individual countries acting on their own. This latter option may in fact lead to progressively lower effective tax rates on corporate incomes.

A first and important step would be to encourage countries to adopt the same concept of taxable income. The definition of taxable income should be a purely technical matter, rather than a political one, as is the tax rate. Tax experts should be able to establish a concept of taxable income acceptable to most of them. Such a concept would determine the best measure of the usable life of assets – in order to establish depreciation rules – the best treatment of inputs (LIFO (Last In First Out), FIFO (First In First Out) and so on), the treatment of interest payments, and so on. Once a broadly acceptable definition of a tax base had been determined, countries would be urged to adjust their own tax base progressively to conform with the agreed definition. This would reduce or eliminate the common form of competition or tax degradation pursued through the granting of tax incentives that erode the tax base and make it difficult to evaluate the effective tax rates applied by different countries. The determination of an internationally agreed tax base would be an activity in which a World Tax Organization could play a significant role.

A contentious issue in the taxation of companies with activities in different countries is the determination of the value of inputs purchased from abroad. If the inputs are bought in the open market from unrelated suppliers, no major issue of valuation should arise because the value of the inputs is determined by the prevailing 'arm's-length' market price. However, if the supplier is a foreign branch or subsidiary of the same multinational company, as is the case with increasing frequency, and especially if the input is so specialized that it does not have a ready, observable market value, then the problem of transfer prices arises. In this case the companies can arbitrarily set the costs of the inputs in order to report higher profits in countries with lower corporate tax rates.

Transfer prices have become a big headache for governments, which have often suspected that the companies manipulate these costs to reduce their global taxes. Suggestions have been made by some experts to change the current method of allocating profits by relying on 'formula allocation' of profits. These formulas, used within federated states such as the United States, Canada and Switzerland, would allocate total worldwide company profits among the various parts of the company on the basis of the value of assets, sales and employment in each of the countries in which a company operates. (See Mintz, 1998.) An alternative would be to stop taxing corporations on the basis of their profits and to start taxing them on the basis of the value of their gross assets. (See Sadka and Tanzi, 1992.) A World Tax Organization could play an important role in advocating these changes by doing the basic work necessary to make them feasible and by promoting the changes among its members.

Personal incomes are assumed to be taxed on the basis of the residence principle, whereby the country where the income is generated (the source country) does not tax it, on the assumption that the income will be taxed in the country of residence of the taxpayer (the host country). In practice this principle is not fully followed because most countries impose some low taxes on the incomes paid out of them. For example, it is not followed in the taxation of corporate incomes where the source principle prevails and it is only partially followed in the taxation of portfolio incomes. Tax treaties often negotiate these arrangements.

In a world of complete honesty or complete and efficient exchange of information the internationalization of economic activities would not create any difficulties and the residence principle should be the guiding one. However, in the real world, neither are individuals completely honest nor is the exchange of information complete and efficient. See Tanzi (1995) and Tanzi and Zee (1999). The result is that, with increasing frequency, foreign incomes evade tax payments and, as already mentioned, foreign incomes are growing at a much faster rate than domestic incomes. This provides an incentive for capital income to move out of the countries where marginal tax rates on it are high and into countries with low or even zero marginal tax rates, such as tax havens.[4]

There is no good solution to this problem. It is unlikely that an efficient and complete system of exchange of information can be developed. This leaves the alternative of using withholding taxes applied at the source as final taxes. This was a recommendation made by the Ruding Commission to the European Community. A recent paper that has analyzed the issue has concluded that, 'on balance ... raising withholding taxes should be seriously considered in a multilateral framework to combat tax evasion' (Zee, 1998). In May 1998 the European Commission proposed that the European Union give its countries the alternative of either imposing a 20 per cent final withholding tax on incomes paid to foreigners or requesting that the taxpayers provide full information for the tax authorities in their countries of residence.

THE FINANCING OF INTERNATIONAL PUBLIC GOODS

In recent years there has been an increasing awareness that public goods or public 'bads' are not confined exclusively within national boundaries but that, at times, they extend internationally and, in particular cases, they may be of relevance to the whole world. This raises the question of how to deal with them.

Traditionally the process of dealing, or not dealing, with international public goods has been the following. For quite some time, there was a tendency to simply ignore them, perhaps under the assumption that they were not important or not important enough to merit attention. When public goods, or more often public 'bads', affected only two or a few countries, as in the case of, say, acid rain or river pollution, the assumption was that the countries would themselves deal with the problem by, for example, the polluter subsidizing the polluted or the (richer) polluted country paying for changes in the (poorer) polluting country that would eliminate the problem.

In cases where the public goods or the public bads are truly international, in the sense that many countries are affected, directly or indirectly, the common solution has been to deal with the problem through internationally agreed regulations. This has been the case for dealing with chemicals that destroy the ozone layer or dealing with the testing of atomic devices. These agreements have been difficult to reach, and in other particular cases they may not be reached, especially when doubts could be introduced about the efficacy of the suggested solution, or when the burden sharing among the countries was not seen by some groups or by some countries as being fair. This may be the case when dealing with global warming.

In some cases, dealing with public goods or bads may require not just regulations but financial resources. Alternatively taxation may be a more efficient solution than regulation. Dealing with a chaos or post-chaos situation (a civil war or a complete breakdown of economy and society) may be an example in which (under the assumption that the solution to these situations is an international public good) money is needed. Dealing with large and destabilizing movements of short-term capital being driven by herd instinct might be a situation in which taxation might be preferable to direct controls over those movements.

There is no doubt that, as the world becomes more and more integrated, as many public goods (peace, environment and so on) acquire an international character, and as the solution to some of them requires financial resources, it would be useful to have revenue sources that do not depend on the willingness of specific countries to contribute to a world fund. One can think of various tax bases that might lend themselves to the possibility of providing these resources. For example, taxes on globally polluting fuels and chemicals might be one possibility. However the administrative, technical and political problems raised by these taxes would be formidable. It is unlikely that these developments might occur without some form of world organization dealing with taxation. Proposals such as taxing airline tickets are not likely to go very far because of the very tenuous connection between the value of these tickets and the pollution associated with them. To have justification, these taxes must bear a direct relation to the environmental effect of the activity.

The possibility of using Tobin-type taxes to provide resources to finance international public goods is worth exploring. An argument for such taxes would depend on their ability to tax short-term and presumably speculative capital movements more than long-term capital movements, thus discouraging large short-term in-and-out capital movement in particular countries. Under the assumption that the international or financial system is a public good worth preserving, these taxes would perform a useful function.

Tax economists, unfortunately, have not shown much enthusiasm for these taxes. For example, two experts who have analyzed them have concluded that 'these taxes would be unlikely to produce the desired effects, would be difficult to design and implement, and would be politically contentious. ... In addition, from an administrative perspective, without a broad international consensus and application, these taxes are likely to be easily avoided' (Shome and Stotsky, 1995, p. 55). Once again, if these taxes have merit, their implementation would be more likely in the presence of a world organization responsible for tax surveillance.

CONCLUDING REMARKS

This short chapter has sketched some of the issues that arise out of the consideration that tax policy that used to be prominently national has been acquiring, in recent years, a progressively more international dimension. This development has many implications that deserve to be studied and analyzed in much greater depth than has been done here. The chapter is largely a listing of issues and a road map for the areas that need close analysis.

The chapter has also introduced the issue of the growing importance of international public goods and the fact that there is no obvious mechanism today that ensures that these goods will receive the attention that they deserve. For sure, when dealing with them requires money, the current arrangements almost guarantee that problems would develop. The time may have come for a serious rethinking of these issues. The purely national approach to these issues is not likely to remain the best alternative.

NOTES

1. On the other hand, impediments based on environmental, health or social considerations may have become more common.
2. According to published reports, this hedge fund had acquired a total gross market exposure of around $1.3 trillion or, say, an amount equal to the combined GDP of Brazil and Korea. Its net exposure was somewhat lower, but still huge.
3. Whether the voting power is weighted by the economic size of countries (as at the IMF) or whether each country gets one vote (as at the UN) would make a big difference.
4. As a consequence the marginal tax rates on the income of individuals have been falling, the global income tax is under attack and dual income tax systems have been introduced in some countries. (See Sorensen, 1998.)

BIBLIOGRAPHY

Eichengreen, Barry (1996), 'The Tobin Tax: What Have We Learned?' in Mahbub ul Haq, Inge Kaul and Isabelle Grunberg (eds), *The Tobin Tax: Coping with Financial Volatility*, New York: Oxford University Press.

Eichengreen, Barry, James Tobin and Charles Wyplosz (1995), 'Two Cases for Sand in the Wheels of Finances', *The Economic Journal*, 105, 162–72.

Group of Ten (1997), *Electronic Money* (April).

Mintz, Jack (1998), 'The Role of Allocation in a Globalized Corporate Income Tax', IMF Working Paper, WP/98/134 (September).

OECD (1998a), *Harmful Tax Competition: An Emerging Global Issue*, Paris: OECD.

—— (1998b), *The Taxation of Global Trading of Financial Instruments*, Paris: OECD.

Raffer, Kunibert (1998), 'The Tobin Tax: Reviving a Discussion', *World Development*, 26(3), 529–38.

Sadka, Efraim and Vito Tanzi (1992), 'A Tax on Gross Assets of Enterprises as a Form of Presumptive Taxation', IMF Working Paper, WP/92/16 (February); reprinted in *Bulletin for International Fiscal Documentation*, 47(2) (February), 1993.

Shome, Partho and Janet Stotsky (1995), 'Financial Transactions Taxes', IMF Working Paper, WP/95/77 (August).

Sorensen, Peter Birch (ed.) (1998), *Tax Policy in the Nordic Countries*, London: Macmillan.

Tanzi, Vito (1988), 'Forces that Shape Tax Policy', in Herbert Stein (ed.), *Tax Policy in the Twenty First Century*, New York: John Wiley.

—— (1995), *Taxation in an Integrating World*, Washington, DC: The Brookings Institution.

—— (1996), 'Is There a Need for a World Tax Organization?', paper presented at the 52nd Congress of the International Institute for Public Finance, Tel-Aviv, Israel 26–9 August.

—— (1998), 'Globalization, Tax Competition and the Future of Tax Systems', in Gerold Krause-Junk (ed.), *Steuersysteme der Zukunft*, Berlin; Duncker & Humblot.

Tanzi, Vito and Howell H. Zee (1998), 'Consequences of the Economic and Monetary Union for the Coordination of Tax Systems in the European Union: Lessons from the U.S. Experience', IMF Working Paper, WP/98/115 (August).

—— (1999), 'Taxation in a Borderless World: The Role of Information Exchange', in Bertil Wiman (ed.), *International Studies in Taxation*, The Hague: Kluwer Law International.

Tobin, James (1978), 'A proposal for International Monetary Reform', *Eastern Economic Journal*, 4, 153–9.

—— (1996), 'Prologue', in Mahbub ul Haq, Inge Kaul and Isabelle Grunberg (eds), *The Tobin Tax: Coping with Financial Volatility*, New York: Oxford University Press.

Ul Haq, Mahbub, Inge Kaul and Isabelle Grunberg (eds) (1996), *The Tobin Tax: Coping with Financial Volatility*, New York: Oxford University Press.

Zee, Howell H. (1998), 'Taxation of Financial Capital in a Globalized Environment: The Role of Withholding Taxes', *National Tax Journal*, LI(3), 587–99.

14. Fiscal federalism and decentralization: a review of some efficiency and macroeconomic aspects

FACTORS BEHIND THE RECENT TREND TOWARD DECENTRALIZATION

Until recent years, issues of fiscal federalism and decentralization had received relatively little attention on the part of economists and other students of economic and political developments.[1] Interest in these issues was confined mainly to specialists. Public finance courses typically allocated no more than one lesson to the topic and, at times, not even that. In his monumental treatise on public finance, 600 pages long, Richard Musgrave dedicated a total of five pages to 'multilevel finance' (Musgrave, 1959, pp. 179–83).

Things started changing in the 1980s and the topic began to attract more attention. By the 1990s the topic had become definitely hot and recently even cartoonists have discovered it.[2] Furthermore professional interest in the subject crossed the US border and became international. In several countries national commissions were established to study decentralization or the possibility of creating some form of fiscal federalism. In others, political campaigns made decentralization or fiscal federalism their centerpiece. Many reasons account for this change; some merit a brief discussion.

Developments in the European Community

The process of creating an entity that will transcend the European member states in some important economic functions has had to face the question of how much economic power to transfer to the European Union. The issues in this debate are similar to those that arise in discussions of the pros and cons of fiscal federalism and fiscal decentralization. In a European Union who would be responsible for income redistribution and for stabilization? And in terms of resource allocation, what specific functions should be performed by the Union and what should be left to the member states? In this discussion, strange words, such as *subsidiarity*, have become important. The European debate has forced many European economists, and not just those who specialize in public finance, to look at the fiscal institutions of countries with strong subnational governments, and at the existing literature, to see what could be learned from them that could be relevant to the European question.[3]

Disenchantment with the Role of the Public Sector

The explosive growth of the public sector of many industrial countries in the postwar period, a growth that was associated with the growing power of the central government due to its increasing role in income maintenance, income redistribution and stabilization, has recently led to strong reactions. At the political level, the 1980s and 1990s have seen a swing toward more conservative attitudes. These attitudes are especially suspicious of powerful central governments. The view that greater reliance should be placed on the market has been accompanied by the parallel view that less power should remain in the hands of the central government. At the technical level some influential economists have questioned the effectiveness of governmental action in stabilizing the economy and in bringing about a better distribution of income accompanied by a reduction in poverty and unemployment. This challenge has reduced the legitimacy of the central governments action and has created a presumption in favor of reducing the size of the public sector while, at the same time, giving more power to both the market and the local jurisdictions. Many countries are now considering a devolution of some functions to local jurisdictions.[4] In terms of resource allocation, various arguments have been advanced to support the view that privatization and decentralization would lead to greater efficiency and to a leaner public sector.

Country-specific Political Developments

Developments in specific countries, such as Canada, China and the former Soviet Union, have forced a reassessment of multi-level finance. In Canada the developments were driven largely by political considerations, with some provinces demanding more independence. In China they were driven by the need to re-establish some control over national public revenue. In the republics that emerged from the break-up of the Soviet Union there was the need to create from scratch fiscal arrangements and especially arrangements that gave significant responsibilities to subnational governments. In the Russian Federation, made up of regions with widely diverse cultural, ethnic or economic characteristics, the need for these arrangements was strongly felt. In these countries interest in fiscal federalism was the logical outcome of the discussion about the political organization that these countries should have after the break-up of the centralized system of policy making. Other countries, such as Ethiopia, have also been driven toward decentralization (or regionalization) by the ethnic diversity of the population and by the belief that decentralization would help keep that country together.

Fiscal Constitutions and Structural Problems

Another group of countries, including Argentina, Brazil, India and Nigeria, in the 1980s experienced macroeconomic problems that required major adjustments in their fiscal accounts, through revenue increases or expenditure cuts. These countries were often constrained in their policy choices by special constitutional or legal arrangements among governments at different levels. As structural and macroeconomic problems became important, and as the need for adjustment grew, so did the attention directed at the legal constraints that, allegedly, limited the central government's scope for policy action.

Although not as significant as the factors mentioned above, one could, perhaps, add that the research work of the World Bank and its lending policy, which have placed emphasis on decentralization, may also have contributed to the present trend.

In conclusion, political and economic developments have heightened interest in the kind of fiscal arrangements that would be desirable in different countries.[5] Should countries establish rules of the game that favor decentralization of fiscal and economic actions? Or is a centralized decision-making process more consistent with good policy? The answer is likely to depend on many, and often country-specific, factors, but at least some of the relevant issues to be faced in dealing with that question can be addressed in a generalized form. Views on fiscal federalism and decentralization in general are constantly changing between nations and, across time, within particular nations. At present fiscal decentralization is fashionable while, for a long time, the opposite was often the case. Whether this is a passing fad or a permanent change in attitudes will in part depend on the success or failure of the decentralization movement.

The next section summarizes the main economic arguments in favor of decentralization, submits some of these arguments to critical scrutiny and concludes with a brief discussion of the conditions that must be met if fiscal decentralization is to succeed. The third section deals with selected stabilization issues, while the fourth section discusses the financing of the activities of subnational jurisdictions. A final section draws some conclusions.

DECENTRALIZATION AND ECONOMIC EFFICIENCY

Before entering directly into the specific discussion of the relationship between decentralization and economic efficiency, it may be useful to distinguish between *fiscal* and *administrative* decentralization. Fiscal decentralization exists when subnational governments have the power, given to them by the constitution or by particular laws, to raise (some) taxes and to carry out spending activities within clearly established legal criteria. Administrative decentralization exists when much of the money is raised centrally but part of it is allocated to decentralized entities that carry out their spending activities under close guidelines or controls imposed by the central government. These decentralized entities act as agents of the central government.[6]

In the discussion that follows, it might have been useful to distinguish between (a) developing countries, (b) transaction economies and (c) developed countries, as the relevance of some of the arguments tends to differ among these three groups, but this would have made the chapter much longer.

Examples of fiscal decentralization are provided by the fiscal federations the United States, Canada, Argentina, Brazil, Germany, Australia, Switzerland, India, Nigeria, and so forth. An example of administrative decentralization is provided by Italy, where the central government raises much of the tax revenue and transfers it to local entities which, under some guidelines, carry out the public spending largely as agents of the central government. In Italy, for example, in 1992, local entities raised about 8 per cent of the total net revenue of the general government but spent about 37 per cent of total net expenditure. Some of the issues discussed in this chapter are of interest to both kinds of decentralization but more particularly to fiscal decentralization.

The main *economic* justification for decentralization rests largely on allocative or efficiency grounds. If the country's population is not homogeneous, and if ethnic, racial, cultural, linguistic or other relevant characteristics are regionally distributed (as they are in Russia and in Ethiopia), one could also advance a *political* argument for decentralization. In this case decentralization may be needed to induce various regions to remain part of a federation. On such grounds, decentralization would be more desirable in, say, Russia, than in Japan.[7] By the same token, the goal of national unity has often pushed non-democratic governments toward the forced elimination of regional differences.[8] In democratic societies the economic and political arguments for decentralization tend to converge. In these societies it has been argued that decentralization strengthens democracy. Most people are more inclined to engage in political activities at the local level because local policies have a more direct impact on their daily life.

The normative, economic argument for decentralization can be based on an ex ante and an ex post case (Cremer *et al.*, 1994). The ex ante theoretical case was best made by Wallace Oates in his classic 1972 book. The ex post case is essentially the one outlined by Tiebout (1956). Oates's *normative* case is based on the realization that not all public goods have similar spatial characteristics. Some, such as defense, benefit the whole country. Some, such as regional transport systems or forestry services, benefit regions. Others, such as street lighting or cleaning,[9] benefit only municipalities or particular districts. Furthermore different geographic areas may have different preferences for public goods. There is thus the need to fit the supply of public goods to the different requirements of different groups. The central government might tend to ignore these spatial characteristics and this diversity of preferences, or it might not be well informed about them and might therefore supply a uniform package to all citizens. Thus this one-size-fits-all policy would not supply a basket of public goods that would be considered optimal by all the citizens. When 'the jurisdiction that determines the level of provision of each public good includes precisely the set of individuals who consume the good' there is 'perfect correspondence' in the provision of public goods (Oates, 1972, p. 34).

In this ideal, normative model, if the spatial characteristics of the public goods differed, at the limit, one might wish to have as many jurisdictions as there are public goods. Thus, in theory at least, one would need a highly decentralized public sector with many subnational jurisdictions of varying sizes. In this ideal or theoretical world, 'each level of government, possessing complete knowledge of the tastes of its constituents and seeking to maximize their welfare, would provide the Pareto-efficient level of output ... and would finance this through benefit pricing' (ibid., 1972. pp. 34–5). Oates's normative policy conclusion is stated through a 'decentralization theorem':

> For a public good – the consumption of which is defined over geographical subsets of the total population, and for which the costs of providing each level of output of the good in each jurisdiction are the same for the central or the respective local government – it will always be more efficient (or at least as efficient) for local governments to provide the Pareto-efficient levels of output for their respective jurisdictions than for the central government to provide *any* specified and uniform level of output across all jurisdictions. (Ibid., p. 35)

The basic and important message of Oates's decentralization policy is that centralization is costly if it leads the government to provide a bundle of public goods that diverges from the preferences of the citizens of particular areas, be these regions, provinces or municipalities. When these preferences vary among geographical areas, a uniform package chosen by a national government is likely to force some localities to consume more or less than they would like to consume. As Cremer *et al.* (1994, p. 5) have restated Oates's 'decentralization theorem': 'each type of good should be provided by a level of government ... enjoying a comparative advantage in accounting for the diversity of preferences in its choice of service delivery'.

This interpretation assumes that subnational governments already exist, so that the relevant question is, which of the existing government levels should be responsible for particular forms of spending? The problem would be much more difficult if one were to determine the degree of decentralization desirable in a world where the spatial characteristics of public goods vary among different public goods and over time, and where the preferences of the various regions may also change.[10] At the limit one could argue that not only should there be many decentralized spending units, but their geographical boundaries and, thus, their number would have to change over time to reflect technological developments that cause change in the spatial characteristics of public goods.[11]

Oates's basic argument can be applied to stabilization policy or even to redistributive policy if the preferences of the population living in different regions are not similar. For example, if the European Union forced the Italians and the Germans to pursue a similar stabilization policy objective for inflation and unemployment when in fact Italians might prefer lower unemployment while Germans might prefer lower inflation, some welfare loss would result; or if Italians preferred higher assistance for invalids, while Germans preferred higher assistance for orphans, a common redistributive package might also imply a loss in welfare as compared to the option in which each chooses the desired package. In both of these cases there is the assumption that the national government would or could choose just one package and that local jurisdictions would base their choices on their citizens' preferences.

In addition to Oates's theoretical argument for decentralization, that is based largely on the spatial characteristics of public goods, decentralization can be defended on the basis of other more practical considerations. Some have argued that a decentralized system can become a competitive surrogate (Israel, 1992, p. 76), thus bringing (to choices in the public sector) some of the allocative benefits that a competitive market brings to choices in the private sector. There are many angles to this argument, one of which is, of course, Tiebout's argument. To the extent that (a) decentralization can help identify the different population groups' preferences for public goods, (b) local governments supply these goods, (c) these groups can be made to pay a tax price based on the benefit that they receive from the public goods, and (d) individuals vote with their feet, by moving to the jurisdiction that best reflects their preferences, the final outcome will approach that of the market mechanism. At the margin the benefit from consuming the public good or service will be equal to the cost in terms of benefit taxes. Such a system would bring a solution that would approach a Pareto optimum.[12]

Another potentially important advantage of decentralization is that it allows experimentation in the provision of the output: when the provision of a public service (say, education) is the responsibility of local jurisdictions, and when these jurisdictions are free to provide the service in any way they see as appropriate, they will experiment with its provision. Some jurisdictions will discover better ways of providing the service and other jurisdictions will emulate the successful ones.[13] The more jurisdictions there are, and the freer they are to pursue the objective in their own way, the more simultaneous experiments may take place. When the service is imposed by a national monopoly, which adopts a uniform approach in the provision of the service, there will be no or little experimentation and, thus, anachronistic or old fashioned methods may continue to be adopted even when better alternatives are possible. This result is often noted by supporters of decentralization, who point to the outmoded curricula of the school systems of countries that have centralized educational systems.

Still another important argument in favor of decentralization is one that emphasizes the fact that, when individuals are responsible for the results of their actions, and thus have property rights over the outcome, they are likely to have stronger incentives to perform better. Therefore, when local officials have direct responsibility in the provision of a public service, and can thus be praised for success and blamed for failure, they will have a greater interest in succeeding. In such cases the community may develop a sense of pride in the successful delivery of the service. Additionally, when the cost of providing a service is borne by the local jurisdiction, there will be more guarantee that the provision of the service will be cost-efficient and will not be extended beyond the point where marginal benefits equal marginal costs. This view, that *accountability brings responsibility*, plays a large role in advocating the decentralization of various functions. As Shah and Qureshi (1994, p. xv) have put it: 'Accountability is promoted through a clearer and closer linkage of the benefits of local public services with their costs.'

Finally, at a time when large public sectors are not considered good for countries, some literature has argued that decentralization is desirable because it is likely to be associated with a smaller public sector and a more efficient economy. This argument has been advanced in various papers over the years, especially following the contribution by Brennan and Buchanan (1980). A recent empirical analysis of this point is available in a World Bank paper by Ehdaie (1994).

The above are powerful arguments which help explain why decentralization has become so popular in recent years. Some writers, however, have advanced counterarguments that either challenge some of the above conclusions or, at least, outline conditions which, in some cases, could make decentralization a less attractive policy. Some counterarguments are discussed in the next few pages. The point of this discussion is not to challenge the conclusion that decentralization may bring benefits, but to identify situations in which that policy may not lead to the expected results *unless some important changes are made in the existing conditions*.

There are many countries that have decentralized fiscal structures. Decentralization has worked relatively well in some, less well in others. It seems to have worked well in Austria, Germany, the Scandinavian countries, Switzerland and the United States, among the developed countries, and in Indonesia and, perhaps, Malaysia, among the developing countries. It has worked less well in some other industrial countries and in several developing countries, including Argentina and Brazil. It is too early to tell how well it will work in the transition economies.

Papers by Rémy Prud'homme (1994), Richard Bird (1994), Wallace E. Oates (1994) and others have suggested that, while the theoretical case for decentralization is relatively straightforward, the practical case may be less so. As Oates has put it (1994, p. 1), 'fiscal decentralization has much to offer, but it is a complicated enterprise'.[14] As we have seen earlier, part of the case for decentralization rests on the spatial characteristics of public goods. Because some of these goods benefit only some areas and not the whole country, there may be a tendency for the central government to underproduce or possibly overproduce them. The reason may be that the central government does not have the necessary information on the local preferences and/or it may not have the right incentives to act on the available information.

The argument related to lack of information has been challenged on grounds that central governments can and do assign officers to local offices. These officers may be quite capable of determining the preferences of the local population.[15] The central governments of unitary countries often have representatives (for example, the *préfets* in France and Italy, or the *intendentes* in Chile) who closely follow local developments and assess local needs. These are often highly trained individuals who, following Niskanen's theory of how bureaucracies work, might even have an incentive to exaggerate the local demand for some public services, in order to increase their own power or importance through a larger budget. Therefore the main question is whether the information that these individuals send to the center is more or less correct and more or less biased than the one available to local policy makers.[16]

Whether the local government is more or less likely to react to the local preferences than the central government depends, of course, on the strength of various incentives and on how political decisions are made. A national government interested in local votes may have a strong interest in meeting local needs; a local government that is not democratic may have little interest in meeting these needs. Therefore one should not automatically assume that subnational governments are made up of democratically elected officials who necessarily have the public (though local) interest in mind. When they do, decentralization has a greater chance of succeeding than when they do not. The basic presumption behind the arguments by the proponents of decentralization is that local democracies are in place and do work. When they do not, the case for decentralization becomes weaker.

Both Prud'homme (1994) and Oates (1994) mention *corruption*. Oates takes an agnostic view on whether corruption is likely to be greater in local governments or in central governments. Prud'homme believes that corruption is a greater problem at the local level, and mentions France and Italy in support of his viewpoint. This is an issue that cannot be settled by empirical evidence, so one must fall back on impressions. My own observations, reading and work on corruption (Tanzi, 1994) have led me to believe that corruption may be a more common problem at the local level than at the national level, especially in developing countries. The reason is that corruption is often stimulated by contiguity, that is, by the fact that officials and citizens live and work close to one another in local communities. Often they have known each other all their lives and may even come from the same families. Contiguity brings personalism in relations and personalism tends to be the enemy of arm's-length relationships.[17] When relationships are no longer guided by arm's-length relationships, the public interest often takes the back seat and some decisions tend to be made to favor particular individuals or groups.[18] It should be emphasized that governance issues are problems for all levels of government in many countries. The conclusion reached in this paragraph is a purely personal one and cannot be generalized to all countries. There are sure to be countries where the local bureaucracy is more honest than the national bureaucracy.

Prud'homme (1994) mentions another factor that may reduce the advantages of decentralization, namely, the *quality of the local bureaucracies* as compared to the national bureaucracies. As he puts it: 'Decentralization not only transfers power from central to local government, but also from central to local bureaucracies ... central government bureaucracies are likely to attract more qualified people ... because they offer better careers ... more possibilities of promotion [and, better salaries]' (p. 9). Prud'homme's conclusion would be strengthened by the arguments made by Murphy *et al.* (1991), who argued that talented individuals tend to choose fields that are wider and that, over the longer run, offer better opportunities for advancement. To the extent that national bureaucracies offer better opportunities to able individuals than do local bureaucracies, they may attract more qualified and more able individuals. However, where qualified individuals are abundant, as is often the case in developed countries, subnational governments may have staff as qualified as national governments.[19] On the other hand, where educational standards are low, so that there is a smaller pool of potentially efficient employees, the point made by Prud'homme carries more weight. This scarcity of local talent may be a problem in decentralization efforts in, say, Ethiopia and other African countries.

Within countries there are often wide differences across regions in the quality of the personnel of the local administrations. For example, in Italy there is a huge difference in the quality of the local public administrations between, say, Emilia-Romagna, where the quality of the local administration is very good – and, perhaps, even better than at the national level – and some southern regions, where it is poor (Putnam, 1993). In Argentina there is also a huge difference between the Province of Buenos Aires and some of the other provinces, and in Colombia between Bogota and Medellin and some other provinces. These differences are in part explained by differences in resources available, but cultural factors, as emphasized by Putnam, also play a role.

Another practical issue is that, apart from exceptional circumstances in which multi-level arrangements can be created from scratch and can thus, at least in principle, be influenced by the available knowledge about the spatial characteristics of important public goods, in most countries the existing local jurisdictions were determined by past political, rather than economic, considerations. The size of states, provinces, regions or metropolitan areas is, thus, fixed and largely the result of historical accidents.[20] These are the subnational governments to which one allocates fiscal responsibilities through decentralization. The chance that the spatial characteristics of the public goods or services whose responsibility is assigned to the subnational jurisdictions will match the areas covered by these jurisdictions, so as to have 'perfect correspondence' 'à la Oates, seems slim indeed. The lesser the degree of 'correspondence', the lower the potential economic advantages associated with decentralization.[21]

Two other aspects may be important in today's world. First, the characteristics of the public goods and services are likely to change. Technology and economic development ensure that new needs for public sector intervention arise continuously and some old needs disappear. For example, the need to protect a city's population from outside attacks and to provide it with information about the time of day was predominant in the past. Walls were built around cities, and clocks were placed on bell towers, to satisfy this need. The 'public goods' provided by these public services are no longer needed. On the other hand, the need to protect citizens from domestic criminals or from pollution have become more important. Second, changing technology, combined with much greater mobility on the part of the citizens, implies that the spatial characteristics of public goods are also likely to change. For example, when mobility is limited, many of the benefits associated with public education are internalized by the jurisdiction that provides the service. However, when mobility is high, extrajurisdictional externalities become important.

The jurisdiction that finances the expenditure may not reap the benefits if those who are educated in its public schools move to another jurisdiction. Similar considerations apply to spending for health and for many other services. On the other hand, this spillover problem can in part be solved through a reciprocity rule, especially if the services can be standardized across regions. In such cases the existence of the spillover does not reduce the advantage of providing the service locally, but the standardization of the services eliminates one of the basic reasons for decentralization.

These two aspects imply that, to be optimal, decentralization arrangements should be flexible over time. Either the geographical areas covered by local jurisdictions – and thus the number of these jurisdictions – should change over time, which may be politically difficult or impossible to bring about, or the continuous re-examination of the characteristics of public goods should lead to a reallocation of some of them across the existing jurisdictions.[22] There is no simple mechanism that allows this process to take place normally. Once the federal structure is determined, local politicians and officials fiercely oppose major changes to borders and/or tasks. As a consequence fiscal federalism is at times characterized by a mismatch between the spatial characteristics of public goods and the existing responsible jurisdictions.

Earlier it was mentioned that a strong argument in favor of decentralization is that it allows subnational jurisdictions to experiment with new methods or new ways to provide the public services. Under certain circumstances, such experimentation can lead to progress for some jurisdictions and to imitation by others through demonstration effects. Of course, in those situations where the quality of the local bureaucracies is not as good as that of the national bureaucracy, and where achieving the public interest is not the guiding principle for the local officials in charge, independence and experimentation by local jurisdictions may not lead to the desired results.

By definition decentralization implies that subnational governments or entities take over some functions from the national government and, thus, come to manage larger financial resources than would be the case under centralized governments. Both the flow of revenue necessary to finance these functions and the flow of expenditure to carry them out increase, at times significantly. This prompts the question of the efficiency of the controls over these financial flows. Are the subnational jurisdictions capable of handling these flows? Public expenditure management (PEM) systems are not very good in many countries. They are particularly deficient in developing countries (and especially in Africa) and in transition economies. This is one of the reasons why there have often been expenditure overruns, and larger than forecast deficits, in many countries.

In their broadest functions good PEM systems must include budget offices capable of making good forecasts of expected revenue and anticipated spending. They must include budgetary classifications that allow the controlling authorities to determine whether the money spent is actually going to the budgeted items and functions. Thus good economic and functional classifications are important. They must include accounting systems that allow the monitoring and control of the cash flows and that provide, in a timely fashion, the needed information on the status of the expenditure and the revenue. They must also provide some controls over other commitments, even when these commitments do not contribute to additional cash spending in the current fiscal year. The skills required to perform these tasks in an adequate way are scarce in most countries. They are far scarcer in developing countries and in economies in transition. It is reasonable to assume that these skills must be even scarcer at the local level in developing countries and in economies in transition.

The decentralization of responsibilities to subnational jurisdictions that have not yet developed these PEM structures is likely to run into difficulties.[23] Decentralization should be accompanied by the establishment of essential, if not optimal, PEM systems to have a good chance of success. Technical assistance missions have often found poor PEM systems and thus a lack of local financial accounting *and* accountability, especially, but not only, in developing countries.[24] Often the most basic statistical information is not available, even on the money spent. There is no information on commitments. When information on cash spending is available, it is often impossible to ascertain the items or the functions on which the money has been spent.[25]

Lack of arm's-length relationships between local government officials and local suppliers or local banks leads to the creation of 'hidden debt': debt which has not yet shown up in the statistical information available. When, for political reasons, local budgets tend to be soft over the longer run, financial difficulties and misallocation of resources are likely to result.[26] This issue is taken up in the next section. In conclusion, the benefits from decentralization may be reduced or may even disappear when the minimum institutional infrastructure in terms of PEM systems is not in place. Brazil, after the 1988 Constitution decentralized spending decisions, and Italy, after the 1979 reform decentralized some of the spending decisions, are concrete examples of this problem. Those who promote decentralization would be well advised to pay close attention to this problem.

Two final points should be mentioned: first is the question of whether there are economies or diseconomies of scale in the provision of public goods; second is the impact of decentralization on the size of the public sector. It is difficult to take a position on whether there are economies or diseconomies of scale in the provision of public goods and services. The answer depends on the particular services or public goods. A good, but dated (and US-specific) survey of the costs of supplying public services is available in Hirsch (1968).

Prud'homme refers to some World Bank studies that have found that economies of scale exist in the provision of some services. However this issue might be less relevant to the choice between centralized and decentralized activities than to the choice of the optimal size of the decentralized jurisdictions.[27] If there are economies of scale in the provision of a public service, *ceteris paribus* the service should be provided by the largest jurisdiction that can fully exploit these economies. This does not imply that the jurisdiction will necessarily be the central government.

Whether decentralization does or does not reduce the size of the public sector is an open question. As mentioned earlier, some literature has argued that more decentralized countries tend to have smaller public sectors, measured by the share of public sector spending in gross domestic product. The main reason for the difference in the size of the public sector (between the industrial countries with large public sectors and those with small public sectors) is the presence or absence of a large centrally funded welfare sector and social security scheme. Countries such as the Netherlands, Italy, France, Germany, Austria, Sweden and Finland have large public sectors because, at some point in time, they decided to have large welfare activities financed by social security contributions. On the other hand, Anglo-Saxon countries, which happen to include three federations (Australia, Canada and the United States), have smaller public sectors because they did not create as large social security and welfare programs.[28] The relation between these historical decisions and the degree of decentralization is difficult to establish.

Furthermore the true impact of the public sector on the economy comes, not just from the spending and financing activities of the government, but also from its many quasi-fiscal activities and regulations. *If* fiscal decentralization increased the number of regulations (because to the regulations introduced by the central government it added the regulations introduced by the subnational governments) and *if* it increased the scope for quasi-fiscal activities, it might increase the impact of governmental activity on the economy even if it did not increase the spending–GDP ratio. Economic regulations are often equivalent in results to either spending or taxing decisions. I am not aware, however, of any study that has shown a connection between, say, fiscal federalism and the extent of regulation in an economy. This might be a topic worth researching.

To conclude this section, under the right conditions, decentralization might be expected to lead to *improved management, information and accountability*. However, as pointed out in the above discussion, these benefits will not take place automatically. If the conditions are not right, decentralization may create additional problems in both resource allocation and stabilization.

DECENTRALIZATION AND STABILIZATION

The previous section dealt with broad allocative or efficiency issues. This section addresses a few additional issues, dealing mostly with stabilization. The relation between decentralization and stabilization has not received the attention it deserves, especially in connection with developing countries. In this section some characteristics of decentralization that may have an impact on stabilization are identified.

Let us assume that subnational governments, with clear expenditure responsibilities, have come into existence and that they have been given the exclusive use of some relatively robust tax bases on which they can depend to finance some or most of their expenditures.[29] Let us also assume that the subnational governments can share other tax bases with the national government. The national government provides the subnational governments with relevant information on taxpayers, or with other technical assistance, so that, within limits, they can profitably exploit these shared tax bases. The subnational governments are run by competent officials who are democratically elected or appointed and are thus responsive to the preferences of the taxpayers. Assume, finally, that constitutional or other legal limitations require that the subnational governments must balance their budgets annually.

The observant reader must have realized that the above description conforms fairly closely to the US situation. In the United States subnational governments generally balance their budgets on an annual basis. Episodes of fiscal stress such as those experienced recently by the District of Columbia and Orange County and, in the 1970s, by New York City, are relatively rare and, thus, they do not change the basic conclusion. Much of the existing literature on fiscal federalism and stabilization has dealt with, or has been influenced by, the US situation. In this literature, the responsibility for fiscal policy has been assumed to rest with the central (federal) government.[30]

Within this context, not only are subnational governments not expected to take an active part in trying to stabilize the economy but, in fact, because they have to balance their budgets on an annual basis, their behavior is fiscally neutral when the economy is on its long-run growth path and fiscally perverse or procyclical during cycles.[31] They raise taxes or cut spending in a recession, and cut taxes or raise spending in a boom. The question asked has been whether subnational governments should not play a positive and active role in countercyclical fiscal policy.

Suppose that in large countries, such as the United States and Canada, business cycles are not strongly correlated across regions, perhaps because some regions' economies depend on the price of particular commodities, say oil for Texas, which can move independently of the country's general economic conditions, or because different regions trade with different partners who experience unsynchronized cycles. Suppose also that, as argued in an earlier section, different regions have different preferences for some macroeconomic variables (some prefer less inflation, others prefer less unemployment). Under these circumstances some economists have argued that a role can be assigned to subnational governments in the pursuit of stabilization policy.[32] The government of the region undergoing the recession may take upon itself the function of stimulating the local economy even though the multiplier associated with its fiscal stimulus may be low.

I have summarized the discussion on stabilization in the existing literature (a) to show that it is very much US- or, perhaps, Canadian- or European Union-specific, and (b) to argue that the issues that are relevant to developing countries are often different from those connected with Keynesian counter-cyclical policy. In developing countries, and in an increasing number of industrial countries, the basic macroeconomic need is not to counter cycles but to bring about a fiscal adjustment that reduces the chronic fiscal imbalance that characterizes many of these countries. The issue then is the relationship between decentralization and *structural*, rather than *cyclical*, fiscal deficits. Does decentralization contribute to structural macroeconomic problems? Does it make it more difficult to adjust the fiscal accounts once a structural deficit has developed?

The experience of many countries points to the possibility that, under circumstances often found in developing countries, subnational governments are likely to contribute, sometimes significantly, to the aggravation of macroeconomic problems, or that they increase the difficulty in making corrections. In several cases local governments have spent more than they have raised in ordinary revenue, thus increasing their debt and occasionally forcing the central government to come to their rescue.[33] In other cases the relationship between subnational governments and the central government has reduced the latter's margin of maneuver. At times this outcome is the consequence of arrangements that have shifted spending responsibilities to the subnational governments without providing them with adequate resources. At other times it is the inevitable result of political forces that push subnational governments toward higher spending or lower taxes.[34] Still, in other cases, it is the result of poor PEM systems which make it difficult to control spending. In many cases wrong incentives and lack of information have played key roles.

When decentralization is based on a clear and comprehensive contract between central and subnational governments that (a) spells out the latters' obligations, (b) assigns to them reasonable resources to comply with their responsibilities and (c) makes it explicit that the local governments must live within the means stipulated in the contract, and that under no circumstances will they get additional resources from the national government, then the situation approaches that prevailing in the United States. In this situation local spending can be increased mostly by increasing the locally controlled taxes. This constraint forces the subnational governments to behave responsibly in a macroeconomic sense and efficiently in an allocative sense. In the absence of 'tax exporting', there would not be an extrajurisdictional externality on the revenue side and the responsibility for any sustained national fiscal imbalance would fall squarely on the central government.

Unfortunately in many countries (a) there is no such contract (explicit or implicit), (b) the assignment of expenditure responsibilities is vague and is occasionally changed by new unfunded mandates, (c) the incentives for the local policy makers and officials may be such as to induce them to overspend or undertax, (d) the budgets for the subnational governments tend to be relatively soft over the long run because of their political power over the national government, (e) the necessary information to guide local governments' policies is often missing, is of poor quality, or is not timely, and (f) the existing PEM systems are not developed and sophisticated enough to allow or facilitate the needed accounting and managerial controls.

When clear and firm constitutional or legal guidelines are missing, decentralization may create a situation where each local government can gain if it can increase its own spending but it can shift the financing cost to the whole country. The possibility that the financing for the extra spending will be paid mostly by those outside the jurisdiction creates an important externality that gives each local government a strong incentive to push for additional resources and for increased spending.[35] When the resources are not available ex ante from the national government, they may become available ex post, after the spending has taken place and the debt has accumulated.[36] The political power of many local governments and the systemic as well as political implications of letting them go broke make it difficult for the national government to resist these pressures.

In addition to the revenue they raise from their own tax bases, from the fees they charge, from the resources they own (natural resources and so on), and from shared revenue, subnational governments have often depended on grants from the central government. Often they can make a strong case for these grants because the national government may require the subnational governments to perform certain functions or to comply with some standards without directly providing funds for them. Unfunded mandates create implicit claims for future grants or for soft budgets. But, as Bahl and Linn and others have pointed out, the design of an optimal grant structure is very difficult (Bahl and Linn, 1992, p. 16).[37] Thus the existence of grants may introduce inefficiencies and may create political pressures to increase their size.

The channels through which fiscal decentralization may aggravate structural fiscal problems are many. Here we identify and discuss three: the assignment of major tax bases to subnational governments, the sharing of major tax bases and the ex post, implicit servicing of debt incurred by subnational governments.

Assignment of Major Tax Bases

Important decentralized countries, such as Brazil, India and Russia, have assigned to the subnational governments, *for their exclusive use*, some major tax bases. For example, in Brazil the general value-added tax (ICM) has been assigned to the states. In India the sales tax has been assigned to the states. As reported by Chelliah (1991, p. 7), the Indian Constitution is guided by the principle that a given tax base should be assigned to only one level of government. In Russia the individual income tax and many excises have been assigned to the subnational governments (Bahl, 1994).

In India, the central government has been left mainly with income taxes, which have never been very productive, with foreign trade taxes, which ought to fall or even disappear over the years, and with highly distorting excise taxes, which are in great need of reform. At the same time the central government is responsible for servicing a progressively more burdensome public debt. Thus, while central government spending has tended to grow, the government's share of total tax revenue has been falling.

In Brazil, between 1980 and 1990, the share in total taxes received by the central government (União) fell from 69.2 per cent to 57.5 per cent. The share of the states (Estados) rose from 22.2 per cent to 27.9 per cent; that of the municipalities rose from 6.6 per cent to 14.6 per cent. The 1988 Brazilian Constitution accelerated the fall of centrally retained tax revenue. This fall contributed to larger fiscal deficits and macroeconomic problems.

If the tax bases that are assigned exclusively to the subnational governments are large and dynamic ones, and if the spending responsibilities of the central governments (for debt servicing, pensions and national public goods) cannot be easily compressed, macroeconomic problems are often inevitable. The three countries mentioned above have experienced macroeconomic difficulties caused, or made worse, by the tax assignments. Similar difficulties may arise in China, where major tax bases have also been assigned to subnational jurisdictions. When macroeconomic adjustment requires that a central government increase its tax level, it will find it more difficult to do so if important tax bases are not available to it. This has been the experience of both Brazil and India. In this situation the central government will be forced to rely on the available, less efficient or unproductive, tax bases. Thus either the level of taxation will be lower than desired or the structure of taxation will be less efficient than it could be.

Sharing of Major Tax Bases

While some tax bases are assigned exclusively for use by particular levels of government, other tax bases may be shared. The sharing may be of, at least, two kinds: different levels of government may independently tax the same base, or one level may collect the tax from a given base and share the revenue with other levels.

Examples of the first kind are the taxing of the personal income tax in the United States and the taxing of sales in Argentina. In the United States personal income is independently taxed by the federal government and by most states. Counties and municipalities 'piggy-back' on the states' income taxes. In Argentina sales are taxed with a value-added tax, at the national level, and with a cascading turnover tax, at the provincial level. When two government levels tax the same tax base, each retains its independence of action even though, of course, if one level increases its dependence on that base it may limit the scope for the other level to tax the same base. At the subnational level the limits on the effective tax rates on a given tax base are generally imposed by tax competition and by the potential mobility of the tax base.

Examples of the second kind are quite common. They exist in Argentina, Brazil, Colombia, Pakistan, Russia and in other countries. In Argentina the federal government collects the income tax, the value-added tax, excise taxes, foreign trade taxes, liquid fuel and energy taxes, the gross assets tax (levied on companies), the personal assets tax (levied on individuals), social security taxes and some minor taxes. Of these the value-added tax, the income tax, the excise taxes, the personal assets tax and the gross assets tax are subject to complicated sharing arrangements with other parts of the public sector. In 1993 federal government revenue, before sharing and transfers, accounted for 81 per cent of all tax revenue. After revenue sharing and transfers, it accounted for 54 per cent.[38]

The Argentine experience captures well the essence of the problem with these arrangements. When faced with the need to correct large macroeconomic imbalances, the Argentine authorities introduced major tax reforms and made highly successful administrative reforms. These policies succeeded in sharply raising the share of taxes in GDP. However part of the potential impact of this effort on reducing the public sector's fiscal deficit was dissipated by the revenue-sharing arrangement. This arrangement required that about 57 per cent of any addition to total tax revenue coming from the central government's effort be shared with the provincial governments, which immediately spent the additional revenue. The attitude of the subnational government has been that economic stabilization is a national public good and is thus the sole responsibility of the national government.

The effort of the Argentine central government was also directed at reducing its own spending through privatization, reductions in its employment, and in other ways. For example, it sharply reduced the number of employees working for the central government, thus continuing and accelerating a trend initiated in the 1980s.[39] At the same time that this was taking place, in part as a result of the additional tax revenue received, the provincial governments were increasing their employment and their total spending.[40] Furthermore the provinces with the lowest own revenue mobilization were the ones that increased most the size of their civil service. Across all provinces, the correlation coefficient between these two variables is about –0.70. It is likely that, at the margin, the benefits lost by reducing central government employment exceeded the benefit gained by the increase at the provincial level. In conclusion the Argentine sharing arrangements have magnified the effort necessary at the central level to reduce the country's fiscal deficit and have probably reduced the efficiency of public spending.

These tax-sharing arrangements, which are limited to specific taxes rather than to the whole tax revenue, also have important efficiency implications on the revenue side. The central government that finds itself in great need of raising revenue, but that has to share the revenue from some taxes (and not from others) with subnational governments, will have a strong incentive to raise revenue (from changes in rates or improved administrative efforts) *from the taxes that are not shared* or from taxes the revenue from which will go mostly to the central government. As a result the structure of the tax system will be distorted and non-shared taxes will acquire a greater weight in the tax system, even when they are less efficient taxes.

There is another side to this problem. The federal government that finds itself in the situation described above will be prone to granting exemptions from the taxes from which it retains a small share of the revenue raised. This seems to have happened in Pakistan in connection with the general sales tax. For this tax the central government has full legislative authority, but transfers 80 per cent of its revenue to the provinces. In other words, the direct revenue cost for the federal government of providing incentives is very low. Perverse incentives have also occurred when some subnational governments have been able to grant exemptions from national taxes, thus passing the cost of the lost revenue to the nation as a whole. Examples of this problem are common in China and were also found in Argentina in earlier years when four provinces had the legal authority to grant incentives against the national value-added tax. In Argentina this led to a considerable erosion of the revenue from the value-added tax, thus aggravating the fiscal crisis. In the above examples, revenue losses, and thus stabilization problems, compounded the efficiency problems. When the sharing is of total tax revenue, rather than of specific taxes, these problems tend to become less serious.

Borrowing by Local Governments

If strictly applied constitutional limitations prevented subnational governments from borrowing, or if the market was able to impose a discipline on the borrowing by subnational governments, or if the national governments never intervened when subnational governments got into trouble, then borrowing by subnational jurisdictions would not contribute to a country's macroeconomic difficulties. Unfortunately, few countries have such strict constitutional limitations; markets have proved remarkably incompetent to discipline borrowing, in part because of informational deficiencies (Lane, 1993); and, often for political reasons, central governments are frequently unable to refuse to assist subnational governments that get into trouble.[41]

There is a lot of variety in the subnational governments' borrowing experience. In Argentina, for example, all levels of government can borrow both domestically and abroad. In 1994 the Argentine provinces were able to finance a deficit of about 0.7 per cent of GDP. In Brazil they can borrow from many sources. São Paulo alone is reported to have accumulated a debt of some $40 billion (*Financial Times*, 25 March 1995, p. 4). In India the states as well as the center can borrow domestically (Chelliah, 1991). In Pakistan, although there are constitutional controls over provincial borrowing, they do not seem to have been effective. In Mexico the finances of its 32 states have been reported as 'precarious' and some states as 'bankrupt' (*Financial Times*, 7 April 1995, p. 7). In Italy borrowing by subnational jurisdictions has contributed to the deterioration in the fiscal situation and has led to the emergence of 'hidden debt'. Some municipalities and regions (Naples, Puglie) have encountered major financial difficulties. These examples could be extended almost ad infinitum.

The reasons for this state of affairs are several and complex. In some cases they may have to do with revenue assignments that could not match the expenditure assignments. However, more often there are more proximate reasons:

1. the lack of good PEM systems within the subnational jurisdictions to monitor and register debt obligations and commitments;
2. the lack of incentives for the local policy makers not to borrow. Often the borrowing gives immediate benefits to those in power while the costs are paid later, perhaps by a different administration;
3. the implicit assumption that, when the chips are down, the central government will step in and foot the bill. As long as the relevant parties (those who lend to the governments and the officials who do the borrowing) believe that the central government will eventually come in, the budget will be soft, and borrowing will be excessive;

4. the lack of good budgetary systems to prepare competent projections for revenue and expenditure; and
5. the multitude of ways 'loans' can be obtained. In the experience of these countries, 'loans' have come from (a) the national government, (b) the central bank – directly, (c) the national or foreign banks, (d) the provincial banks, which in turn borrow from the central bank, (c) the suppliers, (f) the capital market, (g) the pension funds, (h) the arrears on civil servants' salaries and (i) the arrears on payments to utilities, and so forth. At times the 'loans' are voluntary; at other times they are compulsory.

As long as all these possibilities of borrowing exist, as long as there is the belief that the central government will honor the subnational governments' obligations, and as long as the incentives for these governments encourage higher spending, decentralization will contribute to macroeconomic instability.

FINANCING THE ACTIVITIES OF LOCAL GOVERNMENTS

In much of the literature on decentralization the determination of the spending responsibilities, if not the precise level of spending, of the subnational governments precedes the question of how resources are to be generated to pay for the spending. The financing of the expenditure is often almost an afterthought. Yet, for decentralization to be successful, it must relate to the decentralization both of expenditure and of revenue, and these decisions must be made at the same time.

Those who have written on this question have generally argued that local governments should finance their expenditure through 'benefit pricing' or benefit taxation. For example, Musgrave and Musgrave (1984, p. 517) wrote that 'the choice of tax instruments to be used by "local" jurisdictions … should conform to the rule that each jurisdiction pay for its own benefits'. This is necessary because 'benefit taxation – requiring as it does a balance of tax burdens and benefit gains – neutralizes the impact of fiscal operations on location choice' (ibid., p. 518). This is, of course, necessary for the result to be Pareto-optimal.[42] Musgrave and Musgrave recognized that 'the assumption of universal benefit taxation … is unrealistic' (ibid.).

The question of tax assignments by level of government has been discussed by many authors.[43] However, while the general or theoretical discussions of tax assignments are useful, in practice, country-specific factors play a large role.[44] Local jurisdictions raise *whatever taxes they are capable of raising*, often without worrying excessively about the economic distortions that these taxes may create. The search for good taxes that could be exploited by local government has not produced very good results (Bahl and Linn, 1992; Bird, 1986).

The conclusion that the kind of taxes that local governments often raise, especially in developing countries, tend to be of poor quality and thus to generate many economic distortions leads to the obvious question: if decentralization is defended because it improves the allocation of resources on the expenditure side, how much of this efficiency gain is lost when the financing of that expenditure is done in highly distortional ways? This is, of course, a question without an easy answer, but it is one that must be faced when the benefits and the costs of decentralization are discussed. The easier it is to assign 'good' taxes to local jurisdictions, the more justified it is to assign expenditure responsibilities to them. It is also important not to create an imbalance between expenditure responsibilities and the means available to local jurisdictions to carry them out.

The assignment of tax revenue to multi-level governments can follow several options. The first is *to assign all the tax bases to the local jurisdictions* and to ask them to transfer upward to the national government some of the revenue to allow the national government to meet its spending responsibilities. The amount to be transferred upward could be determined by rules, formulas or negotiation. This option is often unattractive and welfare-reducing, for a variety of reasons. It is not consistent with a national policy aimed at redistributing income through the use of the tax system. It is not consistent with a policy that assigns to the public sector the role of stabilizing the economy and that depends on the use of the tax system to help achieve this objective. It may also be inefficient because it would result in an excessive fragmentation of the tax system. It may also provide the wrong incentives to the subnational jurisdictions if they know that part of the taxes they collect will be shared with the national government. There is evidence from some countries (for example China, and Mexico in earlier years) that this policy also leads to inefficient tax administration.[45]

The second option is for the *national government to collect all taxes and to transfer some of the revenue to the local jurisdictions* to allow them to finance their spending responsibilities. The transfer of funds to the local jurisdictions can be done through the sharing of total tax revenue or through the sharing of specific taxes. As argued earlier, the first alternative is clearly superior to the second because it gives the local governments a more stable revenue source and gives the national government more freedom in pursuing its tax policy options. But there are some problems with this option.

By breaking the nexus between decisions to collect tax revenue and decisions to spend that revenue, the concept of the tax price for public spending (that is, the idea that spending decisions carry a specific cost expressed through the taxes paid) is broken. Local officials and local taxpayers may not connect the benefits they derive from public spending with the taxes paid. Therefore they may not exercise the required restraining function on expenditure and the taxpayers will be less willing to support the tax effort.

A third, more common, option is *to assign to the local jurisdictions some taxing power* and to complement, if necessary, the revenue raised locally with some grants from the national government. The taxing power given to the local jurisdictions can be provided by (a) assigning to them the exclusive use of some tax bases, (b) allowing them to share some bases with the national government and (c) allowing the local governments to 'piggy-back' on some national taxes. All of these alternatives are in use in some countries.

If specific tax bases were assigned to the local jurisdictions, the latter would in principle have the option of raising the level of their spending by raising their own tax revenue. Their perception of the benefit and cost of this action would presumably guide their decision vis-à-vis marginal spending and taxing.

The *assignment of tax bases* to local jurisdictions must take into account certain considerations. The first is the importance of objectives (other than raising revenue) being pursued through taxation. The more important these other objectives are in connection with particular tax bases, the less advantageous it is to leave these tax bases to local jurisdictions. For example, the more weight the government assigns to the objective of income redistribution (through progressive taxation) or to stabilization (through the use of built-in stabilizers), the better it is to leave certain tax bases, such as the progressive income tax and the corporate income tax, to the national government.

The second is the mobility of the tax bases. If a tax base can escape taxation at the local level by easily moving to another jurisdiction, that base is not a good candidate for local taxation. Thus the more mobile the tax base, the greater the argument for keeping it at the national level.

Third, the more important the economies of scale in tax administration for a given tax, the stronger the argument for leaving that tax to the *national* government. Economies of scale may depend on informational requirements (for example, the need for a national taxpayer identification number), on technical requirements (for example, the use of large computers) or on other factors. This consideration would call for the value-added tax and for the global income tax to be nationally collected taxes.

Given the above premises, we can quickly survey the assignment of tax bases, starting from the simplest and moving to the more difficult ones.

Import and Export Taxes

Economists generally consider these taxes as inefficient and undesirable sources of revenue, but they still account for a large share of revenue in developing countries. These taxes should always be imposed by the national government to reduce the possibility of major distortions being introduced within the country by differential foreign trade taxes imposed by different jurisdictions.

Taxes on Land and on Real Property

Land and *existing* structures are among the most immobile of tax bases. Land cannot move because of tax factors, nor can existing buildings. Where they are used, taxes on real properties are often, but not always, imposed by local jurisdictions. Of course, while land and existing structures cannot move, *new* structures will not be built if the jurisdiction taxes them considerably more than other jurisdictions. Thus, while old structures cannot move out, new structures may not move in. This limits the rates that can be imposed on properties. Assessment of property values to determine the tax liability often creates major difficulties.[46] Some countries assess the property values nationally but let the local jurisdictions determine the tax rate.

Natural Resource Taxes

Because natural resources are immobile, one could argue that, as with land and existing buildings, natural resources could easily be taxed by the subnational governments in which they are located. However, because (a) natural resources are concentrated in particular areas, (b) revenue from them fluctuates and (c) these taxes, if collected locally, could make a particular region an attractive place to move to as a result of its presumably better public services, it has been argued that these taxes should be assigned to the national government (Shah and Qureshi, 1994, p. 20). One problem with this conclusion is that the subnational governments that control the resource-rich areas are often reluctant to give away their claims to these resources. Major political problems have developed in some federations (Canada, Russia and Nigeria) over who should benefit from these resources. Decentralization is likely to reinforce the local claims over these resources. However, if the political obstacles can be surmounted, these taxes should go to the national government.

Sales Taxes

Among the sales taxes, the single-stage taxes (excises and retail) must be distinguished from the multi-stage ones (turnover and value-added taxes). Excise and retail sales taxes can be assigned to local jurisdictions, provided that neighboring jurisdictions do not use highly different rates.[47] If a jurisdiction uses higher rates than its neighbors, it will encourage its own citizens to shop in the lower-rate jurisdictions. Major factors are the vicinity of the other jurisdictions, the cost of travel and the value of the goods purchased.[48] Generally competition among jurisdictions limits, to some extent, the scope for rate differentials and thus it limits the freedom of action of local jurisdictions.

Retail sales taxes and excise taxes are generally relatively simple taxes. However, in economies with many small sellers, which characterizes most developing countries, retail sales taxes may be difficult to administer, especially if the rates are high. For this reason retail sales taxes are not likely to generate much revenue in developing countries. Local excises, however, have proved to be very useful revenue sources for subnational governments. Gasoline, alcoholic products, cars, hotels and public utilities may provide convenient tax bases for subnational governments.

Imposed with a credit mechanism, value-added taxes are generally rebated on exports and imposed on imports because they follow the so-called 'destination principle'. This principle stipulates that these taxes should be paid by the final consumers and, thus, should not distort trade relations. The application of the destination principle requires border checks by the jurisdiction that imposes the tax. However it is neither feasible nor desirable to impose border checks on trade *within* a country because this would impose excessive costs and would impede trade flows within the country. For these reasons value-added taxes are best left as the responsibility of national governments, especially in developing countries.[49]

Personal Income Taxes

These can be global or schedular. In other words they can be imposed on the total income received by a taxpayer, by combining wages and salaries, interest and dividends received and income from all other activities, or they can be imposed separately on each type of income.

Schedular income taxes can be used by the subnational jurisdictions of developing countries if the taxes on incomes such as interest, dividends, and wages and salaries are withheld at source by those who pay these incomes and the taxes withheld become final taxes. However the tax rates must be competitive, otherwise individuals will invest in other jurisdictions.

For global income taxes to operate well, it is necessary that all the incomes that the taxpayer receives from different sources and jurisdictions be combined before the tax is calculated. The tax administration of the jurisdiction where the taxpayer resides is unlikely to have information about income earned outside the jurisdiction unless this information is provided by the national government. Therefore tax evasion can be significant. For this reason it is better to leave this tax base to the national government, which is in a better position to get the relevant information.[50]

Business activities may be associated with small establishments or with large enterprises. Small, family-type establishments often do not keep good records of their transactions and could thus be taxed on the basis of presumptive principles. For example, they may pay a business tax, which may be assessed on the basis of gross sales, number of employees, floor space, or some other criteria. For this kind of activity local jurisdictions often have as much information as (or more than) the national government. As a consequence these taxes can be imposed as efficiently at the local level as at the national level. Furthermore an argument can be made that they reflect benefits received.

For corporate income taxes on larger establishments, however, the situation is different. Often they have branches in various parts of the country, they may trade with other countries, they may buy inputs from businesses in other jurisdictions and sell their output in other jurisdictions. They are also more sensitive to tax factors. Therefore, in developing countries, it is better to leave this tax to the national authorities.

Other Taxes and Fees

In addition to the main tax categories discussed above, there are many smaller tax bases that lend themselves more easily to exploitation by local governments. These range from relatively important ones (such as those related to the use of cars) to relatively insignificant ones (such as license fees for dogs). A better use of fees for activities that require some use of social services (such as education, health and commercial activities) can provide important resources which come in the form of benefit received and are, thus, consistent with the basic principles behind decentralization.

The conclusion that can be derived from this survey of tax assignments is that there are serious limitations to the tax revenue that local governments can raise on their own if they limit themselves to taxes that are efficient, easy to administer and of a benefit-received nature. Most local jurisdictions raise only a fraction, and sometimes a small fraction, of their revenue needs from own tax sources. Furthermore the revenue raised is often collected with taxes which are relatively inefficient and poorly administered, and which may bear little relationship to benefit received. This conclusion must be related to the question raised earlier: if decentralization is defended, not on political grounds, but on grounds that it improves the allocation of resources on the expenditure side, how much of that efficiency gain is lost when the financing of that expenditure is done in ways that impose significant welfare costs on the economy?[51] This question can only be answered on a case-by-case basis, but is one that deserves to be asked when a policy of active decentralization is pursued.

Besides the revenue raised through own or shared taxes, local governments often need additional revenue that they obtain from grants, from the central government or from borrowing. Earlier we discussed some of the implications for efficiency and for stability of these alternatives. Especially in developing countries one could make an inventory of practices which have distorted the allocation of resources or have created macroeconomic problems. These practices, of course, are not discussed in the theoretical work on fiscal federalism.

CONCLUDING REMARKS

This chapter has reviewed, in a somewhat selective way, some major issues that arise in the decentralization of governmental spending activities. It started with a mention of the factors that have led to the recent popularity of decentralization. With some notable exceptions (for example, the United Kingdom), many countries have been undergoing a process of decentralization of the activities of the public sector. This process aims at providing more freedom for local jurisdictions in order to increase the efficiency and the accountability of public spending. The fact that this process is taking place in many places reflects the prevalent view that decentralization conveys important economic and political benefits. Under the right circumstances, decentralization can be expected to lead to increased efficiency and accountability.

This chapter focuses on some of the circumstances that may derail the process and perhaps lead to lower-than-expected results. It argues that it is especially in the developing countries that, more frequently, the institutional and social underpinnings necessary for decentralization to succeed are not in place. When this is the case, gains in efficiency may be limited or non-existent, and economies that have developed structural fiscal deficits may find it harder to adjust. At times some of the elements of the decentralization process may themselves have contributed to the disequilibrium in the fiscal accounts.

This chapter has also argued that the traditional discussion about the role of fiscal decentralization in stabilization is somewhat off the mark because, in today's world, the problem is not how to counter economic cycles but how to remove structural deficits. This is often the main problem in developing countries and in many industrial countries, such as Canada, Belgium, Italy and many others (Tanzi and Fanizza, 1995).

This chapter has also discussed the taxes that can be assigned to the local governments so that they have the means to finance at least part of their activities. Unfortunately it is not easy, especially in developing countries, to assign to local governments taxes that are sufficiently robust to cover their needs and that are also good taxes. Even when they are good taxes, their administration may not be efficient. For this reason various sharing arrangements concerning taxes collected by the central government have developed. These arrangements are at times supplemented by explicit grants. They make the local governments dependent on the central government for revenue and thus defy, to some extent, the purpose of decentralization. And they constrain the freedom that the central government has in pursuing tax reform.

In practice, and especially in developing countries, local jurisdictions are often in great need of resources additional to those they can get from the sources discussed above. They get these resources through various kinds of borrowing, which they occasionally find difficult to service. This puts pressure on the central government (or the central bank) to step in and finance the debts, and leads to various macroeconomic problems.

Decentralization is a kind of contract that often is not spelled out precisely in all its details and implications. If the constitutional or legal aspects are very clear and are enforced, if the local governments are given access to the necessary resources, if they have adequate PEM systems in place so that they can both monitor and control the pace and the allocation of spending, and if the local bureaucrats are of quality equal to that of the national bureaucrats, decentralization can live up to its promise. Otherwise the results tend to be disappointing.

NOTES

1. On the other hand, in several northern European countries, fundamental changes in the structure of intergovernmental fiscal relations took place in the 1970s.
2. See Herblock cartoon in the *Washington Post* of 9 March 1995, p. A20.
3. For a good discussion of these issues within the European context, see CEPR (1993).
4. Interestingly enough the United Kingdom, which, in a way, led the conservative trend, has gone against the decentralization trend. Especially since 1988, it has sharply reduced the independence of the local governments. The resources raised by these governments fell from 45 per cent of their expenditure in 1988–9 to 15 per cent in 1993–4.
5. The growth of public choice literature has also increased the professional attention paid to decentralization.
6. In practice this sharp distinction is not always possible or significant.
7. To the extent that countries large in area, such as Russia, tend to be less homogeneous than smaller countries, the presumption is that the former should be more decentralized. However even small countries can have a lot of regional diversity, thus creating a presumption for decentralization as shown by Switzerland or even Andorra which, with a territory of 400 square kilometers, has a very decentralized form of government.
8. For example, the policies of Peter the Great in Russia and Louis XIV in France.
9. The classic public goods, such as the clocks on the bell towers, or the lighthouses, are examples of pure public goods with limited spatial characteristics.

10. Technology is likely to change the spatial characteristics of public goods or to create new public goods covering different spaces.
11. Artana and López Murphy (1994, p. 16) have reported that Denmark, in the 1970s, did change the size of its local units, considering them too small. Size was considered important in relation to administrative costs. See also Jorgen Lotz (1995).
12. Of course it is likely that there will be market failure, even in this surrogate market.
13. This emulation may be forced by individuals voting with their feet. In the Scandinavian countries experimentation has been formally legalized with the introduction of 'free municipalities'. A municipality can apply for the right to specific experimentation in a given area (for example, schools) and the outcome is formally evaluated and published.
14. For a discussion of the pros and cons of decentralization, see Boadway *et al.* (1994).
15. However voting at the various local levels and the establishment of various committees may better reveal local preferences and, thus, improve the supply of services.
16. At times, in particular countries, the local representatives of central government authority have been subservient 'kommisare' or party bosses eager to please the central committee. Examples of neglected regional interests and inefficiencies of the central plan under the former Soviets are plentiful.
17. One could argue that contiguity of officials and clients might act as a check on local officials if it brings greater opportunity for scrutiny by those competing for public attention. This argument is not convincing.
18. For example, on 29 March 1995, the *Financial Times* reported that, while Governor Orestes Quércia was Governor of São Paulo (1986–94), 'an efficient patronage system rewarded supporters with government jobs. After the central bank took over [the state-owned] Banespa [Bank], it discovered that the president's office had 1,390 workers on its payroll. The vast majority had no work' (p. 4).
19. The subnational governments in Germany and in the Scandinavian countries, for example, are probably as competently staffed as the national governments.
20. The size of countries is, of course, also the result of historical accidents. In the 1950s some literature dealt with the question of whether there is an optimal size of countries.
21. This point is much more relevant to provinces or states than to municipalities. States may be as different in size as, say, Texas and Delaware.
22. The first of these two options is preferable in theory. The Scandinavian countries provide evidence that this option is not completely absurd.
23. This is the case in several Latin American countries, including Colombia and Peru, and in other regions.
24. This problem also exists at the national level, but it is more serious at the local level. For example, Argentina is putting in place a state-of-the-art PEM system at the national level. At the local level, however, the PEM systems remain primitive in many local jurisdictions.
25. This was the conclusion of a recent mission to a Latin American country. The mission got some (dated) information on the money spent at the local level, but it could not get the information on how it had been spent. This situation is far from rare. The difficulty in compiling an economically meaningful picture on the fiscal accounts of subnational governments (for example, as experienced in the Fund Government Finance Statistics) is not one merely of lack of consistency in statistical treatment, but is symptomatic of a more general problem.
26. The existence of this 'hidden debt' originating in the activities of local institutions has been a major problem in Italy. The treasury minister is occasionally faced with having to meet obligations that he did not even know existed. In Colombia banks accord 'grace periods' to local authorities for interest payments on borrowing that correspond to the terms of office of non-re-electable mayors. In other words this is a fairly common problem at the local level.
27. Thus California and Texas, on the one hand, and Delaware, on the other, cannot both be optimal, given their marked difference in size.
28. In Latin America the more fiscally decentralized countries (Argentina and Brazil) tend to have larger public sectors because they followed the European example in setting up large social security programs.

29. The financing of subnational jurisdictions is discussed in the next section.
30. See Musgrave (1959) and Oates (1972) for the classic arguments. More recently some studies have dealt with stabilization issues within the European Union. See, inter alia, Commission of the European Communities (1993).
31. This procyclical behavior was first described by Hansen and Perloff as far back as 1944. More recently Bayoumi (1992) has provided some evidence. For a good description of these issues, see de Callatay and Ribe (1994).
32. For arguments, see especially Gramlich (1987).
33. This is certainly the case of Argentina and Brazil. In Canada provincial governments have run large deficits and have accumulated substantial debts. The same experience is shared by Italy's subnational jurisdictions or entities. In Brazil the net debt of subnational governments is close to $60 billion at the present time.
34. In some countries a political cycle has been identified at the local level with taxes falling and expenditure rising before elections. Of course such cycles are not limited to subnational governments.
35. This externality is an example of a general problem that has been receiving some attention in the rational choice literature.
36. Once again the experiences of Argentina, Brazil and Italy since 1979 provide relevant examples. In these situations there are always local suppliers available to provide the services on credit or local banks willing to extend loans.
37. See also Ahmad (1997).
38. A good description of the revenue sharing arrangements in Argentina is provided by Liuksila and Schwartz (1997) and by Porto and Sanguinetti (1993); for information on tax assignments in Brazil, see Bonfim and Shah (1994); for Russia, see Bahl (1994); for Colombia, see Ferreira and Valenzuela (1993).
39. In the 1990–93 period, the central government reduced the number of its employees from about 550 000 to about 230 000. Of this decline, 86 000 represented a net reduction and 210 000 transfers to the provincial jurisdictions to accompany the transfer of the responsibility for health and education.
40. Between 1990 and 1993 the provinces increased their spending on personnel from $7294 million to $12 676 million, and their total spending from $14 101 million to $25 696 million (Ministerio de Economía y Obras y Servicios Públicos, 1994).
41. As Lane summarizes his paper, 'Effective market discipline requires that capital markets be open, that information on the borrower's existing liabilities be readily available, that no bailout be anticipated, and that the borrower respond to market signals' (1993, p. 53).
42. This conclusion implies not just that each jurisdiction pays for its benefit but that each resident receives benefits equal to his taxes. Otherwise some taxpayers will vote with their feet and, as long as they do, the result will not be Pareto-optimal!
43. See, inter alia, Musgrave and Musgrave (1984), Oates (1972), Tanzi (1995); various papers or books by Bird (1986), McLure (1983), Boadway, Shah and Qureshi (1994), and others.
44. For the United States the special factors which have contributed to the existing tax arrangements in the local governments are discussed in Tanzi (1995, ch. 3). The role of these special factors implies that the US experience is not easily transferable elsewhere.
45. In China this policy has created a major erosion of the tax system. On the other hand, a variant of this policy seems to work in Germany.
46. Except in a handful of relatively developed countries, these taxes have been very unproductive. This is especially so in developing countries. Most of the revenue from these taxes comes from urban properties.
47. However it is difficult to identify these taxes as benefit taxes.
48. See Tanzi (1995, ch. 3) for a discussion of these issues.
49. Some countries, such as Brazil, have tried to levy value-added taxes at the state level, but the results in terms of efficiency have not been very good. There are many examples of the sharing of sales tax bases and there are examples where these taxes are levied only at one level of government. In India and in the United States sales taxes are collected by the states, although both the federal government and the states collect excises in the United

States. In Brazil all three levels (federal, state and municipal) collect some version of the sales tax. In Argentina the national government collects a value-added tax, which is shared with the provinces, while the municipalities collect a cascading turnover tax.

50. In the United States special factors allow both the states and the counties or municipalities to tax global income by exploiting information available to the national authorities. These special factors are often missing in developing countries.

51. Of course, if decentralization is justified on political grounds, the question becomes irrelevant.

BIBLIOGRAPHY

Ahmad, Ehtisham (ed.) (1997), *Financing Decentralized Expenditures: An International Comparison of Grants*, Cheltenham, UK: Edward Elgar.

Artana, Daniel and Ricardo López Murphy (1994), *Fiscal Decentralization: Some Lessons for Latin America*, Buenos Aires: FIEL.

Bahl, Roy W. (1994), 'Revenue Sharing in Russia', Reprint Series, 61 (February), Georgia State University, College of Business Administration.

Bahl, Roy W. and Johannes F. Linn (1992), *Urban Public Finance in Developing Countries*, New York: Oxford University Press for World Bank.

Bayoumi, Tamin A. (1992), 'U.S. State and Local Government Finances Over the Current Cycle', IMF Working Paper 92/112 (December), International Monetary Fund.

Bird, Richard (1986), *Federal Finance in Comparative Perspective*, Toronto: Canadian Tax Foundation.

—— (1994), 'Decentralizing Infrastructure: For Good or For Ill?', Policy Research Working Paper 1258 (February), World Bank.

Boadway, Robin and David E. Wildasin (1984), *Public Sector Economics*, Boston: Little, Brown and Company.

—— Sandra Roberts and Anwar Shah (1994), 'The Reform of Fiscal Systems in Developing and Emerging Market Economies: A Federalism Perspective', Policy Research Working Paper 1259 (February), World Bank.

Bonfim, Antulio and Anwar Shah (1994), 'Macroeconomic Management and the Division of Powers in Brazil: Perspectives for the 1990s', *World Development*, 22 (April), 535–42.

Brennan, Geoffrey and James M. Buchanan (1980), *The Power to Tax: Analytical Foundations of a Fiscal Constitution*, Cambridge: Cambridge University Press.

CEPR (1993), *Making Sense of Subsidiarity: How Much Centralization for Europe?*, London: CEPR.

Chelliah, Raja J. (1991), 'Intergovernmental Fiscal Relations and Macroeconomic Management in India' (mimeo).

Commission of the European Communities (1993), 'The Economics of Community Public Finance', *European Economy*, Reports and Studies 5, Directorate-General for Economic and Financial Affairs, Brussels.

Cremer, Jacques, Antonio Estache and Paul Seabright (1994), 'The Decentralization of Public Services: Lessons from the Theory of the Firm', Policy Research Working Paper 1345 (August), World Bank.

de Callatay, E. and F. Ribe (1994), *How Intergovernmental Fiscal Relations Affect Macroeconomic Stabilization: An Overview*, Washington, DC: International Monetary Fund.

de la Cruz, Rafael and Armando Barrios (eds) (1994), *Federalismo Fiscal: El Costo de la Descentralización en Venezuela*, Caracas: Nueva Sociedad.

Ehdaie, Jaber (1994), 'Fiscal Decentralization and the Size of Government: An Extension With Evidence From Cross-Country Data', Policy Research Working Paper 1387 (December), World Bank.

Ferreira, Ana María and Luis Carlos Valenzuela (1993), *Descentralizacion Fiscal. El Caso Colombiano*, Serie Política Fiscal 49, Santiago: CEPAL.

FIEL (1993), *Hacia Una Nueva Organización del Federalismo Fiscal en la Argentina*, Buenos Aires: FIEL.

Gramlich, Edward M. (1987), 'Federalism and Federal Deficit Reduction', *National Tax Journal* 40(3) (September), 299–313.

Hirsch, Werner (1968), 'The Supply of Urban Public Services', in Harvey S. Perloff and Lowdon Wingo, Jr. (eds), *Issues in Urban Economics*, Baltimore: Johns Hopkins Press.

Israel, Arturo (1992), 'Issues for Infrastructure Management in the 1990s', World Bank Discussion Paper 171, World Bank.

Lane, Timothy D. (1993), 'Market Discipline', *IMF Staff Papers*, 40 (1) (March), 53–88.

Liuksila, Claire and Gerd Schwartz (1997), 'Argentina', in Teresa Ter-Minassian (ed.), *Fiscal Federalism in Theory and Practice*, Washington DC: International Monetary Fund, pp. 387–422.

Lotz, Jorgen (1995), *Equalization Grants to Local Governments in Denmark and Other Scandinavian Countries*, Washington, DC: International Monetary Fund.

Ma, Jun (1995), 'Macroeconomic Management and Intergovernmental Relations in China'. Policy Research Working Paper 1408 (January), World Bank.

McLure, Charles E., Jr. (ed.) (1983), *Tax Assignment in Federal Countries*, Canberra: Centre for Research on Federal Financial Relations, Australian National University Press.

Ministerio de Economía y Obras y Servicios Públicos (1994), *Cambios Estructurales en la Relacion Nacion-Provincias*, Buenos Aires.

Murphy, Kevin M., Andrei Schleifer and Robert W. Vishny (1991), 'The Allocation of Talent: Implications for Growth', *Quarterly Journal of Economics*, 106 (May), 503–30.

Musgrave, Richard A. (1959), *The Theory of Public Finance: A Study in Public Economy*, New York: McGraw-Hill.

Musgrave, Richard A. and Peggy B. Musgrave (1984), *Public Finance in Theory and Practice*, New York: McGraw-Hill.

Oates, Wallace E. (1972), *Fiscal Federalism*, New York: Harcourt Brace Jovanovich.

—— (1994), 'The Potential and Perils of Fiscal Decentralization', (unpublished).

Porto, Alberto and Pablo Sanguinetti (1993), 'Decentralizacion Fiscal en América Latina: El Caso Argentino', Serie Política Fiscal 45, Santiago: CEPAL,

Prud'homme, Rémy (1994), 'On the Dangers of Decentralization', Policy Research Working Paper 1252 (February), World Bank.

Putnam, Robert D. (1993), *Making Democracy Work. Civic Traditions in Modern Italy*, Princeton: Princeton University Press.

Shah, Anwar and Zia Qureshi (1994), 'Intergovernmental Fiscal Relations in Indonesia: Issues and Reform Options', World Bank Discussion Papers 239 (May), World Bank.

Shome, Parthasarathi (1994), *Fiscal Federalism – Revenue, Expenditure and Macro*

Management: Selected Latin-American Experiences and Recent Discussions in India, Washington, DC: International Monetary Fund.

Tanzi, Vito, Chapter 6 of this book.

—— (1995), *Taxation in an Integrating World*, Washington, DC: The Brookings Institution.

—— (1995), 'Basic Issues of Decentralization and the Tax Assignment', in Ehtisham Ahmad, Gao Qiang and Vito Tanzi (eds), *Reforming China's Public Finances*, Washington, DC: International Monetary Fund, 164–77.

Tanzi, Vito and Domenico Fanizza (1995), 'Fiscal Deficit and Public Debt in Industrial Countries', IMF Working Paper, WP/95/49, International Monetary Fund.

Tiebout, C.M. (1956), 'A Pure Theory of Local Expenditures', *Journal of Political Economy* (5) (October), 416–24.

15. The budget deficit in transition: a cautionary note

During central planning, it was not really meaningful to speak of *fiscal* policy and *public* finance since these concepts imply the existence of *private* finance and thus a significant *private* sector.[1] In that era, all was public in a way. However, many 'fiscal' functions, as defined in market economies, were carried out not by government but by state enterprises. These enterprises often provided their workers with housing, hospital care, vocational training, kindergarten facilities, shops, pensions, various forms of welfare assistance, employment, and so forth. They were also responsible for much 'public' investment. Because the state enterprises were required to hire workers even when they did not need them, *official* unemployment was non-existent. As a consequence no programs existed to protect unemployed workers. In economies in transition, state enterprises are still carrying out many of these fiscal functions and are still hoarding workers. For the transformation to market economies to be completed, most legitimate social functions must be shifted from the state enterprises to the government. As this shift takes place, spending by the enterprises will fall and spending by the government will rise.[2]

In spite of occasional divergent views, most economists agree that, in market economies, the fiscal deficit is a useful guide for assessing fiscal policy. A large deficit indicates that (unless a strong case to the contrary can be made) fiscal policy should become more restrictive. The *concept* of fiscal deficit implies that government activities can be sharply delineated from those of the private sector.[3] Thus expenditures and revenues are either public or private. The *measure* of the fiscal deficit requires that the difference between what the public sector spends and what it collects can be accurately calculated. With full employment, if the public sector spends more, the private sector must spend less, unless the economy is able to attract foreign saving. Thus the existence of a fiscal deficit implies some (unwanted) crowding out of the private sector unless Ricardian equivalence or a Keynesian multiplier can be assumed to operate.

BUDGET DEFICIT LIMITS AND PERVERSE INCENTIVES

There are several reasons for caution when using this concept to guide policy action during the transition. Some of these reasons are conceptual. Others deal with measurement problems. Still others originate from the possibility that strict limits on an inadequate measure of the fiscal deficit may create perverse incentives, which may slow down the transformation.

Transferring Social Expenditure Responsibility

State enterprises in economies in transition continue to dominate economic activity and provide social services for workers and their families. Some of these services are provided in place of higher money wages. Others are provided in place of higher budgetary expenditure. In other words these enterprises continue to perform some functions that in market economies are financed through the government budget.

The transition to a market economy requires that the budget assume the responsibility for those social functions that the country wishes to finance publicly.[4] This transfer to the budget should occur regardless of whether the state enterprises are privatized or not. The faster it occurs, the easier it will be for the enterprises to be privatized or to become economically viable while remaining state-owned.

The transfer of these functions to the budget will increase budgetary expenditure and, unless revenue is raised correspondingly, will also increase the budget deficit.[5] Thus the transfer should also reduce the credit needs of state enterprises. For most of these countries, however, there is little solid knowledge about the potential impact on the budget of a total or partial transfer of these functions.[6] In Russia 'the government appears not to have quantified the dimensions of this problem or planned a solution' (Wallich, 1992, p. 7). The more important are these functions and the faster and the larger is their transfer to the budget, the greater will be the growth of budgetary expenditure. Thus ex ante limits on the size of the budget deficit should explicitly allow for the budgetary cost of transferring some of these functions from the state enterprises to the budget.[7] The possibility must be recognized that a limit on the budget deficit that ignores this transfer might be met by the government *delaying the transfer* of these social functions from the enterprises to the budget. This delay would slow down the process of transformation but would not reduce credit expansion if the banking system continues to react to the needs of the enterprises.

If a decision were made to subsidize some loss-making state enterprises, it would be better economic policy if they were subsidized through the budget rather than through soft and cheap loans from the banking system.[8] However subsidies financed through the budget increase the budget deficit, and cheap loans do not. It would be unrealistic to assume that subsidies to enterprises, whether through the budget or through cheap and soft loans, could be completely and permanently abolished in the short run. Some of these enterprises (especially those in the defense industry) will be able to restructure and become economically viable only if they receive financial support for some time. It would also be unrealistic to assume that those who make or influence economic policy would look at cheap credit given directly through the banking system in the same way as they look at subsidies financed through the budget.[9] Thus the argument that has occasionally been made, that the provision of subsidies through the banking system or the budget is only an accounting issue and would disappear if one measured the fiscal deficit in a comprehensive and economically sound way,[10] ignores the important point that economic policy is not always guided by the most economically correct concepts and that, in any case, the measurement of the all-embracing fiscal deficit is next to impossible under the circumstances prevailing in these countries. Thus the measured (budget) deficit is likely to continue exerting more influence over policy makers and public opinion, both within and outside the countries, than the true but unknown (fiscal) deficit. For this reason policy makers have an incentive to show a smaller budget deficit even when this action may conflict with other important economic and social objectives, such as the speed of transition to a market economy.

If the government raised taxes on state enterprises' profits at the same time that the banking system extended cheap or soft loans to these enterprises, the budget deficit would fall *without reducing monetary expansion*. This implies that focusing on the budget deficit may lead observers and policy makers to miss the underlying cause of monetary expansion and could lead to the apparently anomalous situation (experienced by Poland and, especially, Yugoslavia) of high inflation with the budget in surplus.

The Budget Deficit and Inflation

The relationship between inflation, the budget deficit and the public debt is also relevant to this discussion. To the extent that there is a domestic public debt, an increase in the *nominal* interest rate paid on the public debt will be reflected in government expenditure and in the size of the budget deficit even if the rate of the increase matches exactly the increase in inflation: in other words, even if the *real* interest rate does not change. Given a significant public debt and a potentially high but unknown *future* rate of inflation, it is difficult to predict the effect on the deficit if the government pays a given *real* interest rate on its debt. Given a real rate of interest, the rise in the deficit will be a direct function of the size of the debt and the level of the nominal interest rate which, in turn, will depend on the inflation rate. The effect of a change in the rate of inflation on the conventionally measured budget deficit could be very large.[11]

In the situation described above, a government that has an interest in showing a smaller budget deficit might be tempted to *repress* nominal interest rates, thus creating difficulties for the development of the financial sector and for the allocation of financial resources. Under inflationary conditions, concepts such as the operational or the primary deficit, which attempt to eliminate the impact of inflation on the deficit, may have to be used, but they will only correct the *budget* deficit rather than measure the true *fiscal* deficit. Furthermore these concepts have their own limitations.

The Budget Deficit and the Unemployment Rate

If state enterprises lay off redundant workers in order to improve their efficiency and, as a consequence, the government's spending for unemployment compensation increases, the change will cause the budget deficit to rise. The rise will depend on the level of unemployment compensation per worker and on the *number* of unemployed workers. For a given level of unemployment compensation per worker, the larger the adjustment in the workforce by the state enterprises, and thus the greater the number of unemployed workers, the larger will be the potential impact of this adjustment on the budget deficit. Should the government be excessively concerned about the size of its budget deficit, it may encourage the state enterprises to continue hoarding workers.

The potential impact of this factor on the budget deficits of countries in transition can be appreciated by the fact that falls in output that have, at times, been as large as, or larger than, 50 per cent of GDP have generally not resulted in corresponding increases in unemployment.[12] If these countries had behaved like market economies, they would have experienced unemployment rates not seen since the Great Depression of the 1930s.[13] As long as the state enterprises continue to hoard workers, they will not be able to restructure and become efficient and competitive. It will also be more difficult to privatize them.[14] However, when the enterprises fully adjust their employment to their greatly reduced production needs, and the governments take responsibility for financing the cost of unemployment, budgetary expenditures will go up. This increase must be taken into account in setting ex ante limits on the deficit, but it may be very difficult to forecast.

The Budget Deficit and the Exchange Rate

If a country devalues its official exchange rate, its interest payments on foreign debt *measured in domestic currency* will rise, thus increasing public spending, and government expenditure on imports measured in domestic currency will also rise. Both of these factors would tend to raise the budget deficit.[15] On the other hand, the devaluation will also increase the domestic value of exports by the public sector and the revenue from some taxes. However, if the proceeds from the public sector exports are outside the budget, even if the exporters are public institutions, the improvement will not be reflected directly in the budgetary accounts unless the exporters contribute significantly to tax revenue.[16] In other words the budget deficit will rise, and the rise will depend on the size of the devaluation.[17] Rigid ex ante limits on the measured size of the fiscal deficit (that is, limits on the budget deficit) might encourage the authorities to delay the needed exchange rate adjustment, especially when the external debt is large and the government's imports are significant.

Shifting Expenditures out of the Budget

Another perverse incentive that may arise from the attempt to show a smaller budget deficit or to stay below a too rigid limit is that of pushing expenditures out of the budget and into other parts of the public sector, whether extrabudgetary accounts or lower levels of government. Indeed extrabudgetary accounts have proliferated in many economies in transition, though information on them has been elusive. Also sizable expenditures have been shifted onto local government. In this context it may be worthwhile to quote from a study on fiscal decentralization in Russia by Christine Wallich (1992, p. 3):

> In the fiscal program for 1992, most of the major cuts were made in central government expenditures – centrally financed enterprise investment, producer and consumer subsidies, and defense. These cuts were followed by a decision to delegate an important part of social expenditures (early in 1992) and investment outlays (later on) to the subnational level. On the tax side, the budget envisages a marked increase in taxes, primarily on petroleum products and foreign trade. Thus, virtually all additional revenue will accrue to the *federal* government, while most of the additional social expenditures will emerge at the *subnational* level. (Original emphasis).

Wallich's conclusion is also worth citing: 'The basic strategy has been to "push the deficit downward" by shifting unfunded expenditure responsibilities down in the hope that the subnational level will do the cost cutting' (pp. 3–4).

These are just a few examples of the possibilities that call for caution in the use of the budget deficit in guiding economic policy during the transition. They do not exhaust the possibilities.[18] They all point to the need to ensure that perverse incentives are not created by reliance on narrow concepts of the deficit. These incentives will exist when the deficit covers only a part of the public sector and when the limits imposed on it are too rigid. In this case there will be an incentive to 'park' the deficit where it cannot be measured or to postpone structural adjustments that may tend to increase the size of the measured deficit.[19]

THE NEED TO SEPARATE FISCAL POLICY FROM MONETARY POLICY

A total and sharp separation between fiscal and monetary policy is next to impossible in any economy. There are always overlapping areas. For example, when central banks change the discount rate or engage in open market operations, these actions have an impact on the budget deficit. In general these two policies are less clearly separated in developing countries than in industrial countries. In Latin America, for example, the central banks have, in several cases, engaged in activities that have caused them to experience large quasi-fiscal deficits.[20] In Chile, for example, a quasi-fiscal deficit arose during the 1980s as a result of the central bank assuming the bad debts of commercial banks. This assumption was clearly a fiscal operation that could have been carried out by the budget if budgetary conditions at the time had been more sound. In other cases the central banks assumed the foreign debt of enterprises.

In general the less developed the institutions of a country, the more difficult it is to separate monetary and fiscal policies and the more difficult it is to measure the true size of the fiscal deficit. More often than not it is the weakness of the fiscal institutions (for example, the inability to raise the needed revenue) that forces the monetary institutions to assume a fiscal role. However making the budget deficit look better than it is also plays a role.

Normally economic policy is improved when monetary and fiscal policies are pursued according to their own specific roles. In this case, if an enterprise needs to be subsidized, the subsidy should be given through the budget. If this results in a budget deficit, the deficit should be financed by the country's treasury through the sale of bonds carrying market interest rates.[21]

The budget deficit is a much watched economic barometer. A larger deficit always sends warning signals, both domestically and internationally. Therefore countries have an incentive to limit its size either by genuine fiscal adjustment or by pursuing second-best policies, the result of which may be even more damaging than if the budget deficit had been allowed to rise. In other words the bias is almost always for showing a budget deficit that appears smaller than it would be if the true fiscal deficit were correctly measured. At times this reduction is achieved through policies that do not reduce the real or underlying *fiscal* deficit but only the measured *budget* deficit. In other words gimmicks are used to lower the budget deficit artificially.[22]

During the transition, to the extent possible, it is important to contain the inflation rate without resorting to direct price controls.[23] To achieve this objective the most important macroeconomic instrument for both market economies and economies in transition is credit expansion, not the budget deficit. Once total credit expansion is determined, the countries should be encouraged to continue improving the efficiency of the economy as well as the fiscal accounts. They should be encouraged to reduce particular categories of public expenditure, to make others more productive and to raise government revenue in an efficient way to contain the public sector fiscal deficit. They should also be encouraged to speed up the various adjustments mentioned above, even when these adjustments may result in increases in (measured) budget deficits. Important among these adjustments is the transfer to the government of the essential social functions shouldered by the state enterprises.

Another important point to recognize is that which makes the economies in transition different from normal market economies for given total credit: an increase of the (measured) budget deficit does not necessarily crowd out what, in market economies, is the private sector. Much of the credit expansion goes to the state enterprises and the government, and only a small residual goes to the emerging private sector. A large reallocation of credit between the budget and state enterprises can take place without necessarily affecting the private sector. This reallocation could be fully consistent with the objectives of the transformation. If state enterprises (a) shed redundant workers, (b) transfer to the government responsibility for *essential* social functions, (c) no longer finance *non-essential* social functions (such as vacations for workers), and (d) compensate the workers for a fraction of these reductions through some adjustment in the level of nominal wages, then the net result of these changes could very well be a larger budget deficit *with a more efficient economy*. This change could also be achieved without additional credit expansion if the additional credit to the budget to finance its new responsibilities were compensated by lower credit to the state enterprises to reflect their reduced social responsibilities.

CONCLUDING REMARKS

The chapter has shown that, in situations were the role of the government has not yet been determined, where the budget must assume some responsibilities now carried by state enterprises and where 'property rights' *within* the public sector are ill-defined, the budget deficit, which is calculated by looking at the behavior of *budgetary* revenue and expenditure, has less informational value than is generally assumed. This deficit may often differ widely from the true fiscal deficit for the whole public sector and may even move in a different direction. The true fiscal deficit would include the fiscal activities of the state enterprises and the central bank.

Under particular circumstances, containing the *budget* deficit will not necessarily make more resources available to the private sector and may even slow down the structural reforms necessary to make the transition successful. The above conclusion should not, however, be understood to mean that fiscal policy is irrelevant. If there is a message that follows from the discussion, it is (a) that the most comprehensive and economically sound measure of the *fiscal* (not budget) deficit should be used to guide policy and (b) that the transfer of functions from state enterprises to the government will need to be taken into account in setting limits to the size of the deficit. If this is not possible, the budget deficit should be de-emphasized. In any case structural reforms and total credit expansion must receive the full attention they deserve.

NOTES

1. Recall that, in market economies, public sector activity is largely justified by (private) market failure. See Stiglitz (1989) and Musgrave (1959).
2. This does not imply that the government needs to assume *all* the functions now carried out by the enterprises.
3. It also implies that the fiscal activities of the government can be separated from the monetary activities. For example, the fiscal activities of central banks must be assessed as part of *fiscal* policy.
4. The functions not taken over by the budget should no longer be the responsibility of the public sector and the state enterprises. By adjusting money wages, workers could be given greater discretion over the use of the *total* compensation they receive, while the state enterprises could stop having to provide social services.
5. Throughout this chapter, the term 'budget deficit' is used for that part of the fiscal deficit that is actually accounted for by the budget. This is the measure of deficit normally reported in newspapers and in government reports. The theoretical concept of the fiscal deficit is much more comprehensive and much more difficult to measure (see various papers in Blejer and Cheasty, 1993). It extends to the whole public sector and includes quasi-fiscal deficits.
6. There is no available estimate of the magnitude of these social functions. The World Bank attempted to quantify them for Russia. The assumption is that they are quite important.
7. These limits may be self-imposed or negotiated with international institutions or other creditors.
8. In Russia, the central bank subsidized the state enterprises in particular sectors through subsidized credit and, in the process, created inflationary pressures.
9. For one thing, it is difficult to calculate the subsidy element of subsidized credit. See, for example, the paper by Michael Wattleworth, 'Credit Subsidies in Budgetary Lending: Computation, Effects and Fiscal Implications', in Blejer and Chu (1988). Also subsidies, given through the budget, would most likely be associated with more careful, or at least more politically debated, decisions about which enterprises should be subsidized.
10. This measure would count the social expenditure by state enterprises in the same way as

budgetary expenditures. It would also count the subsidies given by the banking system as public spending. See, for example, Begg and Portes (1992).

11. The relationship between the fiscal deficit, public debt and the inflation rate was discussed in Tanzi *et al*. (1987). For references to the impact of this factor on the fiscal deficit of Latin American countries, see Tanzi (1992).

12. The situation is changing. For example, the unemployment rate in Hungary rose from less than 1 per cent in the first half of 1990 to more than 11 per cent in September 1992. In Bulgaria it rose from 1.6 per cent in 1990 to 14 per cent in 1992; in Poland from 6.3 per cent in 1990 to 13.5 per cent in October 1992; and in Romania from zero in 1990 to 10 per cent in 1992. For the fall in output up to 1991, see IMF (1992a, p. 46). For the estimated fall in 1992, see IMF (1992b, p. 19).

13. Rates of 25 per cent or higher were recorded.

14. In fact privatization may in some cases raise the size of the fiscal deficit if the social expenditures that the government has to take over from the state enterprises exceed the revenue from the sale of the enterprises.

15. If the government is unable to pay the interest on the foreign debt, there will be a difference between accrued and cash measures of the budget deficit. Domestic arrears to and from the government also create differences between cash and accrued measures of the budget deficit.

16. The difficulties of the central governments of many of these countries, in controlling the accounts and the actions of the whole public sector, indicate that the budget may not be the beneficiary of devaluation.

17. This discussion points to the importance of bringing the foreign trade area within the tax net. For example, it is important for imports to be subjected to the value-added tax.

18. For example, a solution to the bad debt problem of the commercial banks and the arrears among enterprises might be delayed by the fact that the solution would raise the budget deficit. Begg and Portes (1992) have argued that, if the deficit were properly measured, these policies would not change its size. However the assumption of the bad debt of the banks by the government, by replacing bad assets with goods assets, would allow them to give more loans that might increase the liquidity of the economy.

19. There will also be an incentive to reduce the cash deficit by postponing payments, thus increasing arrears.

20. See the paper by Fry (1993).

21. When the financial market is not well developed, or when the credibility of the government is not good, this source of financing is not available. However, if the deficit is to be financed through inflationary finance, it may still be better if this finance is directly allocated to the budget and the budget finances the various activities including subsidies to state enterprises.

22. This is not only a problem of economies in transition. In fact it has been a frequent problem in adjustment programs. See Tanzi (1989).

23. However, because of the changes in relative prices during the transition, it may not be wise to aim for an inflation rate that is too low since this would require a fall in prices in some sectors.

REFERENCES

Begg, David and Richard Portes (1992), 'Enterprise Debt and Economic Transformation: Financial Restructuring of the State Sector in Central and Eastern Europe', CEPR Working Paper No. 695, Centre for Economic Policy Research.

Blejer, Mario and Adrienne Cheasty (eds) (1993), *How to Measure the Fiscal Deficit: Analytical and Methodological Issues*, Washington, DC: International Monetary Fund.

Blejer, Mario and Ke-young Chu (eds) (1988), *Measurement of Fiscal Impact: Meth-odological Issues*, IMF Occasional Paper No. 59, Washington: International Monetary Fund.

Fry, Maxwell (1993), 'The Fiscal Abuse of Central Banks', IMF Working Paper, WP/93/58, International Monetary Fund.

International Monetary Fund (1992a), *World Economic Outlook*, Washington: International Monetary Fund, October.

—— (1992b), *World Economic Outlook*, Washington: International Monetary Fund, December.

Musgrave, Richard A. (1959), *The Theory of Public Finance: A Study in Public Economy*, New York: McGraw-Hill.

Stiglitz, Joseph (1989), *The Economic Role of the State*, Oxford: Basil Blackwell.

Tanzi, Vito (1989), 'Fiscal Policy, Growth and the Design of Stabilization Programs', in Mario Blejer and Ke-young Chu (eds), *Fiscal Policy, Stabilization and Growth*, Washington, DC: International Monetary Fund.

—— (1992), 'Fiscal Policy and Economic Reconstruction in Latin America', *World Development*, 20 (May) 641–57.

Tanzi, Vito, Mario Blejer and Mario O. Teijeiro (1987), 'Inflation and the Measure of Fiscal Deficits', *IMF Staff Papers*, 34 (December), 711–38.

Wallich, Christine, I. (1992), *Fiscal Decentralization: Intergovernmental Relations in Russia*, Washington: World Bank.

Index